Golden Leaf

A Khmer Rouge Genocide Survivor

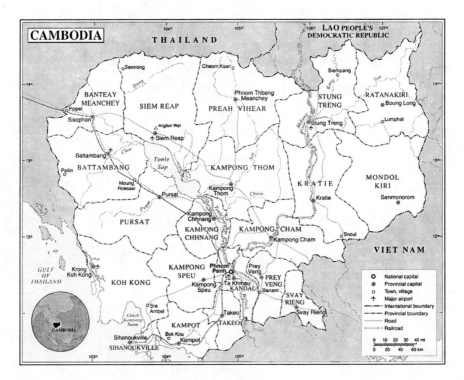

Based on Map No. 3860, Rev. 4, United Nations, January 2004

Golden Leaf

A Khmer Rouge Genocide Survivor

An incredible journey
of an ambassador for peace,
from the Khmer Rouge killing fields
to the Rotary Club of Portland
and the fellowship of the Royal Rosarians,
through minefields, rockets,
bullets, refugee camps,
and Reed College.

A Memoir of
Kilong Ung

អ៊ុង គីឡុង

www.kupublishing.com
USA

Published by: KU Publishing LLC
USA

www.kupublishing.com

All photographs courtesy of the author's family
unless otherwise noted.

Book design: Sucha Production, Inc.
www.suchaproduction.com

Copy edit and proofread: Cory Jubitz
www.thethreecs.com

ISBN 978-0-9823502-0-1
FIRST EDITION

In honor of my family.

In memory of genocide victims.

Dedicated to
a force that makes the world a better place.

GOLDEN WORDS

"Mr. Ung, an accomplished storyteller and author, turns an unbelievably negative experience into a positive by portraying to readers his survival against modern-day genocide. The courage he displays to confront his past and share the story is both provocative and penetrating."
—*Al Jubitz, President, Jubitz Family Foundation*

"Kilong's courageous story reveals the power of the human spirit to survive one of the worst tragedies in recent world history. He gives us hope that goodness will always prevail."
—*Bhavia Wagner, Author of* Soul Survivors: Stories of Women and Children in Cambodia *and Executive Director of Friendship With Cambodia*

"Meet Kilong Ung, a gentle man of fierce intensity whose story will inspire you to make this world a better and more beautiful place in which to live. Conclude as I have that the American dream is merely a launch pad for this survivor of the killing fields."
—*Bob Strader, 2007 Prime Minister of the Royal Rosarians*

"From the jungles, through the landmines and starvation, through the hopelessness and the tragic loss of his parents, to a golden leaf who brings light to the world's ugliness. His story, his suffering: His journey is one that makes every one of us wonder why and how. And yet through the horrors, he was able to use these experiences as a strength to build himself, to provide for and protect his family, and to better this crazy and beautiful world. This is the Kilong Ung that I know. This is the golden leaf who made me a better person. I am grateful for his gift to me and to this world."
—*Chanly Bob, Chairman, Cambodian-American Community of Oregon*

"Kilong Ung's *Golden Leaf* is the epic tale of escape from Pol Pot's Cambodia, a journey so horrific that Mephistopheles cringes with every step. His story represents the stories of many genocide survivors who are left with a Pyrrhic victory. *Golden Leaf* is a must-read."
—*Claxton Welch, Former Dallas Cowboys Player and Super Bowl Veteran*

"Kilong's story proves the height to which the human spirit can reach and the depth of horrors humanity can instill upon itself. Kilong's passion for life is an inspiration for us to remember that most of those in our world are much less fortunate and persevere through difficult circumstances we can barely imagine. *Golden Leaf* gives us visions of desperation and hope. Hopefully, we can use those visions to guide ourselves."
—*Darin D. Honn, Attorney,*
Past President of the Rotary Club of Portland, 2003-2004

"*Golden Leaf* is a memoir that must be read. Kilong Ung takes us deep into Cambodia's recent history and his memories of childhood under the Khmer Rouge. In this compelling and powerful narrative, he seeks to understand the reasons behind the genocide and his own survival.
Ung writes with honesty, courage, and passion, detailing both the horrors of genocide and his coming of age in Cambodia and the U.S. Ultimately, this is a story of resilience and hope."
—*Patti Duncan, Author of* Tell This Silence: Asian American Women Writers and the Politics of Speech

"In his book, Kilong expresses in vivid detail his treacherous journey from genocide survivor to the present in his quest for peace within himself and others of this world. The book will take you through the full range of thoughts and emotions and persuade you that he is eminently qualified to be a leader in the battles for peace in this world."
—*Thomas L. Moultrie, Senior Judge, State of Oregon*

"*Golden Leaf* is a 'must read' for people to learn about the depth of the human spirit and ability to transcend tragedy. Khmer and non-Khmer audiences will gain great knowledge from this book and will appreciate this 'golden opportunity' to learn about the resilience of the Khmer spirit."
—*Tiara Delgado, Writer,* Khmer Post *Newspaper, Long Beach, California, and Documentary-Film Maker*

CONTENTS

CONTENTS

FOREWORD

I met Kilong Ung in 2006, when he joined the Rotary Club of Portland, Oregon. At that time, I had little knowledge of Kilong's journey through life, first as a victim of the Khmer Rouge tyranny in Cambodia and later as a community leader and successful businessman.

Kilong's compelling story chronicles his survival under the Khmer Rouge regime that killed an estimated two million Cambodians, including more than fifty members of his family—among them his youngest sister, grandmother, and parents. After four long years of starvation, beatings at the hands of his captors, and unspeakable conditions, Kilong escapes first to Thailand and then to the United States, triumphing over the worst of humanity to transform himself into an educated, compassionate man. After a twenty-year absence, he returns to Cambodia to visit his remaining family members and friends in an emotional and transformative reunion.

Through *Golden Leaf* and public talks in Portland, where he now lives with his family, Kilong illuminates the darkness of the Khmer Rouge and promotes peace and understanding with his remarkable life story. His tale will mesmerize readers and take them from despair to exhilaration.

—Angelo Carella, Past President, Rotary Club of Portland, 1985-1986,
and Past District Governor, Rotary District 5100, 1994-1995

FAMILY TREE

As of April 17, 1975

Son of Seanho Ung and grandson of Teuklong Ung.

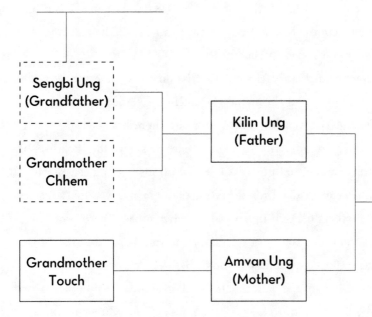

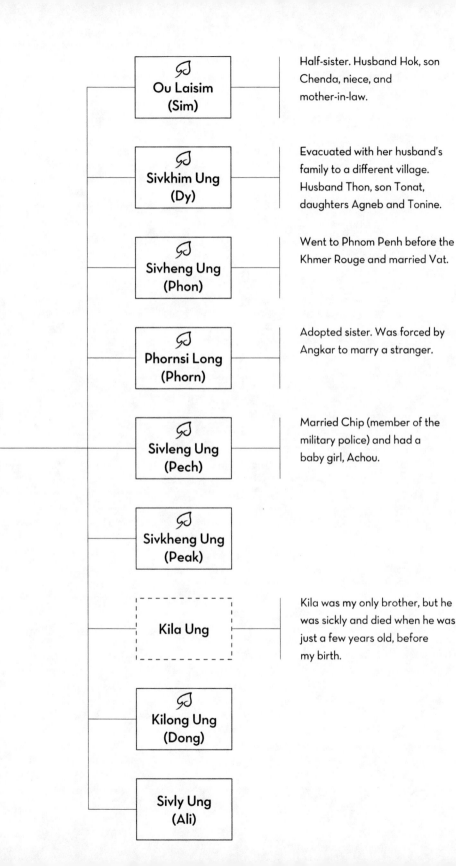

♋ **Ou Laisim (Sim)**	Half-sister. Husband Hok, son Chenda, niece, and mother-in-law.
♋ **Sivkhim Ung (Dy)**	Evacuated with her husband's family to a different village. Husband Thon, son Tonat, daughters Agneb and Tonine.
♋ **Sivheng Ung (Phon)**	Went to Phnom Penh before the Khmer Rouge and married Vat.
♋ **Phornsi Long (Phorn)**	Adopted sister. Was forced by Angkar to marry a stranger.
♋ **Sivleng Ung (Pech)**	Married Chip (member of the military police) and had a baby girl, Achou.
♋ **Sivkheng Ung (Peak)**	
Kila Ung	Kila was my only brother, but he was sickly and died when he was just a few years old, before my birth.
♋ **Kilong Ung (Dong)**	
Sivly Ung (Ali)	

golden leaf (gōl'dən lēf) n., pl. golden leaves (gōl'dən lēvz)

1. a survivor of a heinous act against humanity, especially genocide.
2. **Golden Leaf** (pl. Golden Leaves):
    a. a person who survived the Khmer Rouge genocide:
        "Golden Leaf, A Khmer Rouge Genocide Survivor"
        (Kilong Ung).
3. one who survives against extreme odds.

INTRODUCTION

I was a leaf at the mercy of the wind. The wind carried me from one remote part of the world to another. It blew me through turbulence and catastrophic weather. It took me to a Khmer Rouge labor camp and lingered for an eternity. It dehydrated me and nearly starved me to death. I helplessly watched the most devilish mother of all winds ruthlessly crush my tree into lifeless pulp. Like an almighty Olympian god, when the wind wanted to toy with me, it blew me through minefields, rockets, and bullets. While two million leaves disintegrated, I persevered. Through an extraordinary journey, I discovered myself. I am fortunate, and I don't easily perish. I was a golden leaf. Against all odds, I survived, laid down roots, and became a tree.

I am a member of the Rotary Club of Portland and a knighted member of the Royal Rosarians, official goodwill ambassadors of the city of Portland in the state of Oregon. I graduated from Reed College with a B.A. in mathematics and from Bowling Green State University with an M.S. in applied statistics and operations research. My professional resume includes work for Andersen Consulting, United Data Processing, Step Technology, Corillian Corporation, and CheckFree/Fiserv. The list of corporations that I have serviced includes Nike, Intel, Tektronix, Boeing, Boise Cascade, James River, EB Eddy, MacMillan Bloedel, and Pope & Talbot. As an instructor, I taught computer programming language at Portland Community College and database programming at Step Technology. I served for four years as president of the Cambodian-American Community of Oregon. I managed my own consulting business, Knowledge Unlimited (KU) Consulting.

Before my success, however, I struggled to survive the Khmer Rouge labor camps and became a Cambodian refugee. I struggled to learn English and assimilate into the American culture.

Despite my present success, I forever remain a genocide survivor. I survived the Khmer Rouge genocide that killed two million Cambodians and nearly killed me. The Khmer Rouge starved my parents, maternal grandmother, and youngest sister to death and nearly eradicated my faith in humanity.

In memory of the two million Cambodians killed by the genocide, and in honor of the survivors, I am leveraging my past to make the world a better place, one reader at a time. I invite you to laugh, cry, and celebrate with me as I take you through my incredible journey from the Khmer Rouge killing fields to Portland, Oregon.

សម័យសង្គមចាស់

(sak-mahy sawng-kuhm jah)

PRE-KHMER ROUGE ERA

Once upon a peaceful time in Cambodia, I was born in the provincial city of Battambang, located approximately 280 miles northwest of Phnom Penh. My father's name was Kilin Ung, and my mother's name was Amvan Ung. My father was of Chinese descent, and my mother was a Cambodian (Khmer). From her previous marriage, my mother had a daughter named Ou Laisim (Sim). My parents adopted my mother's orphaned niece, Phornsi Long (Phorn). My parents had a son named Kila Ung, but he died at a young age, before I was born.

Including Sim and Phorn and without counting my late brother, Kila, I had a total of seven sisters and no brothers. All of my sisters except one were older than I. In age-descending order, the full names (and pet names) of my parents' children were Ou Laisim (Sim), Sivkhim Ung (Dy), Sivheng Ung (Phon), Phornsi Long (Phorn), Sivleng Ung (Pech), Sivkheng Ung (Peak), Kilong Ung (Dong), and Sivly Ung (Ali).

There was no official record of my birth, but I believe that I was born in 1960. By the time the Khmer Rouge took control of Cambodia in 1975, I physically looked like a ten-year-old boy to those who knew me and even younger to strangers. I still ran stark naked in the rain, played naked in the mud, and swam nude in rivers and lakes. I completed my provincial seventh-grade education and learned French as a second language. Leading up to the end of my education, my French lessons were replaced by English lessons. For two terms, I had one hour of English per school day, but by the time the Khmer Rouge was done with me, I had no foreign language left in me (especially not English).

Before I started first grade, I ran away from home to Wat Domrei Sor (White Elephant Temple), located just a couple of blocks away from my home. After my parents found me, they spanked me hard. The headmaster monk convinced my parents to allow me to stay at the temple as a child-disciple. During my time living in the temple, I was too young to be a servant-disciple to any monk, and Headmaster Dul took me in as his spoiled disciple. Like everyone else, I publicly addressed Headmaster Dul as Dekun (Reverend or His Holiness) Dul. In private, I addressed him simply as Lok Ta (Grandfather) Dul. I was more like a grandson to Dekun Dul than a disciple. Unlike other people in the temple, I ate when Dekun ate. I was given the distinctive privilege of sleeping in Dekun's quarters. At night, Dekun taught me the Buddhist chanting in Sanskrit, and he put me to sleep. I was infamously known as the spoiled little boy who accompanied Dekun Dul.

I was taught the ways and traditions of the Buddhist monks at a very early age—well before I started first grade. My first- and second-grade lessons were given to me by the second master Buddhist monk. Contrary to Dekun Dul, who was always gentle with me, the second master was a disciplinarian in the classroom. For one reason or another, I seemed to be constantly in trouble. I was often punished for my sharp tongue and excessive questioning of the Buddhist teachings. Although Dekun Dul spoiled me, he never second-guessed the second master's authority to discipline.

By the end of my first-grade year, Dekun Dul showed signs of his old age. At my age then, I thought Dekun Dul seemed like a 200-year-old monk. It was more and more difficult for Dekun to care for me, so my parents took me home.

Although I was back living at home, my second-grade classroom was at the temple. I often visited Dekun Dul on my way home after school. I noticed the progression of his aging. Over time, my visits became less frequent because it was hard for me to relate to him. During my final few visits, he had trouble recognizing me. That was very sad for me, and for years afterward I felt deeply guilty for not continuing my visits.

By one account, I was told that when the Khmer Rouge evacuated the temple, Dekun Dul was left behind, alone, and starved to death. By another account, there was a rumor that the Khmer Rouge executed him on the spot during the evacuation. Having experienced the cruelty of the Khmer Rouge, I would imagine that Dekun was left on his own to starve in the very quarter where Buddhism was taught to me. I will never know the true account of his death; however, my memory of what Dekun Dul did for me continues to be a part of a force that keeps reminding me to remain honest and compassionate whenever I am influenced by a humanly destructive force. This memory has corrected the path of my journey on a number of occasions. I am fortunate to have this memory to counterbalance my nightmares infused by the Khmer Rouge's heinous crimes against humanity.

I was told that there had been a better time for my family before I was born. My father descended from a wealthy Chinese family. Consequently, he inherited a large amount of land and wealth from his parents. A ridiculous dispute with his brother-in-law, coupled with his quixotic pride, caused him to walk away empty-handed and give his inherited land to his younger sister. The demise of my family's fortune began that day.

My father worked for a logging company, managing a logging crew. I was too young to remember the good times when my father owned a logging truck and brought home good earnings; I vaguely remember when my father was laid off and sold the truck. It was before I started first grade. From that day onward, my mother worked very hard selling food to carry the family and keep her children in school.

About a year before the Khmer Rouge took over Cambodia, my father abruptly became sick and partially disabled. I do not know the true cause of his sickness. My mother never told me what was wrong with my father. Some family members told me that my father had a stroke or heart attack, while others said my father drank the wrong kind of alcohol and got poisoned.

My family made ends meet, and we were considered middle-class. With the help of my older sisters, my mother started her daily work around 4 a.m. and stayed up late into the night—often past midnight. With the exception of my half-sister and my adopted sister, all my siblings were in school, but we all helped my mother with the chores of splitting firewood, fetching water, cutting vegetables and meat, grinding nuts and chili, making flour and pickles, and preparing seasonings.

My mother owned a small restaurant that served breakfast, lunch, and dinner. Before school in the morning, I helped bus tables and wash dishes. During our lunch break from school, I delivered meals to our regular clients while my sisters helped around the restaurant. In the evening, I delivered meals, washed dishes, bussed tables, and helped out with whatever was needed.

My mother usually took a couple of hours off in the evening to enjoy live theater and opera. My youngest sister and I were often given the privilege of tagging along if we did our chores well. After her theater break, my mother always returned to her work before going to bed.

Although my mother's life was tough, she seemed happy and proud of keeping her children fed and educated. She appeared to enjoy her friends, family, relatives, and freedom. Live theater seemed to keep her anticipating the next day.

My mother's tough life was a wonderful life in comparison to her horrible life under the Khmer Rouge regime.

By the time the Khmer Rouge took over Cambodia in 1975, my half-sister, Sim, had married a full-blooded-Chinese professional gambler and had moved to a new home in another neighborhood. In addition to her six-year-old son, Chenda, and her husband, Hok, Sim's mother-in-law and her niece lived with her.

My second sister, Dy, had completed her university education and was living with her husband's large family in a nearby neighborhood. She was married to an equally educated man and had three children.

My third sister, Phon, had finished her schooling and was working in the capital, Phnom Penh. She, too, was married.

The rest of my sisters were all still living at home, including my fifth sister, Pech, who was married to Chip; Pech, Chip, and their newborn baby lived under our roof. Chip was a member of the military police.

My maternal grandmother was a Buddhist nun and a hermit living in and serving a Buddhist temple on top of Phnom (mountain) Sompov (ship). She happened to visit our family just as the Khmer Rouge took over Cambodia.

សម័យសង្គមខ្មែរក្រហម

(sak-mahy sawng-kuhm khmair k'raw-hawrm)

KHMER ROUGE ERA

KHMER ROUGE

Like the rest of the country, my family was weary of the civil war between the republic army and the Khmer Rouge. I never became accustomed to the sounds of gunfire or rockets or to the sight of dead bodies. Some days, there were rumors that the Khmer Rouge would invade that night, so my family would sleep in a bunker beneath our home. One night, a rocket hit the governor's mansion and created a huge hole in its facade. Another night, a rocket broke open a concrete wall of the province's penitentiary, and a number of the prisoners escaped. One afternoon, a martyr threw a grenade inside a theater, killed dozens of people, and injured many more. So when the Khmer Rouge took control of Cambodia, people celebrated the end of the war.

The Khmer Rouge took over Cambodia on April 17, 1975, in the middle of the Cambodian New Year. The news got to Battambang around noon. People clustered in small groups around radios, trying to get more details of the historic event. The provincial governor of Battambang had already left Cambodia. Many military officers also escaped Cambodia. Everyone else was led to believe that the Khmer Rouge had good intentions for the country. All soldiers were ordered to put down their weapons and embrace peace. The repeated radio announcement assured people that the war was over and they would see their king again — King Norodom Sihanouk would return and lead Cambodia to peace.

Later that day, just before dinnertime, the Khmer Rouge army marched into the provincial city of Battambang. People were singing and dancing in the streets. The celebration of the Cambodian New Year quickly turned into the celebration of peace.

I was caught up in the revelry — singing, dancing, waving, and welcoming the Khmer Rouge into the city. Rapid gunshots were fired into the sky by the Khmer Rouge soldiers. The celebration continued into the night past my bedtime.

I got up early in the morning to help bus the breakfast tables and wash dishes at the restaurant. The seats were filled by Khmer Rouge soldiers. I was excited to see them up close. Their dusty black outfits and AK-47 rifles lived up to the legendary tales of their guerrilla warfare. I was impressed and mesmerized by their militancy. When they finished their breakfast, they got up and walked off without paying. We were afraid to confront them, and I noticed the sad look and fear in my mother's eyes.

I was in the middle of washing dishes when I heard a few rounds of gunshots across the street. I stopped washing dishes and ran across the street to investigate the incident. When I got there, I saw a half-naked man with his arms tied behind his back. He was kneeling on the concrete sidewalk, and horror was all over his face. He was surrounded by about a dozen Khmer Rouge soldiers, who were yelling at him. They accused him of stealing something.

A soldier slammed the butt of his AK-47 rifle into the man's shoulder. Another soldier harshly butted his rifle against the back of the man's head. Another soldier took out his handgun, cocked it against the side of the man's head, and pulled the trigger. The gun was not loaded; nonetheless, the man was terrorized and urinated on himself. His body shook like a newborn chick's, and he cried like a little boy. He pleaded his innocence, but the soldiers continued their torture in front of the crowd. Children as young as three years old were watching. Unsure what to think, I watched the torture. I watched another soldier hastily pull out his handgun and shoot the man in the chest. I watched the man fall forward to the ground and die. I watched the blood spread on the ground beneath the body. I watched a soldier turn the corpse over. The man lay still with his eyes stuck open, teeth exposed, one leg bent, and body covered with blood and urine.

I ran to tell my parents what I had witnessed. My parents were speechless, but I detected their concern; I also realized my own fear.

That day, the Khmer Rouge ordered all soldiers and personnel of the republic army to go welcome the return of King Norodom Sihanouk and afterward join the Khmer Rouge in reforming the corrupted Cambodia. People suspected that the Khmer Rouge was lying, but there was nothing anyone could do about it. By force or by deception, the Khmer Rouge loaded the soldiers, policemen, and government employees onto buses and took them away to be executed. They also rounded up and executed the educated and the affluent civilians. As a member of the military police, Chip was taken away with his MP buddies on a bus to be executed.

The next day, the Khmer Rouge ordered people to evacuate all the cities.

As the Khmer Rouge was mandating the mass evacuation of Battambang Province, the charge of the family's decision regarding where to go was fully on my mother. Traditionally, the patriarch of the family would preside over any major decision that would affect the family; however, my father was not well enough to be in charge. My brother-in-law had been taken away to be executed. I was not old enough to serve as patriarch. My second-oldest sister, Dy, who now was an integral part of her husband's family, did not join us. My third-oldest sister, Phon, who was the second most educated in the family, was away working in the capital. My oldest sister, Sim, and her family came and joined us. There was a sense of panic about what to take and where to go.

As a young teenage boy, the evacuation and its chaos were exciting. The uncertainty of the future incited my wildest imagination. I imagined that it would be exciting to live on a farm with animals, near rivers and lakes. There was a good chance that I might be armed as a boy soldier to protect my Cambodia against neighboring countries Vietnam and Thailand and the "tiger enemy," the USA. I thought the adults worried too much. I thought my father was crazy to predict that the Khmer Rouge regime would be modeled after China's Maoism.

My excitement turned into doubt and worry when I found my mother sobbing in a room by herself. My anxiety turned even deeper when I realized my mother was trying to hide her emotion and worries from me. I knew my mother well, and I realized then that my mother knew something beyond my comprehension, and it was not good.

After much consideration, my mother decided that we would head northwest from Battambang on Road 5 toward Phnom Sompov, for a number of reasons. One was that my mother had friends and relatives in that area and my family would do well there. Another was to accommodate my grandmother's religious purpose as a Buddhist hermit nun. The most important reason was to give my sister Pech and her baby a chance to reunite with Chip in case he was able to escape execution.

Although I was anxious for adventure, I was sad that I would have to leave my pet owl, fighting betta fish, pigs, fighting cocks, chickens, ducks, parrot, and garden. Even sadder was the fact that I would lose my friends.

Everything seemed to move rapidly. In one moment, I felt wonderfully excited. In another moment, I felt guilty for being excited. In yet another moment, I felt very sad knowing I would have to give up the life and friends I had always known. The uncertainty also brought fear.

Of all the family members, my mother was my main focus. I was acutely aware of her sadness and anxiety. I could not comprehend exactly what her concerns were, but I knew well the magnitude of her worry. My mother was the pillar of my family and the ground I stood on every day. Witnessing the weakening of such a pillar brought me an indescribable anxiety. Up to this point, I had never worried about my future. Leaving the house and our belongings was inevitable, but tomorrow could not come fast enough for me. I could not stand my conflicting emotions, anxiety, and confusion. I wanted to get going and to start the new life right away. I knew the night would not give me good sleep, but I understood how important it was that we stay put as long as possible in case my brother-in-law survived the execution and was able to rejoin the family.

We packed what we could carry on foot. Valuable items such as family china and silver were buried in the backyard with the hope that one day we would return to recover them. The animals were freed from their cages. We killed a few chickens to prepare food for our journey to the farm.

While anxiety ran rampant throughout the city and nearby suburbs of Battambang, the Khmer Rouge soldiers were celebrating their victory with gunshots into the air. I could hear bullets falling on our tin rooftop. My parents warned my little sister, Ali, and me not to play outside as usual, fearing that we might be hit by falling bullets. The confinement and idle waiting made me restless. I sneaked out the window and met up with my friends. We played our usual hide-and-seek and war game together for the last time.

It was one of my most memorable nights. The Khmer Rouge soldiers celebrated their victory by shooting AK-47 rifles into the air. Bullets whistled in the sky and landed on the residential roofs like light raindrops. My friends and I were armed with slingshots, pretending to be the victorious Khmer Rouge soldiers. We crawled through the tight and dark spaces beneath people's houses, combing for enemies. We climbed trees in the dark and pretended to be snipers.

Although we had played war many times, this particular war game was more real. The Khmer Rouge gunshots into the sky created the illusion of the ultimate battlefield, up close and personal. The other boys and I pretended that we were on a cleanup mission. We sought stray enemies with an intent to kill. We pretended that the stray dogs were our defeated enemies—military professionals, affluent people, Americans (aka "paper tigers"), Vietnamese, and Thai.

We shot and killed giant bats in the air because they were enemy fighter planes. We went to the river and sank people's wooden canoes, pretending that they were enemy speedboats, submarines, and warships.

Normally, the boys and I divided ourselves into at least two opposing combat factions that fought each other. This time, however, we united in a single team to fight our common enemies—the enemies of the Khmer Rouge.

It was surreal. Never in my life had I commanded a better company of soldiers. Every boy was enthusiastic, compliant, and fierce. We were armed with our best wooden swords, wooden rifles, wooden handguns, and slingshots. Oh, we could have been the finest militia.

My friends and I knew that it was the last time we would play together.

That night, I returned home close to midnight to find my mother waiting on the front porch. She furiously but calmly stared me in the eyes while puffing her cigarette and sipping her coffee. I had seen that stare often, but tonight's was unmistakably different. There was a mix of anger, fear, sympathy, and emptiness in my mother's stare. Any other time, I would have been spanked and whipped, but this time my mother quietly escorted me to bed and tucked me in. The absence of the usual punishment and the lack of an emotional outburst from my mother, coupled with the staccato sound of gunshots outside, kept me up a bit later into the night before I fell asleep.

I woke up to learn that my brother-in-law Chip had come home. He and a handful of his MP buddies had escaped execution. As soon as he arrived home that morning, the family hustled to get out of the city. No one seemed to care about my existence. I was completely invisible. Uncoordinated, chaotic, everyone was busy with last-minute packing.

With the arrival of Chip, my family decided to change the destination of our journey. Since Chip had escaped from Phnom Sompov, we could not go there. We had to head in the opposite direction—east. We wanted to join my rho farmed east of Battambang. The relatives were well off,

ount on their help. It turned out later to be a horrible idea,

ealthy relatives could be a fatal liability under the Khmer

Rouge regime.

FIRST EVACUATION

We marched in the mass evacuation for two days to reach the village where my father's relatives lived. I felt excitingly more grown up by the minute as the reality of my new life approached. For once in my life, I felt a serious responsibility.

My grandmother cried often during the trip. Her sadness showed as she witnessed dead bodies along the highway and the evacuation of the Buddhist monks. In Buddhism, any form of cruelty to a live being, including animals and insects, is forbidden. Witnessing the monks driving oxcarts saddened my grandmother. She never thought that she would live to see a monk forced into whipping an ox or a buffalo. Out of necessity, everyone—including the monks—did everything possible to survive the brutal evacuation.

Middle-class and upper-class citizens were struggling; my middle-class family was no exception. Our bicycles were rendered useless after a full day of being overloaded, and we had to leave what we could not carry without the bicycles on the first day of our trip.

My father was not able to carry anything. From his sickness, my father was partially blind. He had to rely on his cane and held on to my shoulders for guidance; that put a tremendous burden on me. The heavy load I carried and the excruciatingly slow pace agitated me. My whining and complaining got me slapped and spanked by my mother and my older sisters.

We spent the night alongside the highway, under the naked sky and next to countless strangers. I was unsure of my path to the future. Within a week's time after the Khmer Rouge had entered Battambang, I seemed to mature rapidly inside. In the two days leading up to this night, I felt that I had matured as much as ten years. I had experienced the most profound anxiety among the adults. I had seen brutal execution in broad daylight. I had seen sin committed against Buddhist monks and nuns. For the first time in my life, I had to wonder what would happen to me and my family.

I had trouble sleeping. The night was hot and humid. The mosquitoes were ruthless. The evacuees were noisy. Foul odor from dead bodies along the highway turned the otherwise peaceful countryside sky into a morbidly dark and eerie blanket. Although many families stopped to get a night's rest along the highway, the foot traffic, oxcarts, and bicycles were relentless through the night.

That night, while the adults shared their worries, my little sister, Ali, and I shared (in a whisper) a fantasy about our future. We would be the champions of our family. We would learn to farm, fish, hunt, and trap to feed our family. Lying close to each other, we held hands and whispered ourselves to sleep.

My mother woke me up. She was gentle in rousing me. I woke up to see deep worry and sadness in her face. I wanted to comfort her, but I didn't know how to express myself. All I could do was briefly gaze into her eyes. For that brief moment, she managed to afford me a warm smile, and I found reassurance in that forced smile. I knew then that no matter what, my mother would always be my safety net.

As my mother turned to wake up my little sister, I wrapped my arms around my mother from behind and broke into a sob. She unfastened my arms, turned to face me, and pulled me into her maternal hug. Stroking the back of my head, she assured me that I had nothing to be afraid of. For some reason, I couldn't tell her the truth, that I was not afraid for myself. I couldn't tell her that this new life was exciting for me. I couldn't tell her that my sob was a symbol of my concern for her welfare and her family responsibility. I couldn't tell her that I was sad for her. My sob and the commotion woke up my little sister. She joined in the crying—for what reason, I never knew.

As we reached Phoum (village) Onlong (well, ditch, or small river) Vil (whirl), the midmorning was beautiful. The evacuation traffic lessened because many families had already settled or traveled ahead of my family, which was slowed down by my aged grandmother and my less-than-healthy father. There were noticeably fewer dead bodies farther away from the city. The bodies found closer to the city were mostly from executions; the bodies in the countryside were mostly the result of exhaustion. My family worried about the welfare of my father, grandmother, and my brother-in-law Hok's elderly mother.

I cannot recall who was given charge of my grandmother's well-being, but I was given charge of my father's on this journey. I was frustrated and disappointed that I could not boyishly take full advantage of the exciting journey, but I took good care of my father. I was irritated by my father's philosophical preaching. He was relentless and urgent in sharing his ideology with me. As a boy, I could not appreciate what he was trying to instill in me. His words could not have been emptier. Until that day, I never found my father more talkative. He gave me a private sermon as if there were no tomorrow. He made me promise that I would grow up to be kind and compassionate toward others, especially my own siblings. I made him seemingly countless promises just to appease him, but those promises didn't mean anything to me at the time. I just wanted my father quiet for the rest of the trip. He annoyed me. My father never stopped imparting his ideology to me that day, for he knew that it was his final chance to make his lasting impression on me.

My family got off the highway and traveled along the Onlong Vil River toward Phoum (village) Tavei (a particular bird), our destination. The unpaved road was dusty and crowded by the one-way evacuation. The sound of traffic, especially the ungreased wheels of oxcarts, was deafening. The dusty air was foreign and intoxicating to city folks like my family. Exhausted by the long journey and annoyed by my father's sermon and slow pace, I lost my boyish excitement and fantasy. The hardest work of my life thus far took place that day. I began to see the legitimacy of the adults' concerns and anxiety.

The rest of the trip was uneventful. It was mechanically tiring and long. I do not remember how long my family traveled that day before we reached Phoum Tavei.

I was happy to see my father's distant uncle Ta Nga, a wealthy farmer. Ta Nga was an influential figure in Phoum Tavei due to his wealth. Like my father, he was a kind man. I had met him on many occasions prior to this day and found him very warm, down to earth, and sincere. The villagers liked and respected him for both his wealth and his kindness. Rumor had it that he was one of the Khmer Rouge supporters who often provided food supplies and sanctuary to the Khmer Rouge during its revolutionary movement.

Unlike the city, Phoum Tavei appeared unaffected by the Khmer Rouge's victory. The villagers seemed to go about their business as usual. No one had been evacuated. We were able to purchase what we could afford.

Ta Nga put my family up in one of his spare homes. He did not seem to worry like the city folks did. While we rested from our long trip, he and the rest of the villagers went about their lives as they always did.

My father was incorrigible in his belief that life would get worse. He was adamant that the Khmer Rouge was communist and modeled after Maoist China. His philosophical and political debate put off Ta Nga and the rest of my family members. My brother-in-law Chip sided with my father but was not effective. (The majority of Cambodians did not believe that the Khmer Rouge was communist, even though Khmer Rouge means Red Cambodians, a colloquialism for communist Cambodians.)

Unaffected by my father's seemingly cynical and dogmatic belief, my family settled and started to build a new life. Within a couple of days after our arrival, my family began to gather material to build our own moderate home on Ta Nga's land. The plan for our new home was not much; it was no more than a large straw hut to get us started. We planned to work for Ta Nga and earn money to build a real home in the long run. Unfortunately, that long run never came.

To my father's redemption and everyone else's surprise, Ta Nga informed us that Angkar (the new name for the Khmer Rouge government) had issued an urgent evacuation notice to all people in Phoum Tavei. There was no point in finishing the new home. We stayed in Phoum Tavei no more than a week before we were evacuated again.

SECOND EVACUATION

By this time, money had no value. People traded goods, but would not purchase or sell them. A can of rice, a spoonful of sugar, a handful of salt, or a piece of dried fish had more value than an ounce of gold. Material necessities such as clothes had some value, but luxuries such as jewelry had little or no value. Straw hats (made from palm leaves) and scarves were in high demand, especially among the city folks trying to fit in and to protect themselves from the scorching April sun.

This time, the journey was far more difficult than it had been in the first round of evacuations. People were pushed to remote parts of the country. We traveled on foot through barren rice paddies all day long. We traded bicycles for *dongreks* (fetchers made of bamboo). My father, my grandmother, and Hok's mother rode in one of Ta Nga's oxcarts. My responsibility shifted from guiding my father to carrying two bags of rice with a *dongrek*. This new life no longer excited me. It was hellish. The inhospitably dry rice paddies were hot, rough, and cruel. Barren fields were vast, lonely, and forsaken. It was the first time in this journey that I understood the magnitude of the adults' worry and anxiety. I felt embarrassed, ashamed, and guilty for not heeding my father's prophecy—although there was nothing I could have done to make a difference.

The social tables had already turned by this time. The uneducated and meager folks (especially the farmers) began to show their condescending attitudes toward city folks. The farmers were accustomed to a hard life, the hot sun, and barren fields. This evacuation was a cakewalk for the farmers but torture for their counterparts. While the city folks carried their belongings, the farmers had oxcarts as the proper means of transportation. The majority of the lower class was snobby, rude, and, in some cases, antagonistic. City folks were condescendingly referred to as "Chen" (Chinese) or *thaoke* (big boss, capitalist, oppressor, or fascist).

Prior to this evacuation, we had consumed water either from a treated water source or from collected raindrops. In this April drought, we would be lucky to find any water in this barren farmland.

The *dongrek* burned my shoulder long before we reached our new home, Phoum (village) Chai (flee) Chhke (dog). It gave me blisters on my shoulders; the April sun gave me blisters on my bare back; and the scorching and hard ground gave my bare feet cuts and blisters. I had never endured such hellish torture as this and was very happy to reach and accept a place in the middle of nowhere as my new home.

Phoum Chai Chhke was isolated, surrounded by miles of rice paddies. It was private land confiscated by Angkar. There were a couple of straw huts occupied only during the rice harvesting. Other than a small number of coconut, palm, cashew, tamarind, and banana trees, the land was empty. In winter, Phoum Chai Chhke was surrounded by floodwater that nurtured the rice paddies. Until this moment, it had been a ghost land. Within a few days, Phoum Chai Chhke metamorphosed into a busy village.

COMMUNISM

Angkar decided that my family should be divided into two households. My brother-in-law Hok was registered as the head of one household that included him, his wife, Sim, young son, mother, and niece. My other brother-in-law, Chip, was registered as the head of the other household. Chip's household included Chip, Chip's wife, Pech, and baby girl, my parents, my grandmother, my other three sisters, and me. Nonetheless, we all were registered as one family.

Angkar permitted our two households to build one straw hut with two entries and a windowed divider in the middle. Hok's household occupied the west side of the divider, and Chip's household occupied the east side of the divider.

We cut down bamboo from the nearby woods and built a small bed for my father. We built another, larger bamboo bed for the rest of the family. We did not have privacy, as we shared a single bed. My sisters, mother, and grandmother used sarongs to cover themselves when they changed. My youngest sister and I were young enough that we did not have to care about privacy. We stripped naked to change, but changing was rare and unnecessary, as we had just a few clothes and often got wet and then dried.

For some reason, no outhouse was ever built at Phoum Chai Chhke. Going to the restroom required walking at least three rice paddies outside of the village and digging a small hole in an open field. My disabled father could not walk that far, considering each rice paddy was well over 300 feet long. As my father's caretaker, I carried, emptied, and cleaned his potty every morning and sometimes twice in one day.

At the beginning, there was only one man-made well in Phoum Chai Chhke. The well was dry almost to the bottom. Within days, the shortage of water became a serious crisis. The well could not produce enough water to support the newly formed village. It was difficult for the city folks, but the farming class was familiar with the territory and knew where to find water. I tagged along with the farmers to find water for my family. While the farmers transported their water with their oxcarts from miles away, I had to carry my water for miles with a bamboo fetcher. As a short boy, fetching water across rice paddies and woods was extremely difficult. It took me a couple of weeks before I got used to such tough labor.

We ran out of our personal food supplies by the end of the week. Ta Nga's family at this time had to be careful about sharing their food stores, because they knew that harder times were approaching.

It took the farmers longer to run out of their supplies, because during the evacuation they had the better means of transportation that allowed them to bring more supplies. Consequently, they were arrogant toward the city folks. The tables had turned. The city folks were treated as the newcomers and of the inferior class. The farmers' past diffidence turned inhospitable and condescending. On the other hand, the city folks deliberately tried to keep low profiles. A serious tension between the two classes was lurking, but the farmers had the decisive upper hand by default.

Sometime during the second week, Angkar of Phoum Chai Chhke was fully set up and functional. To no surprise of my father, or, now, to the rest of the family, Angkar called a public meeting to declare Cambodia a communist nation. Angkar now represented the people's commonwealth.

That was the beginning of the Cambodian agrarian utopia. Angkar declared everyone equal. Angkar decreed that everyone must farm. Angkar demanded total patriotism. Ultimately, Angkar pronounced everyone an enemy of capitalism, America, the western world, Vietnam, and Thailand. The people's closest enemies included the republic army and the royalists. It was the law that one either was with Angkar or against Angkar, and there was no middle ground. Money, luxury items, and photos were sources of immorality and corruption. Such items were banned, and anyone found having them would face torture or execution.

The timing of the declaration could not have been better calculated, because the majority of the city folks had run out of food and needed the commonwealth to survive. Even the farmers were in need of the commonwealth. From this day on, no one owned anything, and everyone owned everything. There was no mine, yours, his, or hers; there was only ours. The irony was I could not pick a coconut to eat because it was ours and not mine.

The rationing began that day, the labor camp started the following day, but that night my family's hut was filled with bewilderment. Everyone except my father either pretended to be asleep or tried to fall asleep. My father puffed his homemade cigarette and gazed indifferently into the night sky through the transparent roof. His quiescent but troubled thoughts seemed to stretch lethargically all the way to the moon. Although what had transpired earlier in the day meant little to me as a boy, I could not fall asleep, for I sensed there was something fundamentally wrong with the overall picture. I got up, walked over to my father, snuggled up to him, found my comfort zone, and eventually fell into a deep sleep.

The morning came unwelcomingly quick for my older sisters, brothers-in-law, and the rest of the adults in the village. However, with a restored youthful energy and positive outlook, Ali and I could hardly wait to start our new adventure. It was exciting that people could come and work together.

I took care of my father's potty and gave my father a full-body cleaning with a wet cloth while my mother, my older sisters, and Chip were packing lunch. My grandmother secretly did a quick Buddhist blessing. Ali went to the bottom of the well and fetched the morning-fresh water before the needy villagers emptied the well. As if we were running our restaurant back at home, everyone was busy getting ready to work in the field; however, the air was empty and the emotion was uncertain.

My father, my grandmother, and Hok's mother stayed home. My mother joined other women in her age group to work at the village's central warehouse.

Angkar did not allow Ali to join me and my older siblings, stating she was too young. Not knowing her fortune, Ali was upset and disappointed. At the end of that hard working day, my sisters and I reflected on how lucky Ali was. Instead of experiencing her first harsh labor as we had, she had gotten to play with other children and make new acquaintances.

In the massive crowd, the march to the workplace was annoyingly long. The two-hour walk diminished my adventurous enthusiasm. My lunch bag and the machete became increasingly burdensome.

At the beginning, I was looking forward to clearing the field as a chance to do something interesting and new. However, every step forward and every look in an adult's face made me nervous. The weight of my lunch sack and the machete became noticeable after about an hour of walking on the unmowed field. I had to pick up my feet high to avoid tripping on tall grass, weeds, and little shrubs.

What little boyish fantasy and adventurous enthusiasm left in me were completely gone when I saw the Khmer Rouge guardsmen at the worksite. They dressed in black cotton clothes, black caps, and truck-tire sandals. Their attire was accented by red-checkered scarves around their necks or over their caps. Armed with AK-47 rifles, the guards were unmistakably poised, authoritative, intimidating, and cold. My enthusiasm turned into fear.

My cursory look over at Chip's face told me to keep a low profile. As a former member of the military police, Chip was a man of confidence and assertion. His compliance reminded me of his recent escape from execution and that these armed men were not the expected patriots.

All day, we worked to make the virgin land into a massive rice farm. There were many people chopping, weeding, hauling, and burning to clear the land. The line of workers was thick and as far as the eye could see. I had never seen such a massive number of people simultaneously in one place. My father's accounts of China's Maoist labor camps, which previously meant nothing to me, vividly came to my memory.

At high noon, a rapid round of gunshots was fired into the air. Growing up in the war, the sound of gunshots was not foreign to me; yet, this round was different. It was apprehensively close and personal. I felt an ephemeral sensation of being shot in the back. I shuddered and had an urge to urinate. My knees were weak and my stomach clenched. Chip signaled me to keep cool. Once I collected myself, I learned the gunshots were to let the workers know it was time for their lunch break.

Hok, Chip, Sim, Phorn, Pech, Peak, and I formed a circle in the shade of a gigantic tree to eat our lunches. Halfway through lunch, an uncontrollable gush of emotion took me by surprise. The gunshots had triggered something.

I felt sad for my family. I felt guilty for not being sympathetic to my family's concerns and anxiety. I felt guilty for all the wrong I had done throughout my life. I felt bad that I did not listen to my parents as much as I should. I was upset about having to give up everything I had, including my pets and friends. I was scared and anxious. A mountain had descended upon me, and there were blisters in the palm of my right hand from using the machete. Guilt and trepidation engulfed me. I burst into sobs, but Hok abruptly put a stop to it by threatening to beat the daylight out of me when we got home. The rest of the lunchtime was sadly quiet and uneventful.

The day worsened as exhaustion, thirst, hunger, and muscle ache increased. I thought the end of the day would never come, but it did. Another round of gunshots kindly signified the end of the day. Ironically, it marked the beginning of my journey through hell.

Angkar mandated daily communal meetings. The regular meetings took place in the evening after dinner and before bedtime curfew. They were designed to indoctrinate, intimidate, and control the people. The indoctrination part of the meeting targeted the party loyalists, children, and impressionable people. The intimidation was aimed at anyone who might be resisting the agrarian utopia. The control aspect of the meeting was to clearly communicate an ultimatum to everyone in case the indoctrination or intimidation failed.

With a seventh-grade education, I did not grasp the purpose of these meetings until a couple of years later, when I got to a breaking point; at that point, I gave up my will to live. I knew I was capable of suicide. I knew I was capable of taking down a Khmer Rouge leader in exchange for my life. What stopped me from committing suicide was Angkar's absolute control over my life and beyond. To prohibit suicides, Angkar had decreed that family members of a person who committed suicide would be punished by public torture or heinous execution. No member of my family was capable of being responsible for causing the suffering of another. I was no exception; hence, like millions of other Cambodians, I was totally controlled.

After the often monotonous communal meetings, the crowd was usually broken up into conferences by age group and gender. The children's meetings were co-ed. I belonged in the children's co-ed conference. The purpose of the conference under the open night sky was to get us children fully indoctrinated into the new order. We were empowered to adopt new forms of dialectic tone and culture. We were told that we were the future of the new Cambodia, unblemished by the past national corruptions and undaunted by the worldwide proliferation of capitalism. We were told that the tables had turned and we the children were now in power. We were empowered to help Angkar get rid of Cambodia's past imperfections. One example repeatedly given to us was if we knew that our parents had committed wrongs, such as lying about their past social status or stealing from the commonwealth, then we must proudly and patriotically report them to Angkar. Under a dark sky, in a quiet rice field, each of us was mandated a turn to stand up in front of the other children and practice a speech. The speeches were mainly about patriotism and admonishment. Often in practicing our speeches, we pretended to reprimand our parents for committing offenses against Angkar. We were told that we must teach our parents about personal sacrifices for the common good. In retrospect, I realize this was the worst kind of brainwashing I had ever experienced.

My parents had taught me to respect my elders; my disrespect would certainly guarantee me a spanking, followed by a scolding from my parents. Heartbreakingly, now I had to address my parents with the prefix "Mit" (friend or comrade). My terms of endearment such as "Mak" (mom), "Pek" (Cambodian-Chinese word for father), and "Che" (Cambodian-Chinese word for sister) were suddenly and permanently replaced by "Mit Meh" (comrade mother), "Mit Pok" (comrade father), and "Mit Bong" (gender-neutral comrade older person).

Although I was impressed by the revolutionary idea, I had trouble carrying out the indoctrination against my Buddhist upbringing and my family's teachings. I was troubled by the Khmer Rouge's decree to start treating my parents as my equals.

Late one night, after everyone was asleep, I woke up to find my mother staring blankly at the stars with a lit cigarette between her fingers. Unsure of myself, I timidly approached her. Without uttering a word, she folded me into her arms, held me tight, lifted up the cigarette to her lips, and puffed smoke into the lonely and unpromising air. I felt her heart lazily beat against my face. Her breasts were comfortingly soft. Her new country smell momentarily distracted me from what troubled me. I confided to my mother my struggle and guilt about treating her and other elders as my equals; unintentionally, I made my mother cry. She understood. Her heart was broken right next to my cheek. It forced a violent sob out of me. The commotion woke up everyone in the hut. My father warned everyone to remain quiet, because if we were caught expressing emotion, we would be punished. I did my best to control my crying, but my emotion was too strong.

By the time my mother finished her cigarette, everyone was once again peacefully asleep. My mother assured me that it was okay for me to address her as Mit Meh, my father as Mit Pok, my older siblings and my brothers-in-law as Mit Bong, and my grandmother as Mit Yeay (comrade grandmother). A block of guilt was lifted off my chest. That night, I fell asleep next to my mother's broken heart.

For some months at the beginning, Angkar allowed families to stay together under one roof. Every morning, my family went in separate ways according to gender and age group. We worked and ate lunch separately with our respective age and gender groups. Angkar enrolled Ali and me along with other children in the newly formed school. There was no physical structure to house the school, which was composed of three classes. Each class took place outside in the open field. The children sat on the ground, and the teacher stood in front of the children and taught the Cambodian alphabet. The teaching was unstructured. No pencils or papers were given to the students.

The children simply sat, listened to the teacher, and mechanically repeated the alphabet after the teacher.

Having achieved a seventh-grade level of schooling, I was not that educated; however, parroting the consonants and vowels day after day got the better of me. I tried hard to be good (dumb) and to fit in at the kindergarten-like school, but there was only so much I could take. My humility began to fade. I became bolder, louder, and more articulate. I showed signs of leadership over other children in my class. My boredom drove me to challenge the teacher and to ask tough questions — I tested authority and asked for trouble.

In the evening, all family members returned to the family hut. Sometime before dinner, my mother and grandmother dropped by the village's central warehouse to pick up our ration of food for the day. By this time, a ration consisted of approximately one cup of raw white rice, one-quarter teaspoon of salt, and a few bites of dried mud fish per person. My mother had to be creative with what was rationed to us. Angkar allowed us to grow and pick a limited amount of our own vegetables around our hut. My sisters and brothers-in-law picked and sneaked in wild vegetables on their way from work to help make up for the food shortage. Often, they secretly brought home snakes, rats, fish, bats, snails, crabs, and wild birds.

Family dinner became less and less pleasant, as everyone was tired and cranky. We fought over a bite of food. On the occasions when I caught and brought home a rat, I expected to have a bite more than everyone else in the family. Sometimes, my mother was sensitive to my selfish expectation and yielded to my needs. That caused a stir in the family. One day, my brother-in-law Chip secretly shared a snake with his wife and baby. When the family found out, everyone gave him the cold shoulder. Greed among the family members became more and more obvious.

As food became scarce, my married sisters put priority on taking care of their families over taking care of my family. One thing for sure, they shared their food with my parents. Sometimes they handed food to my parents blatantly in front of other family members and other times clandestinely. Like a nursing mother bat, my mother often woke me and Ali up in the middle of the night and secretly fed us the extra food given to her by my other sisters. My mother would have starved herself before she would have let me and my little sister starve.

Besides arguing over who ate more food, very little conversation took place during and after dinner. On a couple of occasions, Ali told my mother that I had a big mouth in class. Ali worried for my safety. My mother warned me time and time again to tone myself down. Unfortunately, my boredom got the better of me, and I increasingly became bolder, more animated, and more outspoken.

No electricity. No clock. No calendar. No technology of any type. No material possessions. No one cared about time and space any longer. Life became routinely laborious. Freedom slowly became a myth. Holding on to the *songkum chas* (old world) was a capital crime.

FUTURE LEADERS OF CAMBODIA

Life in the kindergarten was routine and went on for quite some time. Then one day, the children were told to leave their families and enroll in an exclusive academy in preparation for becoming the future leaders of the new Cambodia. It was a clear confirmation that I was no longer my parents' son. In fact, I had been told a long time ago that I was Angkar's child and a fellow comrade of my parents.

My sister Ali and I were excited by the opportunity to become the future leaders of Cambodia. Unlike other walks home from school, this particular walk was chatty between my sister and me. We cooked up all kinds of scenarios. We believed that Angkar was going to train us in its military leadership school. I thought to myself that defying my mother's warning about being conspicuous had finally paid off. In my childishly big head, I thought to myself that it was I who had brought this opportunity to the children. It was I who had made us noticeable. It was my leadership that had made our group special. It didn't matter to me that it was made up by me in my own head. Good news was good news.

When Ali and I delivered the exciting news to our parents, they were sad and happy at the same time. They were sad to face the strong possibility that they might never see their youngest two children again, but they were happy that we had an opportunity for a better future. My mother managed to get Angkar to give us enough material to make two cotton backpacks for Ali and me. We did not have clothes or anything else to pack, but the backpacks made us feel proud, special, and official.

It was the first time in my life that I faced the real possibility of never seeing my family again. Nonetheless, the adventure was exciting. My sister and I were anxious during the few days that we had to wait. Likewise, the other children had trouble concentrating at school. During our work hours on the farm, we all talked about the adventure. In a few days, we would leave our families behind. We would become the future of Cambodia. We would be educated in the new order. We would lead Cambodia against all enemies, especially the paper tiger, the United States. I imagined myself in the Khmer Rouge military black uniform and armed with an AK-47 rifle. It was excitingly cool.

The time came. Ali and I joined the rest of the children in rows and columns. There were just children and a few commanding Khmer Rouge officers escorted by their armed guards. The families were not allowed to be at the gathering, as they had already said goodbye to the children over the past few days. Like the other children, I was nervous. I was not sure whether or not this was a trick. I remembered the time when my brother-in-law Chip was ordered onto a bus with his MP buddies to be executed — Chip and his buddies were told by the Khmer Rouge that they were to greet the king and then join the Khmer Rouge to reform the corrupted Cambodia. Here I was, in a similar situation and unsure of what was ahead of me.

I do not remember exactly how many children lined up that day. I think there were at least a hundred. Each of us was given about a cup of rice and a small piece of dried fish to eat on the way. We marched from morning until very late afternoon before we reached the highway. We stayed in a village by the highway. The village was very much like Phoum Tavei. There were big houses built high off the ground on stilts. Each house was surrounded by fruit trees. I clearly remember the mangoes were ripe, and we were allowed to pick as many as we wanted. Like everyone else, the owners of those houses were evacuated deep into the remote areas away from the highway.

No updates, no news, and no supervision. When we arrived at the village, the armed guards simply told us to find a place to sleep and wait for further instruction. We were told that the next instruction could come the next day or next week. No further order or guidance was given. The armed guards disappeared, and the children were left alone. Like the other children, Ali and I were not sure whether or not we were free to explore beyond the perimeter of where we were told to stay.

No adults. No armed guards. No instruction. And the sun was setting.

As evening approached, the anxiety grew. Smaller children started to cry for their families. I gathered other boys to help find food. We killed chickens and ducks that had been left behind by their owners. The girls picked wild vegetables and made food to share. We ate very well relative to our usual rationed meal back in our village. We picked mango, coconut, papaya, banana, and other fruit for dessert.

At bedtime, the older children comforted their respective younger siblings. Ali and I lay down on a hard wooden floor next to each other. Exhausted, I fell asleep and slept all night.

The morning came peacefully, with the happy sounds of roosters, hens, ducks, sparrows, and pigs. Some children were still asleep, some were playing outside, and others were exploring the vicinity. Ali was still asleep. It had been a long time since I had taken as serious a look at Ali as I did that morning. She was noticeably thinner. Her hair was dirty and tangled. I gently woke her up; she woke up with a smile. Her smile was dry, with a touch of sadness. It was not her usual smile, and I pitied her. I reached over and tried to hold her in my arms. She sternly pushed me off, and she reminded me that Angkar banned such affection. Her wisdom choked me up inside. I rubbed my knuckles gently on her head to tease her and divert my sadness. We both got up and went downstairs to join the other children.

Unsupervised, each child was left on his or her own. Ali and I teamed up. I climbed a mango tree and shook down the mangoes. Ali collected the mangoes and put them in our backpacks. We picked other fruit. That day, we filled our backpacks with mangoes, papayas, and bananas. We found rice in the storage unit to make lunch and dinner. We ate chicken. We tried to keep ourselves busy that day by climbing trees, going from house to house looking for useful items, picking fruits, and eating coconuts. The day was long, and nostalgia for my family came and went throughout the day. So did my uncertainty and anxiety.

Another night came and went much the same way as the previous night, but the anxiety among the children was keener. Having slept well the previous night and without the exhaustion from the long trip, I had trouble falling asleep. The village would have been absolutely quiet if it had not been for the loud crickets, wing-flapping bats, and owls. The night was dark and spooky. Some children were snoring very loudly, which made the night even spookier. I was frightened. I tossed and turned. I could not get comfortable. I was cold, then hot, then cold, then hot, then cold, then hot, then ... I finally fell asleep.

I slept hard and woke up only when a whistle was blown at about midmorning. The loud whistle put my heart into a rhythmic shaking. It took me a few moments before I could regain my orientation. I got up, descended the long staircase, and found the children and Ali lined up. Facing the children stood a serious, middle-aged man. I could tell that the man was a very high official because he did not carry a weapon, not even a handgun. He was guarded by a handful of boy soldiers armed with AK-47 rifles. As I joined my sister in the line, other boys and girls came downstairs. Within five minutes of the first whistle being blown, one of the armed boys blew another whistle. All the children were accounted for. The air was unsettled. The man's face lacked emotion, and the boy soldiers were intimidating. My knees shook just a bit, as I was not sure what would come next.

The man simply told us that the academy was no longer available to us. No explanation was given. He ordered us to return to our families immediately. Then we were left alone. No guards, no guidance, and no instruction. As soon as the man and his armed guards disappeared, we went into the house, gathered our backpacks, and headed back to Phoum Chai Chhke. Incredibly, we managed to find our way home without the guides. I felt deeply disappointed by the letdown and loss of hope for a better future. Yet, I was happy that my backpack and Ali's were filled with consolation prizes—mangoes, papayas, and bananas. When we got home, I could not tell whether my parents were happy or disappointed to see us. One thing for sure, everyone appreciated what we brought in our backpacks.

PROMOTION TO ADULTHOOD

Within days of our return, I was told by Angkar that I was too old to be in school. Angkar placed me in the adult workforce. When the order arrived, the first thing that came to my mind was the welfare of my little sister. I wondered if she would manage as well without my presence. I was not as concerned about the difficult path ahead of me as I was about the welfare of my sister. In reality, Ali and the rest of the children had it better than I, as Angkar considered them the future of Cambodia. The adults were used, as slave labor, to develop the nation's infrastructure. The children were the future. In retrospect, I believe I knew what was dealt to me, or rather what was taken away from me, that day. My last hope for any decent future abruptly disappeared. Perhaps it was too much for me to bear as a boy. Perhaps it was easier for me to worry about my sister than about myself. I knew what the adults had to endure in the fields. I knew what I was about to be thrown into.

I know that my mother's heart was indescribably broken when I told her the bad news. "Mit meh min deung jea jouy mit kone yang mej ban te" ("Comrade mother doesn't know how to save comrade son"), my mother said with her face slightly turned away from me to avoid the usual direct eye contact. Her facial twitching, welled-up tears, quivering lips that encased the protruding tip of her tongue, and her lack of eye contact said it all about the condition of her broken heart. My mother would have died for me if she could have.

My father showed no emotion. I suppose nothing came as a surprise to him as far as life under communism was concerned. Knowing that my mother and I were locked in an emotional impasse, my father called out to me, "Ah pong kdor ehng mou onkuy jit pek mou" ("Little testicle [endearing term for a son], you come and sit by me right now"). I was relieved from my mother's maternal sadness. As I sat down next to my father, I saw my mother exit the hut and leave my father and me undisturbed.

As far as I remember, my father talked a lot. For someone with no more than an eighth-grade education, my father was intelligent, knowledgeable, philosophical, and insightful. My father loved to lecture the family and, in particular, me, as I was the only son and the spitting image of him. My father was a typical Cambodian male who was supposed to be tough. If one did not know him the way I did, one would have missed seeing the latent affection that I received from him throughout my life. Until this moment, I had never seen this degree of affection from my father; he squeezed my hand, smiled wearily, and quietly shed tears. No one in my family had ever seen my father's tears. I was utterly crushed.

My father wiped his tears and regained his composure.

"Dong chea kone Pek ... " my father began his lecture. The rest of the lecture did not matter. I understood the emphasis that I was his son, his only son, the signature of the Ung family. That day, I became a man. More profoundly, I became my father.

While waiting to be sent to an all-male labor camp, I was allowed to live with my family in Phoum Chai Chhke, and I was treated as an adult. I began working in the field with the adults who were allowed to stay in the village—these adults were either parents, grandparents, or physically less able.

Life in Phoum Chai Chhke and in the new order spiraled downward. As days turned into weeks, and weeks turned into months, Angkar forced people to work harder with less food in return. Before the first year was over, scores of people were starved, tortured, or executed.

The Khmer Rouge shut down the school, sent the teachers to the labor camps away from their families, and assigned various tasks to the children—ranging from working in the field with their parents to helping with the family chores. My sister Ali was tasked with fetching the water from the village's common well for my family.

As if the Khmer Rouge weren't brutal enough, Mother Nature was not too kind to the Cambodians, either. In addition to the suffering that was inflicted by the Khmer Rouge, my village (along with other villages in the province of Battambang) was punished by a drought. For months, our only source of water came from the lazy drips at the bottom of the well. Every day, Ali collected roughly three pails of water from the bottom of the well to share among our three close families (my parents', my oldest sister's, and my fourth sister's).

One morning, I was awakened by a hunger pang in my stomach—my previous night's supper had been nothing more than a rationed bowl of rice porridge made solely from a tiny amount of white rice and a disproportionate amount of water. I had awoken well before the whistle, so I had some time to just sit there and gaze. Dazed, tired, and hungry, I found myself scanning my surroundings searching for food or a glimpse of hope…a glimpse of anything. Suddenly, I set my sights on Ali heading out toward the well.

Absentmindedly, I followed Ali to the well. Ali was barely eleven years old but a much brighter and more mature child than I was. Just before she reached the well, I was aware of my emotional agony, my pity, for my sister. I noticed her legs, bare from the knees down—dry, cracked, stained, and barefoot. Her entire body was covered only by an old ragged sarong rolled at the waist, leaving the top of her body naked. From behind, through her exposed dry, rough skin, I could see her vertebrae and the back side of her ribcage. If I hadn't been so weak from hard labor and malnutrition, I could have picked her frail body up with one hand.

Her dirty hair could not have looked more beautiful that morning. With one pail in each hand, she turned and forced a tired, heartbreaking smile my way. Ali and I gave each other short smiles in silence. I wanted to run to her, gather her in my arms, press my face to her bony cheek, stroke her dirty hair, and tell her we would be all right.

I could have counted every rib racked up above her bloated stomach. Her chest seemed as if it belonged to a skinny boy. Despite her malnourished face, her big, round eyes and full lips seemed oddly beautiful.

Whatever sibling rivalry Ali and I had had before, none remained. Our fatigued smiles reaffirmed our love for each other. A shot of pain pierced my heart when she turned and descended to the bottom of the well.

Standing on the rim of the well looking down, I saw Ali crouching at the bottom with six other kids and two older women. The well was at least twenty feet deep and was dry, except for about six inches from the bottom. I could not help but wonder, *What if the well collapsed?*

Sad, hungry, nostalgic, tired, and indifferent, I mindlessly left my sister to her task at the bottom of the well. I walked back to my family's straw hut and awaited the whistle to start another day in the killing fields.

Without a clock or calendar, I lost the sense of time. I cannot remember exactly when Angkar moved people from Phoum Chai Chhke to Phoum Khsouy.

Phoum Khsouy means "weak (fatigue) village." Although the village was naturally richer than Phoum Chai Chhke, the name of the village sounded ominous to city folks like my family. The village was very far away from the highway. The term "fatigue village" came from the fact that it was deep into the uncivilized land near the jungle of Tonle Sap Lake. As the fishermen, trappers, and hunters traveled from the highway to the jungle and back, Phoum Khsouy was a good place to rest and replenish food supplies.

Each family was given a minuscule plot of land sufficient to build a hut and a tiny herb garden. The village was rich with coconut, palm, banana, and other fruit trees. Unlike Phoum Chai Chhke, Phoum Khsouy was a mature and established habitat. The village had plenty of natural food resources, since it was closer to Tonle Sap Lake. Unfortunately, everything belonged to the commonwealth, Angkar. Nonetheless, this was an upgrade from Phoum Chai Chhke, because at least there was something to steal to survive.

At night, my siblings and I would go into the darkness and pick bananas, pineapples, and other fruit. We managed to set traps and fish clandestinely. In those days, if we were caught stealing from the commonwealth, we would be tortured or executed. Yet, excruciating hunger drove us to steal to survive.

As difficult as life was, it was still just the beginning of the even tougher life ahead for my family and me. My sister Pech and her husband, Chip, had been living in paranoia. They both had worked harder than most people to prove to Angkar that they were cooperative and productive. In those days, unproductive workers were unmercifully purged. As the fact that Chip was a member of the republic military police became widely known in the village, my sister's family escaped to another village. As fate refused to let up, Chip ended up being executed.

LABOR CAMP

My older sister Peak and my adopted sister, Phorn, were ordered to leave the family and join the other single women in a women's labor camp. Likewise, now regarded as an adult, I was sent to join the single men and older boys in a men's labor camp.

At the all-male labor camp, I was ordered to follow the strictest basic rules. For example, I was not allowed to communicate with the opposite sex (including my own sisters) unless explicit permission was given by Angkar. The basic rules prohibited stealing, speaking in a foreign language, having sexual or romantic relationships, and speaking against Angkar. Vigilance against "the enemies" was everyone's responsibility; failing to follow such decrees could warrant the death penalty.

It did not matter that I was just a boy and physically smaller than my fellow co-workers; if I expected to be fed the same rationed amount of food, I had to pull the same amount of weight as everyone else. Angkar was biased against the city folks, who had to work harder than the farming class to prove themselves worthy of living. I was no exception. Furthermore, I was not just a city boy; I was also regarded as a "Chen" (Chinaman … a "ching") — a double jeopardy. Farming (especially in the rice paddies infested with leeches) incurred a tough learning curve for me, but I mastered the execution of the farming tasks at least as fast as the folks who were from the farming communities. I paid close attention to ensure that I pulled at least as much load as everyone else, regardless of their age, size, and maturity. By the end of the first year, you could not tell me from the farmers. My skin was dark, stained, dry, and cracked. My hair was dirty. My feet were calloused, with numerous cracks. My legs had multiple scars. My teeth were stained and filled with cavities. My skin bore the marks of mosquito bites, leeches, sun rash, and eczema.

My first night sleeping tightly between two boys kept me up most of the night. The boys were filthy and smelly. One young man sleeping a few bodies over was snoring and passing gas all night. An unpleasant odor circulated among the couple of hundred young men and boys under the same straw roof. I was glad that the straw compound had no walls, but the sound of the coyotes brought me chills, loneliness, and apprehension. Staring out into the dark, I wondered if this nightmare would ever end.

WHEN MY FATHER DIED

It was one of the worst days of my life, but, for the life of me, I cannot recall whether it was a cold day, a rainy day, or a hot day. For that matter, I cannot even recall in what month it was, but I clearly remember receiving the news that my father had passed on. It was sometime in 1976.

Right after lunch, as I began to walk toward one of the straw huts, hoping to get a quick fifteen minutes' rest before the afternoon work started, I noticed a gathering of five or six group leaders. As I walked past the men, I had an uneasy feeling, because they abruptly halted their discussion and turned my way. Their blank stares gave me a chill. I knew without a doubt that they had been talking about me. In a world of "no news is good news," I tasted fear and uncertainty. I felt the horror in my stomach. Images of torture that I had witnessed pervasively occupied my mind. I wondered what I had done wrong.

I went into the hut, lay down, and anxiously anticipated a visitor. I watched a young man approach me from a short distance. With unimaginable apprehension, I prepared myself for horrible news. My justifiable paranoia led me to believe that this man came to escort me to my torture or my brutal execution. With his uncommon clean looks, in his fresh black cotton uniform and a red scarf wrapped over his communist cap, he was extremely intimidating. His AK-47 and his thick platform sandals (custom handcrafted from a tire of an army truck) were the ultimate intimidating façade.

The news was delivered to me simply as a matter of fact — accompanied by no sympathy. I was stunned but glad at the moment that the man was not there to escort me to my torture or execution. My selfish elation didn't last long before the reality set in. My father had died. I had lost my father forever.

My fifteen minutes' rest turned into panic. My world was spinning faster than ever. Images, thoughts, fantasies, confusion, pain, joy, liberation, and fear were packed into a fifteen-minute time span. For the first time, at about age sixteen and as the only son, I had become the "man" of the family — even though my appearance was that of a thirteen-year-old boy.

My ultimate thought went to my dear mother. My father was fifty-nine years old, and my mother was fifty-one years old. Nonetheless, my mother looked like an old lady. The Khmer Rouge regime permitted me to see very little of my mother, but when I did, I saw lots of worry and sadness in her eyes. She was altruistically, helplessly, and endlessly concerned for her elderly mother, her children, and her grandchildren.

I wanted to be with my mother to comfort her. I wanted to be home digging my father's grave—the new "man" of the family should be burying his father and comforting his mother.

The thought of my dear mother transformed me momentarily from a cowardly and fearful boy into a compassionate and courageous young man. I gathered enough courage and headed toward the leaders' compound.

As I entered the straw compound, only the top leader was there. In retrospect, I now understand why he was the only one there. The leaders expected my visit. So the top leader was waiting for me. He alone would be handling my dilemma.

Mok was his name—Mit Bong Mok. He lay on the bamboo floor on his right side propping his head on his right hand and elbow. His cold gaze ambushed me as I entered his quarters. My quick glance into his murderous eyes stripped me of the little courage I had gathered earlier. I encountered silence, coldness, and a complete lack of sympathy in the room. A mix of intimidation and humiliation ran through me from head to toe, and I could look no further than beyond his bent knees.

The bastard remained coldly silent. He spoke no words. He initiated no conversation. My father's death was no problem of his; it was mine.

I eventually gathered enough courage to ask the man for his permission to attend my father's funeral—a primitive burial without any religious connotation.

His cold response still lives within me today. He gave me the simplest and most practical, uncompassionate, and unsympathetic answer possible. I was told that I need not go to the burial because I did not have the magical power to bring my father back to life. Oh, what a psychological torture I was in. I was neither granted nor explicitly denied permission. The bastard simply advised me that it was not productive for me to be at the burial.

Then came, "Besides, your father was buried a few days ago."

What little courage I had for pleading my case was decimated. Completely unbalanced and astonished by the second drop of news, I turned and walked out of the compound like a zombie.

I still cannot accurately describe what went through my mind when I found out that my father had died and had been buried only a few miles away without my knowledge. In fact, I cannot recall what happened between that moment and the next day, besides the fact that I became indifferent to my father's death and returned to the field to resume the rest of my hard labor for the day.

A couple of weeks after my father's death, I was given two days off from the labor camp to visit my mother. It took me nearly the entire morning to travel on foot alone through fields and forest from my labor camp to visit my mother, which made a two-day vacation extremely short.

I had a lot of time to myself walking alone through the forest. I thought about what to say to my mother, how to comfort her and how to show my courage. I thought about running away to places rumored to be less harsh than my world. I fantasized about running into a band of clandestine freedom fighters and joining them to save Cambodia from the Khmer Rouge. I thought about tigers, giant coyotes, pythons, and other harmful animals. I also had scary thoughts about ghosts. My wild imagination and yearning to see my mother made the trip seem like an eternity.

When I saw my mother, my heart sank lower than ever. Her moist eyes, controlled emotion, frail body, and quivering lips said it all. If her frail ribcage had been more fragile, her pounding heart would have exploded and broken her ribs into little pieces. Her ghostly appearance took away my self-pity. If it had not been for her face, I would not have recognized my own dear mother.

I wrapped her frail body tightly in my arms and pressed against her beating heart. The bear hug lasted only seconds before my mother pushed me off, grabbed my hand, and led me into the hut to avoid being seen expressing emotion. The inside of the hut afforded us a little sanctity, but we had to be very quiet, as we could not trust our neighbors to not turn us in. Holding back the sound of my cry, I felt a tremendous pressure on my face and in my ears. My whole head was throbbing, and every muscle and nerve in my face was twitching.

After a short burst of emotion, my mother, my sisters, and I were happy to see one another. We spent the rest of the day joking and catching up. Besides the sadness of losing my father and seeing my mother and sisters in poor health, the afternoon was relatively pleasant. Furthermore, Angkar doubled our family food ration for that day as a token of its pity for our loss.

My family stayed up late into the night. My mother and I stayed up all night whispering to each other. Her undivided and most intimate attention was my rightful privilege as the only son in the family. She knew that I had lost more than any member of the family because I was my father's protégé. My mother tried to control her sobs and kept her cry as quiet as possible when she told me that my father held on to his final breath for his entire last day awaiting me to come and bid him goodbye. I was told that my oldest sister, Sim, talked my father into letting go and being free. I was told that he never gave up waiting for me and repeatedly asked for me. He never gave up. His lips moved even when his pleading was no longer audible. His death cheated him of his last, most precious moment with his only son.

I fell asleep just before sunrise and slept through most of the morning. When I woke up, my mother and sisters had breakfast (if one could call it that) prepared. We ate quietly, as there was nothing else left to say. We had caught up. We callously bid one another goodbye and went our separate ways, but not before my mother whispered to me that my father would now always be with me.

On my way back through open fields and spooky forests, I realized I hadn't visited my father's grave, nor had I asked where he was buried. I speculated that perhaps it was not important. Perhaps it was irrelevant. Perhaps I was afraid that the knowledge would have given me a closure that I could not accept. Perhaps my ignorance kept the death of my father less real to me. Not knowing his whereabouts, on top of my mother's whispered assurance that my father would always be with me, was my comfort. I was ready to face the world. In the quiet forest that day, I did not feel alone or afraid. I spoke to my father all the way back to my labor camp. I told him I loved him. I told him he would be proud of me. I told him my regrets for getting into trouble before. I made peace with him, and I took him into my soul as my angel.

My father, my angel, has been watching over me ever since that day.

TWO DEATHS IN ONE DAY

Some months passed since the day when my father left this world and became my angel. I spoke to my father daily. I asked him to watch over me, my siblings, my grandmother, and my mother. I ran into my sisters from time to time on big farming projects, but often there was no news, especially not from my mother. In those days, no news was good news.

How the news about my youngest sister, Ali, and my nephew Chenda reached me is a blur in my memory. I was casually informed by Angkar in the middle of my work in a rice paddy. Nothing to it; it really was a simple message. A few days before, my nephew had died in the morning, and my youngest sister had died in the afternoon. Simply a matter of fact: My mother was alive; my grandmother was alive; everyone else in the family was alive; and there was no need for me to take time off to visit my family. Oh, no need to worry; all my sisters had also been informed. Obviously, Angkar had kindly taken care of all my problems. Angkar went out of its way to make sure I was taken care of and empowered to remain productive. In short, I was not allowed to visit my family.

Sadly enough, I was too callous to care. I was briefly concerned about my mother's state of grief for her loss, but that was about it. It was simply the way of life, and I had to accept it. Every man was for himself. It was my Cambodian heritage at its worst.

Life went on. Crops were produced and harvested but not consumed by the workers. Where the crops went was not my business (nor anyone else's) but Angkar's. Staying productive (by working thirteen hours a day, seven days a week, and 365 days a year) was my business. Ultimately, getting to eat a small bowl of rice porridge (mostly water) at lunch and dinner was my only business. It was the ultimate Orwellian animal farm.

MY ANGEL WATCHED OVER ME

After months of inhumane labor, my unit of men and older boys was reassigned to clear part of a jungle for farming. The jungle was located on the other side of Phoum Khsouy, where my mother was living and working. There were rumors and hope that we might be allowed to visit our families for a day or so on the way to our new assignment. Unfortunately, that was not what Angkar had in mind. All along, Angkar had no intention of allowing us to see our families.

We started to break camp just before sunrise. We were ready to travel by midmorning. We traveled on foot all day and part of the night. It was well after sundown when we reached the main clay road leading into Phoum Khsouy. Within less than an hour, we could have entered the village and reunited with our families. Only then did Angkar inform us that we were not to stop and visit the families. We were to march right through the village in the dark to the assigned labor camp. It would take us all night on foot in the dark to get to the next stop before reaching the jungle.

Disappointed, sad, and hopeless, I whispered to my father, my angel, "Pek, som Pek choy kone phong ..." ("Father, please help son ..."). I asked him to change Angkar's mind to let me visit with my mother a little bit. I told him I was aching to see my mother.

Miraculously, right after pleading to my father, I stepped on a snake. The snake bit the sole of my bare right foot. I screamed in pain. The unit stopped marching, and people gathered around me. A unit leader flicked his cigarette lighter and shined it about my foot. My foot was bleeding and instantly swollen. I was fortunate, because the poison was not the lethal type.

A man was ordered to give me a piggy-back ride to the village. Everyone else was ordered to continue marching through the village in the dark.

My excruciating pain was alleviated by the distraction of my rough ride on the man's back. The night was dark. I was scared, not knowing whether the poison was lethal or not. The ride was rough and long, but I finally was dropped off at the village's primitive hospital. The man left, and I was given a bed and a bowl of warm porridge. The bed and the porridge made everything okay. I was in high heaven. I couldn't have cared less whether I would receive any medical attention, which I did not. My medical attention amounted to an assigned nurse who did nothing more than wash off my wound and wrap it with a strip of cotton cloth; however, the nurse was nice, sincere, and very helpful. She knew my mother, and sent someone to fetch my mother in the middle of the night. The nurse also made an immediate request for my mother to have a few days off from work to care for me.

While waiting for my mother to arrive, the nurse rubbed my back to comfort me. I felt safe and comfortable in the care of a woman who was nearly twice my senior. Unlike women in the field, the nurse was in clean black communist clothing and smelled pleasant. I could tell that she was one of the Khmer Rouge people—not one promoted from the working class. My pain eased. I was distracted, and I really enjoyed the company of the nurse. Safe, mesmerized, and tired, I drifted into a deep sleep.

The pain from my wound woke me up in the middle of the night. In the nurse's place, I found my mother watching me. Strangely enough, I momentarily felt disappointed by the absence of my nurse.

I was very happy to see my mother. I forgot all about the pain and the nurse. My mother undid the cotton cloth bandage and inspected my wound. She managed a smile on her skinny face and told me not to worry. Since mother knew best, I felt completely safe. I went on to tell her about how I had ended up there.

After listening to my story, my mother grinned and reminded me what she had said to me after my father's death. "I told you that your father will always be with you," she recalled. Until then, the presence of my father had been no more than a phantom in my head. It was an epiphany that has continued throughout in my life.

VISITING MY MOTHER

I had not seen my mother for months. In those days, a month seemed like a lifetime since so much could happen. People in the village were dying from disease, starvation, and execution. In contrast to the beautiful nurse, my mother was very skinny. Malnutrition made her hands and legs bloated and her skin cadaverously yellow under the moderate light of a fish-oil lantern. Excess skin made her face sag and her eyes appear lazy and lifeless, but her smile carried the signature of a mother's unconditional love for her son. If I had not been able to penetrate deeper than her tattered skin, I would have mistakenly believed that my mother was at the top of the world and very happy. Despite the horrible world she lived in, her smile was relentless. There were moments when I noticed her smile was forced. Along with her constant smile, her eyes were continually moist with tears. Her radiant smile would have led one to think her tears were happy tears, but her sadness was given away by her nasal voice.

My mother's tattered appearance could not be called pitiful. To this day, I have yet to meet a woman of equal strength, honesty, and integrity. In a world where one would do anything to survive, my mother preferred death over a compromised principle. She would not steal. She would not betray a friend. She would not give up her Buddhism. She would not degrade herself by eating animals such as rats. Behind her relentless smile, lazy eyes, and saggy face, I knew my mother would have given her life for any of her children.

I appreciated the comfort of my beautiful nurse, but such comfort did not measure up to the comfort of my mother. I was, for a time, in a different world—a utopia of my own. Totally forgetting about the pain, my heart ached with joy when I felt my mother's ribcage against my back. Her arms were weak, but she held me tightly as she lay alongside me in a tiny bamboo bed. I told her about my life in the labor camp. She listened quietly, but I knew she silently sobbed. Whenever I drifted off into sleep, she would ask a leading question to learn more about my life in her absence. I felt her sympathetic pain for me, but not once had she admitted her sorrow for me. In place of pity, she showed me love. She softly brushed the back of my head with her face, inhaled the smell of my dirty hair, and whispered that she was proud of me. She continually reminded me that I was a carbon copy of my father—a man of pride, strength, and dignity. I do not know if my mother slept that night, but I finally fell asleep and woke up late in the morning.

When I woke up, my mother and my nurse were visiting with each other as if they were close friends. My mother and the nurse knew each other, but they were not buddies. My mother was in the working class, and the nurse was part of the elite communist party; however, the nurse liked and respected my mother.

As if both women had been waiting for me to wake up, they turned their attention to me. I felt as if I were in a different world. I was, for the time being, in a world in which I mattered. The way that the nurse showed respect for my mother's older age contradicted the reality of the horrible world I endured. It felt surreal, as if time had reverted to the good old days, *songkum chas*.

The nurse got up, picked up a breakfast tray, and brought it over to me. Having had a ration of nearly nothing for months, this was incredibly surreal. I recall what I ate that morning: I had a bowl of thick rice porridge, one dried sausage, and a side of dried pickled radish.

I looked my mother's way. Before I could ask my mother to share some of my breakfast, the nurse happily told me that she had already fed my mother. I was too young to take an interest in the opposite gender, but that morning, the nurse's kindness melted my heart. Her smile, her eyes, her smell, and everything about her made me feel self-conscious. I was embarrassed by my destitute, boyish appearance and feelings of inferiority. The nurse and my mother went on with their chit-chat while I quietly ate with my head down for the entire mealtime.

As much as I appreciated the company of the beautiful nurse, I was happy to see her leave. I was uncomfortable and embarrassed in her presence. "Wasn't she nice?" commented my mother with a wickedly playful smile as the nurse disappeared. I could not muster a response.

Within a week, I was discharged from the hospital. Thanks to the kindness and influence of the nurse, I was given a couple of weeks at home with my mother before rejoining my unit at the new labor camp. The day I was discharged, the nurse talked with my mother but never spoke to me. During her conversation with my mother, she glanced my way a couple of times, but never showed any sign that she noticed me. I was hoping she would come over to say goodbye, so I would have a chance to thank her for her kindness. I could have walked over to thank her, but for some reason, I cowered. I never thanked her for all she had done for my mother and me.

My mother and my oldest sister, Sim, shared a hut as one unit of the household. The household was made up of the family's surviving members: my grandmother, my mother, Sim, Phorn, Peak, and me. Phorn and Peak had been separated from the family and were working and living in a women's labor camp. Pech's family had escaped to another village.

I could hardly recognize my grandmother. She was more emaciated than my mother. Her speech was not as audible as I remembered. Her physical and mental capacity had diminished. Like my mother, she would not steal or compromise her diet to eat food such as rat meat. It was obvious that the communist utopia had taken its toll on my grandmother.

In the midst of the starvation, family separation, and death, it was extraordinary to witness my grandmother's immutable faith in Buddhism. My life in the labor camp was mechanical, focused, and apathetic—surviving was first on my mind in the morning and last in the evening. This night was very different. I was puzzled by my grandmother's determination and commitment to her faith. It was beyond my boyish comprehension that there could be anything other than surviving. I could not imagine holding on to principle, dignity, pride, and religion in a time like this; yet, my mother and grandmother did it.

My grandmother silently uttered the Buddhist chant. As a former student of a head Buddhist monk, I understood the silent words from her lips. I knew what she uttered. I felt a strength belied by her physical appearance. I felt peace emit from her body. Yet, I was privately annoyed and disrespectful of my grandmother's clandestine religious practice. What god would be worthy of a prayer if people were dying helplessly? As a boy who suffered as a man, inwardly I mocked my grandmother's unpractical practice of her faith. In my own thoughts, I resented her for putting me at risk by her practice. Nonetheless, I loved my grandmother, and her annoying prayers brought me a much-needed nostalgia and dream of normalcy.

My mother put me next to my grandmother that night. I had slept next to her often in the past, but I had trouble adapting to her new strange, fusty smell. There was a moment or two when I noticed her physical condition and recognized that her final days were coming. As I always had in the past, I childishly caressed my grandmother's breasts. Her breasts were saggy and deflated. There was little familiarity left to my hand. In place of fondness, I pitied my grandmother. Conscientiously, I moved my hand away and placed it on her back while she remained facing me. My fingers explored her back; I felt her ribcage and vertebrae.

My grandmother's shaved head looked like a ghostly skull illuminated under the temperate rays of the moonlight that penetrated the holes of the hut. That night, I felt eerie, sad, and loving all at the same time. I cried myself to sleep in silence.

My mother woke me up to eat lunch. She told me that the nurse had stopped by while I was asleep and brought us a dried fish, a tablespoon of salt, and a couple of coconuts. It had been ages since I had eaten a coconut, even though coconut trees were ubiquitous in Cambodia. A taste of salt was heavenly. I had the lunch of a lifetime. I could not believe my fortune. Perhaps I had my father to thank for it.

I lost track of how long I was allowed to stay with my mother. It was not months, but it was weeks. I was allowed to work with my mother at the central warehouse during my recovery from the snake bite.

BURYING MY GRANDMOTHER

During my short visit, I saw the health of my mother and, especially, of my grandmother worsen. As my snake bite got better, my grandmother got sicker. Her clandestine nightly prayers became more audible as her health deteriorated. Her speech became utter nonsense, and she uttered strange words. No one was laughing; everyone knew the significance of her strange behavior. Having lost enough people in my family and having witnessed daily death in the village, I accepted the reality that my grandmother was dying. I felt guilty for not having the same degree of sadness for her as I did for my father. It could have been because she was old and ready to die. It could have been because I had time with her during her final days. Perhaps deep down I knew her Buddha had been listening to her prayers, or perhaps I simply became callous to death and loss.

In place of sadness at my grandmother's last breath, I felt my maturity and internal strength. Never mind that I was just a boy; in my father's absence, I was my father. I was the pillar of the family. I took charge of my grandmother's burial. I was the shoulder that my mother cried on. I was the man who notified Angkar of my grandmother's death. I was the man of my remaining household.

Finding someone to help me bury my grandmother was not easy. I had asked at least five men living nearby. Only one man had enough strength to help. The man was a family friend from the old days; he was my father's age and was not well. Hard labor and starvation had taken a toll on him like it had on everyone else in the village. Furthermore, as a former prison guard, he was a dead man walking.

The man and I cut down a four-inch-diameter bamboo stalk. We harvested reeds and made them into a sling. We wrapped my grandmother's body in her tattered blanket. My mother kept a few of my grandmother's clothes for her own use; I wrapped the rest of the clothes with my grandmother's body. I also placed my grandmother's ivory Buddha statue on her chest. The wrapping was clumsy, but we properly folded my grandmother's arms and clasped her hands into a praying position—a Buddhist tradition.

My mother cried, but I was too busy playing man of the house to have any sorrow over my grandmother's death. I worried about whether Angkar would find out that my mother was emotional. I worried about whether Angkar would think that we were prolonging the burial. I worried about whether the man would change his mind about helping to bury my grandmother.

By midafternoon, the man and I had wrapped my grandmother and placed her in the sling. We slid the bamboo stalk through both ends of the sling and hoisted it with our shoulders. Being much shorter than the former prison guard, I felt more of the weight slant toward me; as I marched in the front, my grandmother's body barely cleared the ground.

As funerals were not allowed, only the man and I went to the gravesite. There was no formal cemetery; basically, we just had to find a spot in the field outside of the village and dig a grave. To get there, we had to cross a shallow stream. As short as I was, we were unable to keep my grandmother's body above the water. The load got heavier, and I had difficulty dislodging my feet from the deep mud at the bottom of the stream. I was grateful that the man had volunteered to carry the shovel.

I was relieved to step out of the water. The load briefly became slightly lighter, as some of its weight was transferred to the middle when the ground gave me the necessary elevation to match the height of the man still walking in the stream.

We arrived at a small mound situated at an intersection of four rice paddies. Such a mound was the only part of the land (besides dikes, villages, and roads) that remained above the flood during the farming season.

While the former prison guard rested, as if he were a very old man, I dug my grandmother's grave. I was aware that there were existing graves on the mound, and I was careful not to dig up an existing grave. There were at least five or six existing graves on the mound.

After a short rest, the man left me alone to finish my task. He was not insensitive; he was just being practical. His service was no longer necessary, and he needed to return home to rest. It was common in those days that someone in his poor health condition would die and be buried only days after having helped to bury a body.

I was alone on a quiet prairie digging my grandmother's grave. I was aware of my uneasy feeling; I was afraid of ghosts. I deliberately kept my back toward the open field and my front facing the village. Occasionally, I looked up to reassure myself that I was just outside the village. The breeze was much too peaceful for my comfort. The chirping sound of the birds was a distraction and a reminder that I was alone.

Physically, I was busy digging, but mentally I was not focused. I was afraid of my grandmother's body and feeling guilty for being afraid. I could not help but feel disrespectful for being afraid. I was tired and wanted to quit digging, but fear kept me going.

Time could not have passed any slower. An image of my grandmother in her white Buddhist nun outfit meditating in the middle of a dim and quiet room made the vast prairie an eerie place. Knowing that there were other bodies buried in the same mound made me feel utterly alone and horribly frightened.

My grandmother's grave was not deep. I had just enough strength left to dig a grave sufficient to keep her body beneath the earth's surface.

I rolled my grandmother's body into the fresh and shallow grave. A mix of trepidation and love bore an insurmountable guilt into the very center of my heart. So much for being the man of the house, so much for being my father's son, so much for being my father, so much for being the pillar of my family, so much for being the shoulder on which my mother cried. At that moment, I was a frightened boy who had no courage to look directly into the vast open field behind me.

As I placed dirt on my grandmother's body, fear confined my peripheral vision to within the perimeter of the grave. I was afraid to look directly at my grandmother's wrapped and disappearing body, but I was more afraid to look up. I was acutely aware of my surroundings. I heard every bird, bee, and insect. No thanks to the strong prairie breeze, the rustling sound of the dancing leaves kept my ears tuned and my mind scattered.

When the last scoop of dirt completed my task, I lifted my head, took one quick glance at the eerie field behind me, and ran for the woods. As if I were fully wound up, I dashed through one rice paddy after another. I burst into sobs as I ran. Alone, I cried at the top of my lungs. I cursed. I screamed. I took hard swings at the wind. I kicked the tall grass, bushes, and air. I exploded without knowing whether I was sad, angry, or scared.

No one heard me in my madness. I could not stop crying when I reached the edge of the woods. I could not go into the village crying. I sat down on a fallen tree. Only then did I realize my body was light. My head was hurting. I was empty physically and emotionally. My chest was pounding, but eventually the pounding subsided.

It did not take long before my senses came back. I appreciated the chirping sound from the surrounding birds. I wiped my tears and nose with my bare hands, and smiled in my own ultimate privacy. I was proud of myself. I congratulated myself. For the moment, it did not matter that I had just lost a grandmother whom I had loved more than life itself. What mattered was that I had accomplished an extraordinary task.

At that moment, I was the man of the house, my father's son, my father, and the pillar of my family. I was the worthy shoulder on which my mother cried. Overwhelmed, I cried again. I sobbed a happy cry, gathered my courage, entered the woods, crossed the stream, and returned to my mother.

DEATH OF MY MOTHER

About a week had gone by since I had buried my grandmother. My mother told me that the former prison guard had died, but I did not care, because daily death (outside of my family) had become a way of life. My village, Phoum Khsouy, was part of the Battambang Province's harshest area, which was notoriously known as Dombon Bourn (Section Four). Worse yet, Phoum

Khsouy was the harshest village of all villages in Dombon Bourn. Nonetheless, my life was better here than with my unit at the labor camp. Here, the food ration was twice as much, and work was not as inhumanely laborious. Instead of two tablespoons of rice, I enjoyed four tablespoons of rice per meal. Instead of working harshly thirteen hours a day, I worked between eight and ten hours a day. The actual farming was easier than digging a canal, putting up dikes, constructing a water reservoir, building a dam, or clearing a forest.

My mother's health progressively and rapidly worsened. She cut back on her tobacco smoking because her chest hurt when she coughed. Her droopy face and her lazy eyes defied her young age. I often saw tiny streaks of unemotional tears flowing from the corners of her lethargic eyes. I was aware of her effort to keep her mouth shut, and despite dry, cracked lips, she still forced a smile for me.

My fatigued mother never failed to mother me. Losing herself to starvation and poor health did not stop her from taking care of me. At night, she stayed up until I fell asleep. Her calloused palm, stroking my back at night, comforted me and annoyed me at the same time.

In my younger days, I had played with my mother's breasts while she put me to sleep. This night, I fondly caressed my mother's hip. It was more a bone than a hip. I was sadly fascinated by her protruding skeletal hip bone. I kneaded it; I traced the curvature of the bone. I ran my hand along her leg to feel the measure of her knee, leg, and hip bone. My mother was emaciated. Her skin was saggy. Indifferent, like a baby, I played with my mother's saggy skin. I twirled it. I stretched it. I gently rubbed it against my mother's bone beneath it. At times, I looked in my mother's face, seeking her reaction to my childish exploration of her body. If she had any reaction, she did not show it. Perhaps the sensation in her skin was diminishing. Deep down, I knew my mother was approaching her last days, but I never acknowledged such a thought.

Even after a few years of starvation, hard labor, and losing precious loved ones, my callous heart still managed to ache over the manifestation of my mother's dying days. I was saddened by my mother's suffering, but in some way I had self-pity, fear, and guilt. My mother was my last anchor, her absence would leave me untethered and permanently orphaned. My thought of being an orphan brought me self-pity, trepidation, and loneliness. I felt guilty for having these selfish feelings while my mother was dying, because I was taught early in life by my family's deep belief in Buddhism to put other people's welfare above mine.

The nurse managed to convince Angkar that my mother needed to be taken to a more advanced hospital. I was allowed to walk behind the oxcart that carried my mother to the hospital. After nearly an all-day trip, we arrived at the hospital.

Angkar had converted Wat (temple) Kompong (dock, pier, or port) Preah (god) into a hospital. It was located next to the highway that stretched between Battambang and Phnom Penh. The hospital was dirty, poorly managed, and morbid. Prior to the Khmer Rouge regime, in addition to providing a place for religious ceremonies and prayers, a temple also served as a cemetery; it was a gate to heaven and hell. In its converted form, Wat Kompong Preah was very much a gate to hell—a purgatory.

I was not allowed to stay with my mother after we arrived at the hospital. Once my mother was securely laid in bed, Angkar ordered me to join a labor camp located not too far away from the hospital. That was the last time I saw my mother.

The news of my mother's death was delivered to me in the same manner as the deaths of my father, youngest sister, and nephew, but this time the news reached me within a couple of hours. Nonetheless, it was delivered as matter-of-factly, and I was told again that there was no need for me to go see my mother's body. I do not know exactly where the body was buried.

WORKING NEAR PEAK

Nothing was sweeter than the sound of a whistle at high noon; the Cambodian sun was scorching hot. Everyone was tired and hungry from digging and moving dirt to build a giant water reservoir. The entire workforce of thousands of people had been up working since three o'clock that morning. Every smoker got a brief break at midmorning to roll and smoke one cigarette. As part of the non-smoking minority, I did not get a break except when I faked my restroom stops.

My team leader had noticed my hard work the last few days and decided I deserved a lighter job for a few days. Today and for the next couple of days, I was assigned to dig and fill dirt containers (*bonkees*) for the others to carry up to the top of the half-finished reservoir. It still was a backbreaking job, especially with an absolutely empty stomach and under the relentless sun. Nonetheless, I was very happy to be a digger rather than a carrier. As a carrier, I would have to walk back and forth, up and down the reservoir wall with a fetcher made of bamboo (*dongrek*) on my shoulders along with two *bonkees* full of moist clay dirt.

It had been a very long morning. I witnessed and endured so much in just one morning. At three o'clock that morning, my 200 teammates and I had been awakened by the morning whistle—the sound I loathed so much. What I hated the most about the morning whistle was not that it started another day of hard work and suffering, but that it mercilessly roused the hunger in my empty stomach. There is no way I can accurately describe what it was like to wake up to an excruciating hunger. As I am getting older, my memory of my horrific experience during the Khmer Rouge regime is fading, but the one thing I will never, ever forget—even on my deathbed—will be my hunger pangs.

About half an hour after that evil, annoying sound of the morning whistle, everyone was at the worksite. Knowing the intensity of the labor that awaited me at the worksite, half an hour was no more than a blink of an eye, yet it was long enough for me to have all kinds of pictures run through my head.

One recurring thought I often had during my march to work was what would happen to my family should I be brave enough to end my life with suicide. I often pictured the Khmer Rouge torturing my older sisters while holding up my dear mother's face to watch the horrific act. I often imagined the Khmer Rouge cutting up, cooking, and feeding pieces of the flesh from my fresh carcass to my mother and sisters before they were tortured and killed one by one. It is hard to believe, but in retrospect, I am grateful for such imagination. I suppose if one lost hope to live, then such imagination could be an ultimate incentive to survive.

Sometimes I replayed in my head the good old days before the Khmer Rouge came to power. Oh, those were the days. My youngest sister, Ali, and I used to get in trouble with our parents for having too much fun at the rivers where we bathed at midday and in the evening. For adults and "good" kids, a bath at the river was a bath at the river. To Ali and me, the river was our playground, castle, moon, ocean, pirate ship, Apollo 11, battlefield, underground kingdom, and so on. In the water, we were the kung fu masters. Our bodies were weightless. We could fly and master the most difficult spin kick, which only a 2,000-year-old kung fu master could do. We were the most magnificent whales swimming in the biggest ocean known to mankind. We landed on the moon centuries before the American astronauts set foot upon it. At the shallow water where the stronger current flowed, we were the dam that held power over the farmers downstream.

No different from any other morning, this morning I thought to be my last on earth. At the rate that people were dying from famine, torture, and execution, such a thought was not uncommon. I am sure I was not the only soul having such a thought.

All things considered, that morning was a relatively good morning. My work was easier; I had a couple of breaks by pretending to have diarrhea. The best part of the morning came when I secretly exchanged a long glance and a sad smile with my older sister Peak as she labored nearby. At our village, opposite sexes weren't allowed to communicate openly with each other in any capacity or circumstance. This ordinance applied to everyone, including a brother and a sister.

These last couple of weeks, labor reinforcement had been needed, since the completion of the reservoir construction was behind schedule. Without additional workers, the rainy season would arrive before the completion of the reservoir, and all the completed work would be lost. My sister's company was one of the reinforcing companies.

Often, male and female companies weren't allowed to work so closely together. Running behind schedule was our blessing since we had not seen each other for over a year. Just as sweet as the sound of the whistle at high noon, my sister's smile made my morning. I know mine made her morning as well. There was so much emotion all rolled into one. I was so happy to see her, yet I felt empty. She was so close, yet I could only yearn for her to fold her arms around me. I was acutely aware of the sympathy in the eyes of her teammates working in her proximity. I remember one of my digging partners' elbow kindly jabbed at my side to warn me of the danger I was bringing to my sister and myself. As if I were watching an old film of Charlie Chaplin—black, soundless, choppy, and quick, with joy and sadness all rolled into one—I noticed one of my sister's teammates patting her back in sympathy.

A long glance was enough for me to appreciate the sight of my sister. I was happy that her company was less harsh than mine, for it provided her better clothing. Unlike my tattered, sun-faded black cotton shirt and pants, her communist-black, long-sleeved cotton shirt seemed relatively new. She was covered by the shirt and the black cotton skirt that draped down to her ankles. Except for her face, her entire head was covered by a communist red cloth (*kroma*) and a sunhat made of palm leaves. In comparison to her calloused heels, her slightly sun-blotched face, with a sad but sincere smile full of love, was beautiful. If one were in my shoes at that specific moment, only then would one understand the ultimate love between two siblings.

When I felt sorrow for my older sister that morning, I felt as if I were the biggest man in the universe. I felt sadly good. Then, when I felt her sorrow for me, I felt a tremendous pain in my heart. All kinds of foolish ideas ran through my head, and murder-suicide was among them. Nonetheless, this was a better-than-usual morning, for I had seen my sister, alive.

A wake-up whistle in the morning was usually followed by a few more whistles, but a whistle at high noon needed no additional whistles. Like everyone else, there was nothing that would get my attention like a midday whistle. This whistle was no exception. After throwing a glance, along with a fatigued smile, at my sister, I put down the picker, wiped the sweat off my forehead, placed my right hand in my back pocket to make sure my spoon was still there, and headed toward food.

At mealtimes, the workers were to sit on the ground in groups of ten. No one washed his hands before eating. Dirty and hungry, I found a group to join. My fellow workers and I were no different from the pigs at feed time. No encouragement was necessary when it came to food. I and nine other workers, a mix of older boys and young men, squatted around a pot of stew.

Usually, food ration in the dry season was better than in winter. No one ever understood why, since we seemed to produce an awful lot of rice, vegetables, fish, and meat — much more than we could consume. We were always told that although we produced more than we needed, the rest of the country was not able to make ends meet; therefore, we had to share. I was not as educated and intelligent as I am now, but I was not a fool, either. I knew the Khmer Rouge was lying, but I was afraid like everyone else to not conform to that theory. In winter, the pot would be filled with rice porridge made up of merely a cup of white rice and a pot of water from the rice paddy.

On this particular day, the stew was made from mostly water, but it contained a couple of fish about the size of my thumb, a bit of salt, a handful of *trokoun* (a type of wild vegetable), and sour tamarind. By today's nutritional standard, the entire pot could not contain enough nutritional value to feed a child.

Everyone had a spoon tightly gripped with anticipation. Each worker knelt on one knee ready to start eating. (If one paid enough attention, one could actually see a few hands in each group twitching as if they were about to commit a false start on eating.) This was my moment. I had the ultimate spoon, and I was fully alert. I was ready. Like the other guys, I planned to get more than my share of the food. The only thing between my stomach and that delicious stew right at that moment was the sound of the starting whistle—or lack thereof.

The whistle was blown, and nearly half of the stew was consumed by the time the sound of the whistle subsided. The eating was done in ten minutes.

Like everyone else, I was grateful for the one-hour lunch break. After finishing the lunch so quickly, we usually had about forty-five minutes before the afternoon work started. Everyone was encouraged to take a nap to recharge for the rest of the day's work; however, few people rested. This was the most precious time of the day, for I could roam freely within half a kilometer of the feeding area—momentary freedom. To this day, I understand that when time is precious I can accomplish a lot.

That particular afternoon, I knew exactly how I wanted to exploit my freedom. With a pick on my shoulder, I headed straight out toward a dike. Over the last few days, I had scoped out a rat hole alongside the dike. The tracks were fresh; the droppings were indicative of a good-sized rat.

I managed to catch a couple of fat rats and clean them up before the sound of the whistle called everyone back to work.

With two rats hanging from the left side of my waist, I continued digging dirt and filling *bonkees*. I would not dare put down my rats unguarded. Having managed to get two rats in one day brought both envy and jealousy upon myself. If allowed, I would be barbarously killed and robbed on account of those two dead rats. I knew this for a fact, because I often felt this way toward someone when I was not able to catch anything and he had managed to catch a bird, a snake, a turtle, a frog, a monkey, a fish, a squirrel, or an eel.

Yes, I was selfish—until I exchanged a glance again with my older sister working nearby. I remember a sense of euphoria. This day was just getting better. Not only was I two rats up on most people today, but I knew my sister was going to be well fed tonight. Without attracting much attention, I covert-

ly tossed one of the rats at my sister's feet. My sister picked it up and quietly
rolled it inside the waist of her skirt. I knew that I had to share my other rat
with a couple of my nearby working comrades to keep this transaction secret.
I didn't care. This was one of the moments defining my becoming the man of
the family. I felt as if my feet were big enough to fill my father's shoes.

BUILDING A DAM

The Khmer Rouge changed me in more ways than one. At some point, I learned
to smoke tobacco so that I would have more breaks from work and a tobacco
ration—courtesy of Angkar to all smokers. Being a smoker made me feel more
integrated into the labor camp, and less like a city boy. The fear of the Khmer
Rouge soldiers, their AK-47 rifles, and their cruelty transformed me from a
city boy who was afraid of snakes, leeches, ghosts, and even darkness into a
person who caught snakes with his bare hands, commanded a pair of water
buffaloes more than a few times my size, cultivated farmlands, and moved
earth to build a huge reservoir. More incredibly, I became part of the human
force that dammed a river.

There were thousands of young men and women among a smaller number of middle-age men and women gathered along the Songke River to be
indoctrinated and given an orientation on why and how we would build a
hydro dam. Chronically hungry and tired, I was apathetic to the reasons for
and logistics with which the dam would be built; nonetheless, I was hoping
the indoctrination and orientation would go on forever. I would rather sit
there with my apathy, hunger pangs, and fatigue than endure slave labor.

My temporary "relief" came to an end as the meeting came to an end. We
picked up our tools and formed teams of four workers. Two people would dig
and fill *bonkees* with dirt; the other two would serve as the fetchers who would
transport dirt to the water. The team would work out a system of rotation so
everyone would have a chance to dig, which was relatively less difficult.

A group of men placed big, heavy logs vertically in the water despite
the modestly strong current. The logs were pounded into the bottom of the

river one log after another, forming a line across the river. They were placed approximately three feet apart.

Another group of men and women brought in smaller tree boughs and placed them horizontally against the logs. The logs and the branches served as the foundation for the temporary dam. We then built up dirt in front of this foundation to construct the temporary dam so that the permanent dam could be built behind it after the water below had completely receded.

Manual digging and transporting dirt intensified on both sides of the river. On the first day, we managed to place all the logs needed across the entire width of the river, which was wider than a football field. Lots of dirt was thrown into the river, but none was seen above the water.

For a couple of weeks, we worked very hard but seemed to accomplish very little relative to the overall completion of this monumental dam. One *bonkee* of dirt after another was dumped into the river by the thousands of workers. Yet, the temporary dam remained in its skeletal form — only outlined by the logs that ominously stood in defiance against the increasingly strong current.

The first day's excitement and morale boost by the indoctrination now faded into mechanical work. Dirt seemed to contribute nothing to the overall effort. The current got stronger as more dirt was dumped into the river. The food ration became more meager. So far, the river had the upper hand, and the workers became more exhausted.

We worked long hours with little food. Fortunately, we were free to bathe in the river during our brief lunch break, after dinner shortly before our evening meeting, and at bedtime. Most people usually headed to the river to catch fish, collect clams, or dig up eels during these breaks. The soldiers knew about these activities at the river, but, for some reason, they turned a blind eye. Perhaps there was a modicum of humanity in them after all. This was good for those like me who were capable of gathering additional food for personal consumption, but not so for the other people. Unfortunately, some people would only eat what was rationed to them. That made them weak and less productive on the field. Consequently, they would be outcast and assigned to less favorable tasks. I empathized with these people because from time to time I, too, was in this predicament due to sickness or fatigue.

A long time had passed; I don't even know what year it was when I worked on the dam project. However, I remember the excitement when we completely dammed up the Songke River. Once a city boy, I was now a part of the force that stopped the river from flowing. I felt an amazing sense of victory. I even thought the Khmer Rouge might know what it was doing for the country.

As the workers watched the water downstream of the dam recede, the celebratory mood came abruptly to an end as we were told that we had only finished the first phase of the project. The completed dam was only a temporary dam. The final dam would be built behind the temporary dam with steel and concrete.

There were rumors that the workers would be allowed to visit their families for a few days after the dam was completed. The younger boys naively had their hopes up when the temporary dam was completed. The rumors never materialized, and I spent the night listening to the boys quietly crying out their disappointment. As if the boys' clandestine tears flowed into the river overnight, the river began to rise on the upstream side of the dam.

Ever since the dam project had started, each morning had been nothing but routinely mechanical, but this morning, something extraordinary happened: The dam blocked the water upstream and allowed the water downstream to recede. To my knowledge, no one had ever seen the bottom of the Songke River. Like thousands of other workers, I raced down the riverbank to the bottom of the river with excitement. At the bottom, I gazed with awe and amazement at the monumental dam. I was unaware that the water was quietly, slowly, and steadily rising on the other side of the dam.

Recall that during the first phase of the project, dirt was manually transported from nearby land to build the temporary dam. To the contrary, the second phase required digging from the bottom of the now-dry riverbed to build the foundation for the permanent hydro dam. That translated into manually transporting dirt from the bottom of the river back to the previously dug land, a process that was the reverse of phase one.

Good jobs such as mixing cement and pouring concrete were not given to city folks like me. The Chinese-like and the educated Cambodians were given the grunt labor—digging and carrying dirt from the bottom of the river—very harsh.

Bamboo cut in the form of fishbones was connected together to form ladders along the side of the temporary dam. The workers carried dirt up the unstable ladders to the top of the temporary dam, which served as the path to the landfill.

Carrying a heavy load of dirt on my shoulder up an unstable bamboo ladder never failed to make my fatigued legs tremble. Sometimes, I looked down and wondered when I would fall; it seemed inevitable. Sometimes, I looked up and wondered if I could reach the top given my exhaustion. Oftentimes, I was simply mechanical, taking one excruciating step upward at a time. From time to time, I got scratched by a bamboo branch that made up a step of the ladder. Bruises and scratches were just part of my daily life in the camp. A day without a scratch could be considered a great day.

Often, I was less like a human and more like a mountain goat or a rhinoceros. Like the hooves of a mountain goat, my bare and calloused feet helped me skillfully climb the ladder up and down without falling. My rough rhinoceros skin protected me against minor bumps and scratches. Nonetheless, I was human and not immune to accidents and injuries.

Once, with a heavy load on my shoulder, I slipped and fell from near the top of the ladder. Instinctively, my right hand gripped the fetcher to prevent the load from falling off my shoulder; Angkar would definitely chastise me for dropping the load. With the load securely on my shoulder, I descended in freefall until my left hand gripped a bamboo branch, about halfway down the ladder—a few more feet down, and I would have hit a co-worker and caused a domino effect down the ladder. I accidentally smashed my left shin, hard, against the ladder.

The fall shook me up, but in shock, I felt no pain. I collected myself and continued climbing the ladder. Not until I reached the top of the ladder and stepped onto the top of the temporary dam did I feel my injury. At first, I felt only a little pinch of pain register. Then I looked down and saw a dent on my left shin where it hit the ladder. The dent was slowly changing, as I watched, into a swollen bruise. I was shaking but happy to know that my shin bone was not broken. I limped and continued to work for the rest of the day.

I continued to work for a few more days, but my injury became increasingly disabling, and I had to declare myself sick. In this twisted utopia, being sick was a taboo. Even with the extreme swelling on my shin, I was made to feel as if I were pretending to be sick, especially during the meal breaks.

A SICK DAY

Unlike the usual lunch whistle that brought pleasure to my day, today's whistle saddened, humiliated, and infuriated me. A serious infection on my left shin prevented me from working. Unable to work, I was not allowed to eat. According to Angkar, a sick person was not supposed to be able to eat—if one were well enough to eat, then one would be well enough to work. A sick person was usually labeled as a lazy person who did not want to pull his own load. Punishment for being sick ranged from food deprivation to public hazing—and occasionally execution.

I once witnessed a man with his head held down in a river as punishment for his alleged crime of pretending to be sick. He did not drown, but I am sure he would have been better off dead.

I sometimes had a recurring nightmare in which I was this poor man. In my nightmare, my arms were tightly and painfully tied behind my back. A hand, strong as steel, held the base of my neck and pushed my face deeper and deeper into a murky river. Sometimes, a couple of black, slimy eels penetrated my nostrils. Sometimes, I died and my soul watched my supine body float in the silent river. Sometimes, my executioners laughed at my corpse, and other times they cannibalized my body. The nightmare varied, and I always woke up sweating and momentarily lost.

There I was, with four or five other sick people, resting in a straw compound without walls. One or two of the sick people could have been pretending; however, being malnourished and overworked, a person should have been well qualified as being sick—the Khmer Rouge disagreed.

My back was aching from being in one place all morning, yet I dared not sit up to ease my sore back, because I was afraid I might invite a false perception that I was not sick enough to miss work. A long line of workers were passing the compound, approaching the kitchen area for their lunch break. With my high fever, throbbing pain on my left shin, excruciating hunger pangs, and bruised self-esteem, I swallowed my frustration, humiliation, and anger. I hid myself in a faked sleep.

The one-hour lunchtime went by, but not without seeming like an eternity. Within the hour, I contemplated my horrible journey to this point in life. I recollected a few painful moments cursed upon my family during these horrible past few years. Much tragedy had happened to my family. In comparison, my life was not terribly worse than the lives of my siblings, parents, and other family members. Yet, at that particular moment I could not care about what had happened to everyone else; I was at the top of self-pity.

I missed my mother as if I were a toddler. I had a deep and painful yearning. I wanted her to come alive, cradle me, place a wet cloth on my feverish forehead, feed me rice porridge with salted egg, sing me a Khmer lullaby, spoil me, tickle me, and hold me tight against her breasts. I wanted so much to wrap my arms around her body. I wanted so much to play with her hair. I missed playing with her underarms. I wanted to smell her, suck her thumb, and toy with her knees. I wanted so much to play with the small, soft rolls around her waist.

Within that hour, I missed my mother in ways unfathomable. I missed even the things about her that I disliked. In my younger days, she used to scrub my dirty skin with a rough wet cotton cloth. I missed that. I missed the guilt trip she gave me when I ran away at age five to live with the head Buddhist monk in a temple nearby. I missed her spanking me for being a troublemaker at school. I missed the feeling of jealousy that my mother had loved my youngest sister more than me. I missed the annoying lecture after a spanking. I missed the morning humiliation when I wet the bed. I missed the nagging. I ached to relive my early childhood. I wanted to trade my life for a chance to relive my early childhood moments. I wanted so much a chance to do everything perfectly right by my parents. I prayed to Buddha that I would do right by my parents should I be given another chance.

Taking my mind back into my childhood had helped pass the hour; unfortunately, the hour did not pass fast enough. My imperfect and annoying bladder would not let me escape the hour in peace. I needed urgently to urinate.

I didn't have to go far to urinate. I hopped on my right leg toward a mango tree standing about twenty-five feet away from where I was lying. All eyes from the kitchen area were on me. The hopping aggravated my wound, and the excruciating pain permeated my entire left leg. I hobbled the equivalent of the last mile of an uphill marathon, forcing back the tears that welled in my eyes. I felt not a sense of relief but a sense of triumph when I finally reached the mango tree. I placed my bent right arm above my head against the tree trunk to support my forward lean against the tree. With all my weight on my right leg, my left leg off the ground, and using my left hand, I fertilized the tree. Ironically, the tree that I urinated on seemed far more fortunate than I at that moment. In contrast, the tree was healthy. No one ridiculed it. Unlike me, it stood erectly strong with pride and poise. I, on the other hand, couldn't even concentrate on my urinating. The infection was the least of my agony. I worried about what others would think. I had every right to be anguished, for most eyes were on me probing how sick or how fake I was. I understood the power of mob mentality.

Hobbling back was painful and difficult, but I was glad that I could finally bury my face, shame, and agony in my soiled pillow.

I was relieved when finally the lunch hour was over. I once again could rest in peace. Peace? How much peace could one have with an infection throbbing like an active volcano and a stomach rumbling like an earthquake?

The moment the kitchen staff were gone to collect food to get ready for dinner, I got up and hobbled over to the kitchen and got a coconut shell full of water. After I clumsily cleaned my wound with the water, I hobbled to a nearby field and harvested a handful of grass seeds and leaves believed to be the ingredients for medicine. I chewed and mixed the ingredients to produce the assumed medicine. I wrapped my wound with the medicine using a large mango leaf and a long piece of vine as a Band-Aid.

Still hungry, I returned to the kitchen—my other last mile of a marathon. There lay a few sacks of uncooked rice. I thought of stealing some rice, but I did not go through with it, because I was sure the kitchen staff had noted the amount of rice.

In retrospect, I now realize that one of the reasons that a number of Cambodians survived the Khmer Rouge regime was the fact that there was always food around if one were willing to eat just about anything. As luck had it, a gecko presented itself on the kitchen wall. It didn't take me long to drop and kill the poor animal with a piece of firewood. Although the kitchen was closed, there was still ample burning coal in the fire pit. I tossed the gecko into the lazily burning coal. My infection throbbed next to the hot air around the pit, but I didn't care. I was about to have a nice healthful meal.

It didn't take long before the gecko was cooked, yet the waiting was a nerve-wracking experience. If I were caught out of bed catching food and cooking it, I would face a punishment of unpredictable severity. Nonetheless, my first bite justified the risk. No steak from a five-star restaurant could compare to that gecko that day. With the exception of its guts and eyes, I ate every bit of that unfortunate gecko, including its well-roasted skin—the phrase " tastes like chicken" didn't even come close. This was my top sirloin…my New York steak…my prime rib…my lobster…. It was nothing less than the most delicious meal I had ever tasted.

My injury eventually healed, but I went back to work long before I had completely recovered from it. I was given only a few days to rest during the peak infection of my injury. When I could work, I did, since each of my sick days brought me humiliation and more hunger.

WHEN THE DAM BROKE

In my few days of absence from work, the dam project had progressed nicely. The foundation was finished. People were pouring concrete to construct the dam wall. Since the evacuation, I had not seen industrial construction utilizing steel and concrete. I had been a part of a workforce that built a water reservoir, but it was built with clay.

Some time had passed, and the permanent dam was near completion. It was within a week's time of when the center gap would have been closed. Unfortunately, the pressure against the temporary dam was overbearingly strong, and the dam broke.

It was midmorning when workers at the top of the temporary dam began yelling at the workers at the bottom of the river to get out of the river. I ran up the riverbank. I was nearly at the top of the bank when the temporary dam gave way to the pressure, broke, and violently let a gush of water rush through it. Within minutes, the dam was gone, a majority of the permanent dam was broken, and a number of my fellow workers were washed downstream.

In the midst of the havoc, I found myself safely standing at the top of the riverbank with other workers, shaking and helplessly watching people drown.

The rest of that day was unusually unstructured. The workers were left alone to a free afternoon while the leaders waited for an order from their superiors and tried to figure out what to do next.

ARRESTED FOR ATTEMPTING TO STEAL A COCONUT

The morning after the dam broke, the workers were told to return home to Phoum Khsouy. We were told to assemble in front of the warehouse in Phoum

Khsouy after a few days of family visits. After we loaded all our tools and food supplies onto oxcarts, we were discharged.

The men and bigger boys walked faster than those who were my size or smaller. Eventually, the group broke off into smaller bands. People wandered off in small groups, as we did not have to meet up for another few days. A handful of young boys and I were the last group meandering through rice fields and villages toward Phoum Khsouy.

The boys and I came upon a small abandoned village. There were a few unoccupied huts, but the village was rich with fruit trees. We looked around, but there was no one in the village. Everyone went their separate ways. I was hungry and decided to climb a coconut tree. Stealing was a crime punishable by torture or death; however, I was confident that there was no one around to catch me stealing the coconut.

I scaled the tree. Halfway up, someone screamed in an intimidating voice at me. When I looked down, I was staring into two barrels of AK-47 rifles. The soldiers who were pointing the rifles at me were at most my age. I was close enough to see their facial expressions. It was absolutely clear to me that if I did not come down fast, they would not hesitate to shoot me. My legs and arms weakened and trembled involuntarily in panic. I had no idea how I was going to descend without falling off. I closed my eyes, relaxed my grip on the tree trunk, and let my body slide down freely. It happened so fast that I did not even feel the abrasions on my legs, arms, chest, and stomach.

After I reached the ground, one AK-47 barrel was immediately pointed tightly against my forehead, and another AK-47 barrel was pushed sadistically against my back. At this point, I still did not feel the scrapes and burns on my skin. I was oblivious to my surroundings. At that moment, there was only me, two AK-47 barrels (not even rifles, just barrels), and the two Khmer Rouge boy soldiers.

The soldier behind me kicked my back and pushed me to the ground with his foot. In place of the AK-47 barrels, one soldier's foot was on my back and the other soldier's foot was on my right cheek pressing my left cheek to the ground. The soldiers screamed at me. The screaming intimidated me; I did not feel pain on my left cheek.

After my wrists were securely tied behind my back with a thread of fresh vine, I was ordered to stand up. Only then did I realize that I had wet myself. I had neither pride nor dignity left in me. The cuts, scrapes, and burns inflicted serious and deep pain on my skin. But pain, pride, and dignity were my secondary concerns, because I knew that the worst was yet to come.

After a short walk, escorted by the two soldiers and with my wrists tied behind my back, I was brought to join a handful of boys and young men who were shackled outside an abandoned hut, under a large mango tree. The shackle was made of two long pieces of wood put together to form a contraption with holes barely large enough to fit human ankles. The contraption was chained to a tree so that the prisoners could not get up and run away with it. The prisoners were guarded by three or four other young soldiers.

One of the guards unlocked the contraption and ordered me to sit down at the end of the line, where a vacant shackle hole awaited me. My left ankle was shackled; my wrists were still tied behind my back.

By noon, I was hungry. The soldiers were eating their lunch and giggling. They tossed chicken bones with some leftover meat toward the prisoners. With one ankle anchored to the contraption and both hands tied behind, no prisoner was able to pick up the bones to gnaw on. My fellow captives and I struggled unsuccessfully to pick up the bones. We quickly became a joke for the soldiers. The soldiers' small talk and giggles burst into laughs and ridicules. More food was mockingly thrown our way.

After a protracted lunch, the soldiers untied our hands and gave us their leftover food. The soldiers disappeared until the following morning. Throughout the afternoon, the tree ants descended the mango tree to eat the garbage. Like the Khmer Rouge soldiers, the ants were nasty. They bit me and my fellow captives. We were fortunate to have our hands untied and free to kill the nasty ants. I ate practically every tree ant I killed. The ants' citrus taste inside my empty stomach gave me a stomachache.

My fellow prisoners and I urinated and defecated in place. The odor of fresh urine and feces tortured my nose. I wanted to vomit, but there was nothing in my stomach to throw up. I kept my eyes cast away from my fellow captives.

As if lifeless, the prisoners did not talk to one another. When I looked into my fellow prisoners' eyes, I saw the complete lack of spirit. Besides silence, there was nothing to exchange among the prisoners — no empathy, no sympathy; nothing. Every boy and man was for himself.

To quench my thirst, I cupped my hands together, urinated into the cupped hands, and drank my own urine. Drinking my own urine neither disgusted nor humiliated me; my thirst made the odor and flavor of the urine quite acceptable.

At night, there were vicious mosquitoes, a heartless wind chill, creepy howls of the coyotes, and lonely darkness. The solitude of the night intensified the odors of the urine and feces. My back ached and my buttocks were numb from my sedentary and prolonged position. When I lay down, I could not bend my restrained left leg. My overall range of motion was extremely limited. My sleep was interrupted multiple times throughout the night by the hungry mosquitoes, the cries of the nearby coyotes, and the sick coughs of my fellow captives. More than once, I awoke to the sad cry of a boy just a couple of years younger than I.

Shackled, cold, and tired, I was in hell. It would have been much more hellish, however, if my hands had not been free to brush off the mosquitoes, cup my own urine for drinking, tend to my excoriated skin, and scratch my itches.

Shortly after the sun was up, the soldiers returned. They kicked and slapped me and my fellow captives. They called us thugs and traitors. A knuckle to the back of my head sent a surge of pain down my spine to my bladder and triggered a spurt of urine through my shorts.

To my pleasant surprise, the soldiers freed me and the boys but kept the men shackled. The soldiers shooed us away as if we were dumb sheep. A soldier kicked my buttock, backhanded the back of my head, and told me to get the hell out of there. My instinct told me to hurry and get out. I did not care what happened to everyone else. I took off running, thinking that I had a fifty-fifty chance of being shot in the back by an AK-47. A blast of my urine soaked my shorts as I ran for my life. Without turning back, I ran, anticipating a bullet piercing the back of my head. I heard the ridiculing laughs of the soldiers behind me fade as I continued to run.

I have no idea how long I ran, but when I stopped and looked back, I was alone in the middle of an open field. Everything but my pounding heart was peaceful. A strong breeze, oblivious to my hellish life, sent waves over the rice stalks. The birds went about their own peaceful way of life singing their happy songs. Lonely trees harmoniously orchestrated their respective leaves against the breeze. My fatigued legs shook like those of a newborn fawn. I went down on my knees, leaned forward, put my hands and forehead on the ground, and sobbed.

I thanked my father for watching over me and bringing me to safety. I cried out my self-pity, shame, and anger. I screamed in vain at the top of my lungs. I picked up hard pieces of dry clay and violently threw them at the ignorant trees, the oblivious birds, and the insensitive breeze. At that moment, if I had faced a weaker person, I would have ripped him to pieces. I hated humans. I had just escaped death and thanked the spirit of my father for keeping me alive, but ironically I wished I had died. I hated the world, I hated me, and I hated my lack of dignity. I collected myself and went on my way to Phoum Khsouy.

Sadly, Phoum Khsouy no longer gave me any sense of home, as I no longer had my parents to anchor a place that I could regard as home. The center of my family was now my oldest sister, Sim. I loved all my older sisters and especially Sim like I loved my mother, but no sister could take the place of my mother. Coming home now was just a motion and not an emotion. After a good night's rest at Phoum Khsouy, I reported to the rendezvous point and rejoined my unit. Although I shared the news of my arrest with my oldest sister, I kept it a secret from my fellow workers, because my life could be in danger if any commander of my unit knew about it.

A LUCKY DAY

Rampant starvation, hard labor, lack of freedom, torture, and unjust execution made life under the Khmer Rouge regime unpredictable and outright horrible. Every morning was the start of a fresh chance that life could end. Throughout a given day, there were continual chances of torture, humiliation, solitary confinement, and execution. Nighttime was no different, except it appeared calmer. Normally, a given night would be blessed with deep sleep due to the exhaustion from hard work during the day, but my deep sleep was usually encroached upon by nightmares.

Rarely would life ever receive favorable fortune under the regime; however, this day was my lucky day.

Soaked under the drizzling tropical rain, digging and tossing dirt with a shovel to strengthen rice paddy dikes, I was approached by a Khmer Rouge boy commando in his intimidating black uniform—which appeared even blacker and more intimidating in wetness. Approximately six feet away, standing on a firm dike and holding his left hand to keep rain from his eyes, the commando pointed at me and signaled me to come with him.

As usual, I thought the worst. My day had finally come. No one among hundreds of my co-workers would dare look directly my way. Everyone pretended to see, hear, and sense nothing. As I was escorted through the laboring crowd, I could imagine the worst communal thought from my co-workers. If they were to pool a bet, everyone would bet on the high chance that I would be either corporally punished or executed for a wrong I had done.

As the crowd disappeared into the distance and the oblivious rain, I wished the commando would walk either in front of me or beside me—even now, his calculated arm-length distance behind me continues to haunt my nightmares.

Whenever I slowed down, hoping he would come up to walk beside me, he would politely ask me to pick up my pace. His unexpected politeness gave me no comfort. To the contrary, it felt like a cruel mockery and precursor to my death. Walking in front of him, I thought I was being escorted to my execution.

The walk seemed to be protracted. My awareness of the surroundings was at its pinnacle. I heard practically every step behind me swishing the mud. I counted the raindrops. I studied the length and angle of each raindrop.

I imagined numerous scenarios in which I would be either tortured or executed. I imagined what it would be like to be buried alive. I wondered if my spirit would be sad watching the disposal of my bloody body. For my own comfort, I silently told the spirits of my departed father and mother that I was looking forward to our reunion. I told myself that the Khmer Rouge was about to help me reunite with my parents, grandmother, youngest sister, nephew, and other relatives who had passed on by either starvation or execution. My self-comforting and bravery were short-lived. As my fear and anxiety returned, I asked the spirit of my father to protect me as I would ask a doctor to sedate me before my most painful surgery.

I felt my warm urine percolating in my pants.

I continued counting the raindrops. I tried digging my bare callous heels into the clay surface of the dike so I would not slip. I practiced digging different parts of the bottoms of my feet, searching for optimal traction on the slippery surface. I realized my cotton shirt had a big tear in the back. My black cotton pants were now gray, with one leg half torn off. I wondered whether I would be buried with my clothes on or naked.

My warm urine once again seeped down my pants.

About an hour later, the walk—which seemed like the walk of my life-time—ended. In front of the commander's straw hut, the commando told me to wait outside. He entered the hut. Moments later, he waved for me to come in. At the door, he handed me a cloth to dry myself off.

As I was led to face the commander, my stomach had a mind of its own. My nerves were beyond control. If I had had any food that day, which I hadn't, I would have defecated in my pants. My bladder was involuntarily triggering urination, but unsuccessfully, for no urine was left within me—a tiny dignity saved.

With an unusually friendly smile, the commander signaled me to sit at his lunch in progress. My fear and anxiety were momentarily diverted by the food in front of me. It had been at least three years since I had seen such food luxury—not to mention sitting close enough to taste it.

In those days, if a ration of rice porridge in one meal contained one tablespoon of rice, the meal would be considered standard. Between two and five tablespoons, and the meal would be very good. Add one or two sprinkles of salt, and the meal would be great. An even better meal would include some degree of sugar and a mouse-bite of a dry salted fish. A modicum of any protein such as beef or pork would be a luxurious meal.

In front of me, there was a grilled fish garnished with shredded young ginger, freshly sliced garlic, shredded onion, and freshly picked mint leaves. Making up the remainder of the five-course meal were half a roasted chicken, half a steamed chicken, smoked cobra, and stir-fried beef with Chinese broccoli.

No explanation for why I had been summoned had yet been given to me; however, at the moment, I neither cared about the reason nor feared my surroundings. I was enthralled by the seduction of this regal lunch. The delicious aroma captivated my undivided attention. My uncontrollable hunger ruled my body, heart, and soul. For a bite of this food (or even a taste), I would kill.

Without a word, the commander gestured for me to put some food on the plate that was neatly placed in front of me. I filled the plate with steamed rice with uncertainty. I timidly asked if anyone would be eating with me. The commander smiled and told me to enjoy my lunch. I did.

For the duration of my life under the regime, there were no other meals worthy of a comparison to this meal. I was in high heaven. I ate practically everything in front of me. My stomach was full and stretched beyond its normal capacity. I was painfully uncomfortable. However, the pain was gratifying. I would have welcomed such pain every day if I could have.

I was so focused on my eating that I was completely oblivious to my surroundings. I did not realize I had been left alone in the room. Only after I had completely finished my meal did the commander re-enter the room. With a reserved smile, he asked whether I had enjoyed my lunch. Politely, with a fearful undertone, I of course responded with a grateful yes.

The commander ordered his assistants to clear the floor. As the assistants went back and forth between the room and the kitchen, I envied their positions in contrast with my hard-laboring position.

At last, the commander sat down face to face with me. My fear and anxiety returned. The commander's relentless friendly smile induced intimidation rather than amity in my mind. Understanding my apprehension, the commander made an effort to put me at ease. He started the conversation by mentioning that he had been told I could read and write. He told me that he had heard of my good handwriting.

In place of his intended reassurance, his knowledge of my education amplified my fear. People were executed for wearing glasses. All levels of educated people were targeted for elimination. My fear appeared justified at the moment. I did not like where the conversation was heading. My paranoia was forming into a reality. I completely forgot the pain from my overeating. I panicked. I denied the fact that I had good handwriting. I denied the fact that I could really read and write. To make my denial credible, I hesitantly admitted I could at best read and write with great difficulty.

The commander took my denial for humility. He told me he would like me to do paperwork for him. I was stunned, uncertain, and, above all, relieved.

For the next couple of months, my time on the field was often shortened by a couple of hours. Practically every morning, I would be called to inscribe letters, passes, and other papers. I was never again fed the regal meal, but on occasion, I was given a few bites of leftover food, which was much more nutritious than my rationed rice porridge.

That day, all things considered, was my lucky day ... a very lucky day.

COUNTERFEIT PASSES

Before the Khmer Rouge ruled Cambodia, my parents had always reminded my sisters and me to pay special attention to good handwriting, and all my older sisters had good handwriting. In particular, my sister Phon had exquisite handwriting, which inspired me to work on my own.

My good handwriting paid off. As the commander's ad-hoc secretary boy, I learned how the official documents were written and signed. In fact, I had hand-signed low-level documents such as visiting permits, travel documents, and requests of supplies on behalf of the commander.

While working in the labor camps, I met and made friends with a boy named Trou. Trou was no more than a couple of years older than I. In a time when I could not trust anyone, the friendship and trust between Trou and me were unquestionable. We shared secrets and stole food together.

Trou was always a rebel, and the Khmer Rouge leaders had their eyes on him. He was rancorous toward the Khmer Rouge — his father, a high-ranking republic military officer, had been executed by Khmer Rouge soldiers.

Trou was a bad influence and liability to me, but I appreciated his dedicated friendship, respect, and trust. With conviction, he often talked to me about escaping or starting a revolution against the Khmer Rouge. He was serious, but I could not take his seriousness beyond my amusement. He and I were a pair that commanded the respect of our fellow workers. We often worked as a team, leveraging each other to be more productive than most workers. I had good people skills, and Trou had the reputation of a mentally unstable person. We both were hard workers and always watched each other's back. Together, we were a pair not to be messed with by our fellow workers. I believe that if it had not been for our productivity, Angkar would have purged us, because we were somewhat of troublemakers — by the Khmer Rouge standard.

One quiet night, Trou encouraged me in a whisper to forge a pass for both of us to visit home. At first, I did not take him seriously, because he often talked about escaping and overthrowing the Khmer Rouge. I thought that Trou was all talk. Every opportunity he had, he was relentless in his pursuit to convince me to forge the pass. His persistence began to weaken my resistance. I went from thinking that Trou was all talk to believing he was serious. I went from being amused to being scared and, finally, to being Trou's accomplice.

One day, I forged a signature on two passes that would allow Trou and me to visit Phoum Khsouy for a couple of weeks. I was diligent in making sure that the passes were properly stamped. The passes also noted that Trou and I were outstanding workers who deserved two weeks off. As a commendation for our exemplary work, Trou and I were to be rewarded with extra food rations during our visit at Phoum Khsouy.

The following day, armed with our counterfeit passes, Trou and I sneaked off after the morning work and headed for Phoum Khsouy. I was excited and scared at the same time. This was a crime that would definitely earn me torture or death. Once we were away and alone, I realized that we had not thought out our plan thoroughly. We had not thought about what explanation we would give to our supervisors for our two-week absence. You can imagine my anxiety about not having a way to go back to the labor camp.

For the first time, I realized that I did not really know Trou. Unlike me, Trou did not seem to worry about the return. He only cared about visiting his family. He brushed off my concern and told me to worry about it after our time off. Still unsure whether I was hanging out with the right person, I managed to get excited about my two-week visit with my oldest sister, Sim.

When we arrived at Phoum Khsouy just before dark, Trou and I parted to join our respective families, but not before we agreed to meet after two weeks to decide our next move, as returning to our labor camp now was not an option.

My sister Sim was happy to see me. The counterfeit pass did not fool her. She recognized my handwriting. Like my mother, she knew me well. After a few tricky questions, she got me to admit that the pass was counterfeit. She was scared at first, but eventually she accepted the reality. Like Trou, she was a risk-taker, so she was quite happy to take me to the warehouse, present the pass, and bring home two weeks of food ration.

My sister and I lived well for those two weeks. We had plenty of rice and dried fish and small amounts of salt, sugar, and honey. Additionally, my sister was given some time off to visit with me, the exemplary worker. At night, my sister and I sneaked out and stole bananas, coconuts, pumpkins, and corn. We really lived well, knowing that we might not see each other ever again. Going back to my labor camp would be a sure death sentence. The only remaining option was to hide out. Whatever step I would take, my sister and I knew that this would be our last visit for the rest of our lives.

We reminisced over our past, and we caught up. We spent every moment with each other. I slept with her as I always had with my mother. We talked late into the night until we became senseless and fell asleep.

I learned that after Pech's husband Chip was executed, Pech was forced to marry another man, whom she did not love. (Rumor had it that one of the reasons that Chip was executed was because this man was well connected with the Khmer Rouge and wanted Pech for himself.) The arranged marriage provided her better living conditions. After the wedding, her husband moved her to Phoum Tavei, where life was less harsh. I also learned that the husband was able to pull some strings and allow Pech to bring Peak along to help her care for Chip's daughter.

My two-week visit was full of anxiety because I was unsure whether I would get away with the counterfeit pass. On the other hand, I enjoyed the exceptional amount of food. Sometimes, my visit seemed like an eternity due to my anxiety; other times, it seemed to pass too quickly. At the end of my visit, Sim suggested that I escape to Phoum Tavei and join Pech and Peak. Although my sister and I believed that we would never see each other again, our farewell was not difficult, as we were accustomed to goodbyes.

ARRESTED FOR RUNNING AWAY

I met Trou at our rendezvous point. After I told him my plan, he wanted to go with me to Phoum Tavei. He told me that he would follow me to the end of the earth. That day, Trou became my brother. We would die together as brothers. At that moment, I had nothing left but Trou, and likewise, all Trou had was me. Accomplices and brothers, Trou and I headed to Phoum Tavei. We crossed rice paddies and wooded areas without encountering one soul. We speculated that perhaps we could go as far as Thailand. We thought about going into the woods and creating a stronghold to build a force that would eventually liberate Cambodia from the Khmer Rouge.

On our way, we avoided occupied areas such as Phoum Chai Chhke. When necessary, we would stop and hide. We had a good sense of where labor camps were, and we managed to circumvent them. We had enough food to last us at least two days. For the first time under the Khmer Rouge regime, I felt a taste of freedom—in a vast countryside, Trou and I were two wild animals. I tasted happiness. I felt power. I recognized my ownership of the earth. I understood and envied the animals and the birds in the wilderness.

Trou and I finally arrived at the edge of Phoum Tavei. We were so close that we could see the rooftops. My sisters were supposedly under one of those rooftops. All Trou and I had to do was cross a creek into the village and find my sisters. A better life was within our reach. Unfortunately, fate had a different plan for Trou and me.

Both Trou and I were dusty from our long trip. I wanted my sisters to see us more presentable. So we stripped naked and jumped in a pond with clear water, lilies, and lotus plants. At ease and excited, we did not just wash ourselves. We played as if we were back in the era before the Khmer Rouge. We were being ourselves. We swam, laughed, and splashed. We were free.

Our boyish water play and sounds of happiness attracted the village patrol guards. Four young guards with AK-47 rifles surrounded the pond, pointed the barrels at Trou and me, and ordered us to get out. We got out and got dressed. When asked where we had come from, we lied and told the guards we had come from Phoum Tavei. We would have been charged with a more serious crime if they had known we had come from the frontline labor camp. Unlike where we had come from, the rules in Phoum Tavei were relatively lenient. I believe the guards thought that we were just a couple of workers trying to skip work.

We were brought to a place where there were more guards and about fifteen other people about our age who had also committed wrongdoings. For some reason, Trou and I were not scared, but we noticed the anxiety in the eyes of our fellow arrestees.

One boy about my age had been caught stealing rice. From where Trou and I had come from, he would have been tortured or executed. Instead, he got a couple of knuckles to his head, three or four kicks to his buttocks, and a couple of hard slaps to his face. To these people, that was torture. Trou and I looked at each other and instinctively knew we had it good here. I smiled inside, and for sure so did Trou.

The guards admonished the arrestees. Trou and I still thought we had it good here; sticks and stones might break our bones, but words did not hurt us. We had it good. I liked this place, and from Trou's bright eyes, I knew he agreed with me.

At lunchtime, each person was given a ration of one bowl of solid rice, a piece of dried and salted fish, and a cup of fish soup. The disappointed eyes of the other people told Trou and me that this was a reduced ration as a punishment for those who did wrong by Angkar. I liked this place.

The arrestees were told that as part of the disciplinary actions, they had to be separated from their families and join the men at a harsh labor camp. What these folks considered a punishment, Trou and I considered a normal life. Therefore, we still thought we had it good here. So far, we were ahead.

Separation from one's family was not a punishment for us. Labor camp was not new. In fact, judging from how one boy was punished for his stealing, we knew that their definition of a harsh labor camp would be nothing compared to our actual labor camp. Trou and I could definitely enjoy this type of food ration. We actually had a good time during this ordeal.

When asked for names, we made up new names. I gave the guards "Mab" as my name, meaning "Fat," and Trou gave a name that I cannot recall. My name fit, because my whole body was swollen from years of malnutrition.

The next day, we joined a labor camp located halfway between Phoum Tavei and the labor camp from which Trou and I had deserted. There, Trou and I gained the respect and admiration of the camp supervisors and guards. We worked as hard and pulled at least as much load as the men. We helped and mentored the boys. We were always smiling and whistling, while other boys and many men were struggling. Obviously, these people had not endured the type of work and slavery that Trou and I had endured. Trou and I were jointly given the responsibility of team leaders. We were the poster-child workers. There was no reason why we would not be perceived as great workers, as the labor camp was relatively easier: The work was easy, food was better, and leaders were less intimidating and abusive. It was the first time that I enjoyed working that hard under the Khmer Rouge.

One day, my newly adopted unit was called to aid another unit nearby. To my pleasant surprise, I was planting rice next to my sister Phorn. Until now, my sisters and I had given up all hope that Phorn would still be alive after the Khmer Rouge had arrested her a while back.

Prior to her arrest, the Khmer Rouge had forced Phorn to marry a stranger. I cannot say for sure if the arranged marriage later turned into love, but it did not matter. Phorn had a husband. Then the Khmer Rouge found out that her husband was a Catholic and a marine in the republic army who once fought against the Khmer Rouge. His skin was peculiarly pale white. People gossiped that he was of western descent and a member of the CIA. Consequently, the

Khmer Rouge executed him. Even though my sister was forced into marriage, the Khmer Rouge arrested her anyway—charging that she had been tainted and corrupted by him.

I was so happy to see my sister. Unlike my previous units, this unit was much more lenient and did not criminalize me for talking to my sister. I told her my story, and she told me hers. We exchanged news and caught up with each other's life stories. She was glad to see Trou with me. In some way, it was a comfort to her knowing that I had Trou as a friend and confidant.

As happy as I was to see Phorn alive, I was sad to see her broken. Something horrible had happened to her at the prison that she did not tell me about. She did not have to tell me. It did not matter. Something horrible had happened to her, but she was alive. That was good enough for me; shit happened, but life had to go on.

As poster-child workers, Trou and I thoroughly enjoyed our new labor camp, but our newly found good life came to an end.

One afternoon, while working in a rice paddy, Trou and I noticed a man in an olive-green uniform. The man walked past us and toward the makeshift office of the labor camp director. We recognized the man and knew that our time there was over. He was the commander for whom I had scribed. We knew the purpose of his presence.

To no surprise of Trou's and mine, the camp director sent the guards toward us. The guards called out for the boys named Dong and Trou. Trou and I (Dong) pretended not to hear the calling. While everyone stood still listening to the call, Trou and I kept on working and pretending not to hear our names. The guards did not notice us, but the commander did and yelled out to the guards to escort us out of the rice paddy. The camp director was surprised to find out that we were the Dong and Trou whom the commander sought.

The commander and a few of his armed guards escorted us back to our labor camp. We walked all afternoon without uttering a word. I was a bit scared, but having gone through so much, I just accepted my fate and simply counted on my father to keep me and Trou safe. In silence, I spoke to my father all the way to the camp. We arrived at the camp after nightfall, and only a few people knew of our return that night.

As a punishment, Trou and I were told to go to sleep without dinner. I was very hungry, and my stomach ached. After years of starvation, hunger pain simply became part of life, and I eventually fell asleep.

The punishment was extremely lenient. The next day, we resumed our regular life in the labor camp with the rest of our fellow workers. Trou and I could not believe our luck and were pleasantly surprised by this mercy.

I missed the better life that Trou and I had just experienced, but working thirteen hours a day for seven days a week quickly got me back into my routine. Once again, I was mechanical and productive—sometimes under the scorching sun, sometimes in the rain, and sometimes just in an empty space. Nonetheless, life went on.

សម័យក្រោយសង្គមខ្មែរក្រហម

(sak-mahy sawng-kuhm k'rouy khmair k'raw-hawrm)

POST-KHMER ROUGE ERA

LIBERATED

One day in 1979, I woke up to an unusually peaceful morning. No whistle. No wake-up bell. No roll call. The morning would have been utterly silent if it had not been for the birds' singing and chirping. The bright sunrays piercing through the trees made the morning magically peaceful.

In the midst of this extraordinary serenity, I was lost, confused, and panicked. I thought I had slept through the whistles and bells. The first thing that came to my mind was that I would have to face punishment for missing work. I gravely worried that I would not be allowed to eat.

I sat up and looked around, trying to figure out what was happening. Then I noticed that all but a few of the guys were still asleep. I noticed the same confusion and panic reflected in the guys who were sitting up. To the guys who were awake, I quietly shrugged my shoulders and secretly signaled with my left hand, signifying a question about whether anyone knew what was happening. The guys reflected a similar signal to let me know that my guess was as good as theirs.

I woke up the other guys sleeping next to me. More guys were now awake, dazed, and confused. No one seemed to know anything.

My curiosity finally overcame my fear. I got up and stepped out of the straw hut in a manner as if I were sneaking out. Once outside, I looked around and found more guys coming out with uncertainty in their eyes.

No Khmer Rouge leaders in sight. The chaos continued for at least an hour.

One guy began to scale a coconut tree to pick the coconuts. Just about everyone warned him that he might be punished or killed should the leaders show up. As the young man reached midway up the coconut tree, more guys began climbing other coconut trees.

The confusion and chaos escalated. The guys started to loot the kitchen. Fruits were picked. Gardens were looted and destroyed.

I grabbed whatever I could. With sticks and rocks, I shot and killed a hen. I went into the chicken house and gathered as many chicken eggs as I could.

By about noon, without realizing we were celebrating our freedom, the guys and I were singing songs from the days before the Khmer Rouge came into power. We were singing the love and sentimental songs that were banned by the regime. We were beating pots and pans as if they were drums. We feasted on our looted spoils.

Like caged birds that suddenly became free, the guys and I were utterly lost. Other than engrossing ourselves with the looting, singing, and feasting, we did nothing. We did not realize we were deserted in the heart of our freedom. Years of commands and strict instructions had made us robotic, and we could not decide what to do.

The guys and I sat around and talked about the good old days. I felt good. I felt bad. I felt guilty. The good feeling was foreign, strange, and unnatural. I felt like a traitor to the regime. I contemplated the worst outcome of my unpatriotic behavior. I imagined the best outcome and everything in between.

My stomach was in pain from overeating. My body was skinny, the bottom halves of my legs were swollen, my arms were stringy, and my stomach was bloated as if I were pregnant. Since that morning, I had eaten four coconuts, a few raw chicken eggs, half a papaya, half a flame-broiled chicken, and a few guavas. I was in an excruciating heaven. I went into the hut and fell asleep.

My peaceful nap was interrupted by noise outside the hut. I got up and went

outside to find out what was going on. Only then did I find out that the Khmer
Rouge soldiers had run away in the middle of the night because they had
become aware that the Vietnamese army was coming.

The Vietnamese army.

"Chuy mai heuy," was my exact thought. (The literal English translation of
my thought would be culturally too graphic, but in a lighter English translation, it means "Oh, crap!")

Given the long acrimony wedged between the Vietnamese and Cambodian
histories, heritages, cultures, and nations, I was dubious whether I was safer
in the hands of the Vietnamese soldiers. The stories of cruelties inflicted on
the Cambodians by the Vietnamese came to mind. What would become of me
and my countrymen when the Vietnamese soldiers arrived?

A new wave of panic, chaos, and fear consumed the guys and me. We were
afraid to leave because the Khmer Rouge might return to punish us. We were
afraid to stay because the Vietnamese soldiers were coming.

It was midafternoon when one of the guys directed our attention to the approaching of two soldiers on horseback. Unlike the Khmer Rouge, the men
were in plain green army fatigues, including green caps, but like the Khmer
Rouge, they were wearing the communist sandals and red-checkered scarf. I
was confident they were Cambodians by their dark skin.

They greeted us and immediately put us at ease. The fact that they were
armed with machetes instead of guns helped us relax. They introduced themselves as freedom fighters aided by the Vietnamese army. When asked the
whereabouts of the Vietnamese soldiers, they told us the Vietnamese soldiers
were a few days behind, and, with the help of the Vietnamese soldiers, the
freedom fighters were liberating Cambodia from the Khmer Rouge regime.
We were told not to be afraid.

Until this day, I had been deprived of food and freedom. I had been forced
to labor inhumanely on the farmland thirteen hours a day, seven days a
week, and 365 days a year. Per my survival, I ate field rats, field mice, snakes,

beetles, tree ants, bees, lizards, vines, leaves, and roots. Overnight, I went from being a slave of my own government to a free person ... and then a recruit of the Cambodian liberating army backed by the Vietnamese army.

As I listened to the two soldiers trying to recruit the guys and me to join the army, I went from being a coward constantly in fear of the Khmer Rouge to being an angry and bloodthirsty avenger. I joined the army. I felt patriotic. I felt manly. I felt worthy of being my father's son. I felt my rage. I was on my way to do worse than what the Khmer Rouge had done unto me, my family, my friends, and my countrymen. I was on my way to chop off their heads, rip off their ears, slice open their stomachs, cut off their penises, rape their women, and kill their babies.

I was on my way to claim justice.

Trou and I joined an organized mob that was made up of young men and older boys. The mob was armed with machetes, picks, and sticks. It went from village to village seeking any hidden Khmer Rouge. We did not find any Khmer Rouge, but we found and looted the food supplies deserted by the Khmer Rouge. We burned homes that had been occupied by the Khmer Rouge.

Weeks later, the mob's leader told us that the Vietnamese army was ready to officially integrate us into the Khmer army aided by the Vietnamese army to fight against the Khmer Rouge. Obviously, Trou, I, and our fellow mobsters were excited. Raised in wartime, I glorified a dream of being a soldier, shooting an automatic AK-47 rifle, and stabbing the enemies with my bloodstained bayonet. I could hardly wait to torture and kill a Khmer Rouge follower—yes, their babies, too, must be uprooted. Within days, I would be initiated into an army that would sanitize Cambodia.

The morning came when the mob leader blew a whistle to gather a meeting. We were told to file into a line and start marching toward the Battambang main airport, Veal Bek Chan (field of broken dishes). The mob formed a very long line and walked very slowly. Trou and I were inseparable. We were about two-thirds of the way back in the line. It was one of the happiest moments of my life since the start of the killing fields. Likewise, it was Trou's happiest moment. For all the time that I had known Trou, I had never seen him more excited.

Trou and I agreed that it was our destiny to be soldiers and fight against the Khmer Rouge. We both knew that it was our calling, and we were ready. We imagined various scenarios of our futures in the army. The majority of the scenarios were based on torturing and killing Khmer Rouge soldiers, and saving the world that they oppressed. I could hardly wait to trade my machete for an AK-47 rifle and a bayonet. I could hardly wait to be in a republic army uniform. I was ready to torture and kill. It was not vengeance; it was my destiny.

My destiny to become a torturer and a killer abruptly ended when a hand from the middle of nowhere grabbed my arm, and pulled me out of the slowly moving line. To my utmost surprise, I turned and stared at the face of my sister Pech. I quickly turned to look at Trou's face. I knew what Trou was thinking at that very moment. We both realized that there was no way in hell we would reach our destiny. My sister ordered me and Trou to step out of the line.

Although Trou and I thought we were mature enough to join the army, we were just two boys to my sister. Trou and I were disappointed. We had waited for so long to have a shot at claiming our justice. We were only hours away from being deputized as the champions of justice. Unlike me, my sister valued peace and family reunion over vengeance and justice. I was disappointed, but I was also happy to see my sister. I reluctantly surrendered to her wish. It would not have mattered, anyway, because my sister would have beaten me senseless if I did not listen to her. I was not the only one scared of my sister. Trou, too, listened to her. Pech told him where his sister was and ordered him to go find her. Trou went his way, and I went with my sister. A new destiny awaited me.

My sisters Sim, Phorn, and Peak had seen Trou and me marching, and Pech had pulled me out of the line. I was disappointed that my sisters kept me from joining the army, but when I saw all my sisters together along with Pech's little girl, my disappointment completely vanished. My sisters and I cried. We hugged. We broke open wide our dammed emotions. Once again, we were a family. We were orphans, but we were a family. Together, we would start a new life, as a family.

For weeks, it was still dangerous in Battambang. The battles between the Vietnamese armies and the Khmer Rouge unpredictably took place in pockets of western parts of Cambodia and, in particular, the province of Battambang. We were not able to return to the city until days later.

While waiting to safely return to the city, we teamed up to find food and take care of Pech's little girl. As a family, my sisters and I were the parents of the toddler. As the only male of the family, I took on the role of a father to the girl. When we needed food too close to the battlefields, I would be the one to go find food for the family.

We slowly edged our way toward the city. We pushed as far into the city as we safely could. Some people took more risk and went in deeper, while others took less risk and lagged behind. Without an adult male in the family, my sisters and I were afraid to go too deep into the city; eventually, we settled in a big abandoned house in a suburb within the city limits. We only stayed for a short time, perhaps weeks, but during those weeks, I became bolder and ventured farther to find food and other necessities. Sometimes I went behind the enemy lines, where the food supplies were not yet looted. Dodging bullets, running for my life, and maneuvering around unexploded rockets and landmines became a normal part of my life. During the day, I was an adult; at night, I curled up like a baby yearning for the warmth and comfort of my parents. Nightmares permeated my sleep. Unbeknownst to my sisters, I woke up every morning with my shorts wet with urine. It did not matter whether the morning was cold; I woke up before my sisters and jumped in a nearby river to get rid of the urine smell.

One afternoon, I came home to find that Pech had left the family to seek a better opportunity that held the potential to help all of us. Although everyone in the family was responsible for taking care of Pech's little girl, Pech had named Peak as the mother in her absence.

RETURNING HOME

Within days of Pech's departure, my sister Sim ran into an old friend of hers, Siphan (Phan) Un. His family was squatting in a small abandoned house near the main hospital in the city. Living with him were his wife, aged father, and younger brother named Bunthan (Than) Un. He invited my family to share the house. My sisters and I moved in with his family. We only intended to stay temporarily with the family until we could safely move back into our home.

A few days after we moved in, I went to see what had happened to my home, located about five miles away, on the other side of the city. When I got there, I stood in the middle of the land where my house would have been if it had not been demolished by the Khmer Rouge. In place of my house, there were squatter shelters.

Before April 17, 1975, I had planted a coconut tree in my backyard in the center of an old automobile tire. At the time when my family was evacuated, the coconut tree was a few feet tall. Now, as I stood in the middle of my land, I could see the tree was at least a few times my height. Without my home, I was a little disoriented, but the tire indisputably marked my coconut tree. I knew my tree. My nostalgia reminded me that my family was broken. My pet owl and parrot were gone. My childhood was gone. My days of playing hide and seek and war games were forever gone. The air was heavy, choking, and short of oxygen. My stomach hurt. My face throbbed. My jaw tightened, and my sinuses became congested. My heart was empty. I stood there and cried. The squatters watched me, but I did not care.

Unable to return to our own home, my sisters and I adopted the new family as our own. The younger brother, Than, was a dark, handsome young man. Than got along well with me, and he adopted me as his little brother. He and I teamed up to find food for our newly formed family. We risked our lives together and depended on each other to find food near the battlefields and behind the enemy lines. We bonded as brothers. We kept each other safe. During our overnight trips to find food, we shared many dark nights under the stars and often under flying bullets and rockets. We helped each other maneuver around the minefields. As the only male among my siblings, I really enjoyed having Than as a big brother. In many ways, he filled the void of my brother-in-law Chip, who was killed by the Khmer Rouge. Having Than watching over me near the battlefields and in the minefields was a comfort to my sisters.

During one of our lootings, Than and I found a pair of oxen and an oxcart. With the oxcart pulled by a pair of oxen, we were able to bring home more food and other necessities. The cart enabled us to get into and out of the enemy lines quicker. Consequently, we were able to bring home higher-quality food.

Weeks turned into months, but we knew nothing of my sister Pech's whereabouts. In the meantime, Than and Peak became romantically interested in each other. Naive and idealistic, I had trouble accepting their romance but thought my sister deserved her happiness and, more important, a man to help her raise Pech's daughter.

One day, my long-lost sister Phon unexpectedly showed up. She had come home to find our family and was told by our old neighbors the whereabouts of my other sisters and me. A couple of years prior to the fall of Cambodia into the atrocious hands of the Khmer Rouge, my third-oldest sister, Phon, left my family in Battambang and went to Phnom Penh for a desk job. Now, to her surprise and horror, she found out for the first time that our immediate family had lost our parents, our grandmother, two brothers-in-law, our youngest sister, and one nephew to starvation and execution. We told her that our home was completely demolished, our land was squatted upon, and we were living with a family friend. As we exchanged our bad news of losses, Phon told us that her husband had gotten sick and died shortly after her family was evacuated out of Phnom Penh.

Phon had reunited with a childhood friend. The friend worked for the new government at the department of municipal utilities. She had helped Phon get an office job with the department. As part of the job benefits, the government provided modest housing for Phon. Phon took my other sisters and me into her home, just blocks from my birthplace.

Word that my sisters and I had returned to the city traveled fast. Within days, long-lost friends and neighbors came to visit us at Phon's quarters. My second-oldest sister, Dy, got in contact with the rest of the family for the first time since the evacuation. Like Phon, Dy was surprised and saddened by the news of our family's loss. In addition to their losses, both Dy and Phon must have felt an incredible guilt for not being there to share the suffering with the family. I was young, but I understood and empathized with their guilt. We spent days and nights sharing the stories of our lives. Our family shared pain and loss. We were incomplete, but we were a tighter and more loving family.

Than and I continued to team up and find food together. We also took turns taking care of our oxen. On my turns taking care of the oxen, my nephew Tonat would come along and help me. Tonat was Dy's firstborn. When the Khmer Rouge took over Cambodia, Tonat was just a toddler. So I was a stranger to him when we first reunited, but as we spent time together herding the oxen, he and I bonded as nephew and uncle.

ESCAPING TO THE THAI BORDER

After nearly five years on my own under the Khmer Rouge regime and as the only male left in the family, I thought I was the patriarch, the man of the family, the one who made decisions for the entire family—as the Cambodian tradition would have it. Although I was now the youngest in the family, the deaths of my parents should have allowed me as the only male to have the dominant influence over any decision that might affect the family. That thought lasted for a short while, until the day when my sister Phon came home and took charge of the family.

After a couple of weeks in Battambang, Phon had made friends with Dy's cousin-in-law, Vann Mealy Metta Touch (Mealy). As their friendship quickly developed, Phon and Mealy collaborated on a plan to escape into Thailand.

The fact that I was the only male left in the family and traditionally to be consulted on any family decision did not matter at all to Phon. Her mind was made up, and she was ready to escape from Cambodia. Mealy was the added influence. I had no input in the matter. Phon simply pulled rank and ordered me to prepare for an escape into Thailand.

Phon also pulled rank on Peak, but Peak's heart was with Than. Peak's wish to be with Than created friction within the family. Sim and Phorn sided with Peak and Than, but Phon was not giving in. Dy, feeling not as much a part of the family due to her separate life during the Khmer Rouge, was neutral. I was caught in the middle. A stalemate would fall on me to break the tie.

Phon had been known to be the most stubborn in the family, but she was one of the kindest sisters to me. She had always seemed to understand my imperfection more than anyone else in the family. Being educated, knowledgeable, and smart, she commanded my respect and admiration.

On the other hand, my other sisters had suffered alongside me during the Khmer Rouge. In a sense, we had become one.

In the battlefields, beneath the flying bullets and behind the enemy lines, I watched Than, with his broken heart. He risked his life, and at the end of each trip, he gave me a larger portion of our findings so that my family—and particularly Peak—would be well fed. It was obvious that he cared about my sister and his heart was broken facing the possibility of losing her. A traditional man, he would not impose on my family's wish and interfere with our internal affairs.

In the end, it was up to me to make it right. I spoke with Phon and asked some very tough questions. Was it our place to decide Peak's future? What if she got killed during the escape? Would we then be able to live with our decision? How about the broken hearts of the two lovers? I was eventually able to convince Phon that Peak was old enough to live her own life.

The decision was made. Phon, Mealy, and I would cross the border, but not before the wedding of Than and Peak. The wedding ceremony was quickly organized and held. It was not much, but it was the first wedding free of the Khmer Rouge decree. I was so proud of my family. Many friends and relatives came together. It was profound. The wedding was not just the union of the two lovers; at the wedding, people reunited. For most people at the wedding, it was the first reunion since 1975. We celebrated the reunion and shared our respective loss and grief. It was simultaneously sad, joyous, beautiful, and reflective. For me, it was the wedding of a lifetime, and no wedding besides my own could match it.

My other sisters had difficult choices to make. For one reason or another, mostly due to their respective family commitments, they all decided to stay. My heart was once again broken, because we had just reunited and had yet to reconcile our feelings of loss, let alone celebrate our reunion; now, we would once again be separated.

Mixed emotions were flying around in the family for a few days before our escape. Some emotions were easily shared and spoken out loud among the family members and close relatives. Deep and not easily understood emotions were kept hidden; without a word, we exchanged deep hugs, longing stares, prolonged hand-clasps, and excruciating sobs.

To compensate me for my share of the oxen we jointly owned, Than gave me a piece of gold to take with me. The gold piece was as small as the tip of my little finger.

I yearned for the trip to happen, which made the few days waiting rather long. I was excited because something new and adventurous was about to happen in my life. The wait was unbearable. The prolonged farewell by family and friends was even more unbearable. I experienced all ranges of emotions, but mostly guilt and sadness.

In one sense, the wait was over far quicker than I anticipated. Emotionally, I was not ready to leave. I did not feel I had said everything I needed to say to my sisters nor heard everything I needed to hear from them. I did not share with them enough hugs, longing stares, prolonged hand-clasps, and excruciating sobs. I felt as if my heart had been cut out of my chest or a chunk of flesh had been removed from my stomach.

Throughout the entire trip, I went back and forth between elation and guilt. In fact, to this day, I still struggle to reconcile my happiness and guilt.

Mealy, Phon, and I traveled on foot toward Thailand. Mealy and Phon each brought a few changes of clothes. I only had the clothes that I was wearing. We didn't have any money, because the Khmer Rouge had abolished the monetary system and the country was still in a chaotic war. We counted on selling the gold piece in Thailand.

We tried to be inconspicuous on our journey. We traveled only in daylight. Morning was the best time to travel, because there were more people out searching for food and other survival necessities. We walked in the morning on a war-ruined highway and settled in just off the road in the afternoon. We pretended to be squatters, which was not difficult, because we had to rest and eat. We weren't able to bring along our traps for obvious reasons; we needed to travel light. We did our best to catch fish, eels, frogs, and grasshoppers by hand along the highway. Food was scarce because everyone was scavenging for whatever was available.

After days of clandestine travel, we met and joined other escapees. There were approximately thirty people in the group, which was made up of people of various ages, including a few babies. Everyone's anxiety (including mine) escalated from day to day as we temporarily squatted in a huge abandoned farmhouse near the Thai border.

Mealy had been enrolled in a university in Phnom Penh before the Khmer Rouge took over Cambodia and knew English. As the only English speaker in the group, Mealy monitored an underground radio broadcast in the English language. Mealy told the other escapees to wait a week or so because the Thai government was sending the Cambodian refugees back into Cambodia through the treacherous mountain Phnom Dongrek, protected by minefields. A rumor was also flying around that scores of Cambodian refugees had been shot dead by Thai soldiers as they refused to be repatriated back into Cambodia.

We waited and waited while Mealy continued to monitor the situation.

While waiting for an opportunistic moment to resume our escape, a neighboring family from my hometown arrived and joined with us. A daughter of the family, who was also a friend of my sister Phon, told us that our sister Pech was in a nearby town, Svay Sisophon.

Since Phon had not seen Pech since 1975, we wanted to go back and find Pech. We also hoped that we could convince Pech to come along. At the very least, we wanted to say our farewell, since we had no hope of ever seeing her again. So Phon and I decided to head back to Svay Sisophon.

After an entire day on foot on a dusty road, we arrived in Svay Sisophon. It was not difficult to find Pech. Pech was well and romantically involved; she did not want to leave. All three of us stayed up practically all night crying and catching up. Phon and I returned to the farmhouse the next day.

Days, perhaps a week or two, went by as Mealy continued to monitor the situation. We continued to maintain the appearance of squatters. We caught fish by hand and hunted birds with slingshots. We traded some fish for salt and rice.

One morning, the anticipated good news arrived. Concerned by the Thai government sending Cambodian refugees back into Cambodia through a landmine-infested mountain-range border, the international community had decided to expedite the process of moving all refugees out of Thailand.

The opportune time had come, and we planned to begin our border crossing the next day.

LAST MEAL BEFORE ESCAPING INTO THAILAND

That afternoon, Mealy and I went out to find food. We were hoping to catch some fish by hand at a lake located about a kilometer away from the farmhouse. Along the side of the lake, we saw a man walking with his retriever trotting playfully behind him. Apparently, the man was better off than we were. He had on his shoulder a long fishing pole, a few traps, and a crossbow. By our standard, he dressed well and appeared native.

The man barely noticed us and gave us a brief and stingy glance—as if Mealy and I were a disease—as he and his dog passed us by. Ironically, his dog gave us a much kinder greeting. It came and tried to lick my hand. The man rudely called his dog away, but not before I managed to secretly spit into the dog's mouth.

In Cambodia, it was common knowledge passed down from generation to generation that a dog would follow you as if you were its master if you spit into its mouth. I had never seen proof of this until that afternoon.

I noticed the dog's hesitation as its master repeatedly called it. There was something peculiar about this dog. Oddly, I felt a connection with the dog because it kept looking into my eyes. It responded to the call of its master, ran a little bit toward the master, stopped, and turned to stare at me. This ceremonial behavior was repeated until both the man and the dog disappeared into the distance.

Mealy and I went on our way in the opposite direction. It wasn't long before the dog returned and caught up with us. Mealy and I looked at each other, and without a spoken word, we knew we had ourselves a good meal. Suddenly, we both began to walk really fast, as if to get away from the dog. However, in actuality, we wanted to get to the camp before the man came looking for his dog. The dog kept up with us through the wooded area, across a field, and to the farmhouse.

That early evening, Mealy and a few other men slaughtered the dog, and the women prepared a meal. We celebrated our luck and the good news. The quiet festivity went on for a couple of hours after nightfall. Then we went to bed, but anxiety kept us up most of the night tossing and turning. I might have slept an hour or two just before my sister woke me up for the trip.

THAI BANDITS, VIETNAMESE, AND KHMER ROUGE

Having never been outside of my third-world province, let alone the country, I felt an indescribable excitement… elation. As the group was preparing to start the trip, I imagined crossing the border to a very exciting world, a world at least as exciting as the one I knew before the Khmer Rouge destroyed it.

I imagined electricity, running water, automobiles, colorful clothes, and food.

I had fond memories of Coca-Cola. While I was growing up in Battambang, before the Khmer Rouge era, soft drinks such as Coca-Cola were not for the poor kids. Whenever I was given some, I took a long time to drink it and repeatedly swished it around in my mouth before swallowing it; I loved feeling the fizz go down my throat before I burped.

My memories of Coca-Cola reminded me of Dy's wedding. At the wedding, my parents provided an extravagant amount of Coca-Cola for the guests. I remembered my friends, my cousins, and me playing outside the wedding tent; we were playing with the full bottles. We opened the caps, put our thumbs over the opening of the bottles, shook the full bottles, and sprayed the drinks on one other. We then licked the syrup off ourselves. Each of us took home a few empty bottles, because we thought the Coca-Cola bottles were really cool; I took one bottle to school to brag about the fact that there was plenty of Coca-Cola at my sister's wedding.

My mind wandered ...

Totally forgetting about the minefields, the Vietnamese soldiers, the Khmer Rouge, and the vast scary unknown world I was about to face, I could hardly wait to start the trip. The short wait seemed like an eternity. I was annoyed by the babies who cried constantly, the women who had to pack their small belongings, and the old folks who moved ever so slowly.

I kept looking at the eastern horizon, anxiously hoping that the sun would not be rising soon. We would have to postpone the trip if we could not make it across the open fields into the woods before dawn, because the Vietnamese soldiers were patrolling the fields to prevent the Khmer Rouge's attack and the escape by the Cambodian people into Thailand.

I was ready. I was more than ready. I had my little piece of gold tucked snugly in one of my nostrils. I had on my cotton shorts, my cotton shirt, and my two-inch platform sandals I had made from a tire of an army truck. I was going somewhere into the future — an uncertain future, but a future nonetheless.

The wait was long, but the march in the dark across the fields was even longer. I was annoyed by the babies, women, and old people. I kept thinking that my sisters had sacrificed their opportunity to come along partly because they might have felt their families would slow us down. Yet, here I was, burdened and slowed down by strangers. I was angry but kept it to myself because I knew my sister would not approve of such selfishness.

I was angry, but I was glad to reach the woods. Then I was frightened when four armed men approached us.

I knew immediately that the men were neither Khmer Rouge nor Vietnamese soldiers because of the way they dressed and the weapons they carried. Similar to the Khmer Rouge, their uniforms were black. However, the uniforms were of a far better quality than the cheap cotton uniforms worn by the Khmer Rouge. Their western military boots, caps, backpacks, canteens, and M-16 rifles were distinctively non-communistic. Their clean-cut hair and smooth, dark skin were the definitive contrast to the Khmer Rouge's wild hair and rough skin and the Vietnamese soldiers' simple-cut hair and light skin. Their uniforms were definitely different from those of the Vietnamese soldiers. The Vietnamese soldiers wore lower-quality green fatigues, less sophisticated black army boots, and simple light green hats or caps. The M-16 rifles were a clear indication that the men were neither Khmer Rouge nor Vietnamese soldiers, because both armies were armed with AK-47 rifles.

A few of my former neighbors were able to communicate with the men in Thai. As it turned out, the armed men were Thai bandits who regularly went deep into Cambodia waiting for any Cambodian escapees with valuable belongings. I was acutely aware of the piece of gold hidden inside one of my nostrils.

My former neighbors managed to convince the bandits that they had wealthy relatives in Thailand and the relatives would financially reward them if they would lead us safely into Thailand. So, led by the bandits, we resumed our journey down a narrow path through a jungle protected by landmines and unexploded ordnances.

We were not running, but we were quietly marching as fast as we could. Two bandits led the way. The other two bandits did their best to bring up the tail, made up of the old people and families with little children and babies.

As the bandits took full charge of the trail, my neighbors seemed to be second in command. They did their best to translate the communications between the bandits and the other escapees. I noticed gripes and resentment directed toward them by the slow people as they tried to speed up the crowd. I was annoyed and hoped that we would at some point ditch the slow people.

The sun had barely reached a 45-degree angle above the horizon when the Vietnamese patrols fired bullets and small rockets at us. Chaos, terror, and panic... there were screams in Cambodian, Thai, Chinese, and Vietnamese. Every man for himself, I ran as fast as I could. I neither slowed down for people who stepped on mines nor cared what happened to anyone else (including my sister) at that moment. The sound of the mine explosions and screams for help from other people only urged me to run faster and farther.

The sounds of the firing guns, flying bullets, intimidating rockets, exploding landmines, and screaming chaos faded. My adrenaline subsided, but my heart was still pounding. Silence once again emerged as more and more people filed in and gathered into a group. Many old people, small children, and families with babies were noticeably missing.

When my sister and Mealy caught up, I simply regarded it as a matter of fact that they had survived the shooting. Oddly enough, I was more concerned about missing the bandits than missing my sister, Mealy, and my neighbors—the bandits served as both the guides and the protectors.

Then I was disappointed that through the chaos I had lost my sandals. However, I was glad that my clothes were untouched and my gold was still tucked securely in my nostril. I was whole and ready to move on.

All four bandits showed up unharmed, along with my neighbors and their families. Overall, only about two-thirds of the people survived the vicious attack.

We must have run for well over an hour, or so it seemed.

Everyone marched on, quiet and happy to be alive. Every time a baby cried, I wanted to strangle it. I wanted to kill the baby's entire family for putting me at risk. My heart pounded every time a bird made a startling chirp. My eyes constantly scanned my surroundings. I walked forward, backward, and sideways. I looked up. I looked down. I looked left and right. My head was constantly turning, whether I walked straight, forward, backward, or otherwise.

My sister and I did not exchange a word. No one else seemed to be interested in any conversation, either. Like me, everyone was in a constant lookout mode.

We stopped for lunch near noon. We had lost much of our travel food during the ambush. To my surprise, the bandits took out cans of sardines from their backpacks to share with us. The sardines were a priceless luxury. Everyone crouched in a circle. I was annoyed and angry at a crying baby. I began to eat, and suddenly, the gold piece dislodged itself from my nostril and landed on the soft ground between my crouching feet. My heart was pounding once again. I immediately and instinctively moved my right foot to place my big toe over the gold piece. I discreetly lifted my head to see whether any of the bandits had noticed the gold piece. Inconspicuously, I picked up the gold piece with my right hand and lodged it back into its rightful place, my nostril. I was quite aware that the gold piece was now muddy, but I was relieved that it was once again safely cached. Throughout the entire lunch, I was neither able to completely tame my pounding heart nor able to enjoy the sardines. The luxurious sardines became just another lunch.

Grrrrr! I could have put my nefarious grip around that crying baby. I could have killed the stupid mother as well.

Despite the baby's crying, the lunch was completed undisturbed. We must have traveled far enough from the Vietnamese patrol. We were deep into the jungle, not knowing whether we were in Cambodia or Thailand. We passed big trees, small trees, bushes, and open fields and crossed a few narrow creeks. There were no rivers in our path. The path was somewhat beaten down. The bandits told us to stay within the path to avoid stepping on the landmines.

The repetitious scenery of the jungle made me feel like we were going in circles. I had doubts that we were going in the right direction. I imagined stepping on a landmine and dying. I imagined being ferociously eaten by a tiger. I imagined getting lost and becoming a cannibal. I imagined being killed by a cobra. I imagined being alone in the jungle.

I was scared. I was afraid of what would come next. I was doubtful that the bandits would keep their promise. I thought that they would most likely sell Mealy and me into slavery and Phon to a brothel. I thought my neighbors' relatives in Bangkok would not pay a reward on our accounts.

I started to regret escaping Cambodia. I doubted Phon's wisdom and decision to escape Cambodia. I wished that I had asserted my rightful influence as patriarch of the family. I wished that I had not been seduced by the idea that life would be better in another world. I had done just fine back at home looting for food from day to day in order to survive.

It was late in the afternoon when a group of about fifty Khmer Rouge guerrillas appeared from nowhere and surrounded us. These guerrillas had been driven out of power by the Vietnamese army and deep into the jungles along the Thai border, where they lived and fought the guerrilla war against the Vietnamese and new Cambodian armies. They regarded any Cambodian who had not been evacuated by them into the jungle as their enemy. They had been brutal when they were in power, but as guerrillas, they were known to be more brutal against any enemy, Vietnamese or not.

To these grubby guerrillas, we were their enemy. We were the ultimate traitors. I was certain that they were going to kill us. Without a doubt, they would torture us before they killed us.

The guerrillas were mostly boys between eleven and thirteen. They were led by a few young men. They wore their usual intimidating faces without smiles, but a few of them uncharacteristically wore an exaggerated application of white power makeup on their faces. The white makeup made them look silly, morbid, and psychotic. Their utter silence, bare feet, AK-47 rifles with bayonets, machetes, and black cotton uniforms with red scarves were foreboding.

One of the guerrillas' leaders ordered us to sit down in a close bunch. The guerrillas formed a circle around us with their AK-47 rifles pointed threateningly at us. They escorted the Thai bandits away from us into the woods. Then they ordered us to divest all of our belongings in one pile. Phon, Mealy, and I had nothing valuable other than the gold piece hidden in my nostril. I lay low and kept my gold piece while everyone else formed a pile with their stuff: plastic rain cloths, sandals, watches, jewelry, rice, dried fish, dried beef jerky, Thai bahts, U.S. dollars.

The women were escorted into the woods supposedly to be searched for any hidden valuables. During their absence, I imagined horrible torture like rape being done to them.

My concerns for the women's safety (especially my sister's) were a much-needed distraction. During the women's absence, I totally forgot about my own safety and fear. All I could think about was the women's welfare. I feared for them. I was anxious for them. I temporarily became a man. I thought of ways I could rescue them. I thought of being a hero and disarming a couple of the guerrillas. I thought of taking the AK-47 rifle from the youngest guerrilla, who seemed to have his eyes fixed on me—perhaps he read my thoughts. My heroic imagination went wild, producing enough adrenaline for me to kill at least one of the guerrillas with my bare hands. My adrenaline urged me to act, but my cowardice and selfishness kept me spinelessly safe.

After a short while, the women were escorted back to join us. To my relief, they appeared unharmed. Their mental and physical faculties appeared normal and calm. There was no obvious sign of abuse of any kind. I looked into my sister's eyes in search of any sign of abuse. I found none.

The return of the women brought fear back to my attention. I felt a few drops of my urine percolating in my cotton shorts. My stomach was churning as if I were ravenous. I thought this time that death—which I had escaped many times—would surely come to me.

My fear forced me to stare blankly at the ground. I waited for my gloomy fate. I shut down. I heard nothing. My peripheral vision spanned no farther than my two big toes. I prayed silently to the spirit of my father for protection. I thought my time was coming.

I have no idea who said it was time to get up to go. As I indifferently got up and lifted my head to look around, I noticed the Khmer Rouge guerrillas gather the confiscated items and disperse into the woods.

I was relieved and puzzled but grateful to be alive. From the looks on the faces of the other escapees, I knew I was not alone in feeling bemused but extremely happy to be alive.

The Thai bandits did not return. We were momentarily helpless. Without anyone to lead the group, each family resumed the trip together but independently. Everyone was still shocked by what had just transpired. No one really knew how far we had to travel to get to Thailand. We hoped to get there soon, because the Khmer Rouge guerrillas had taken all the food. We went without food and water for the entire afternoon, because we dared not step off the beaten path into the minefields.

Exhausted, sore, thirsty, and hungry, we finally emerged from the jungle into a rice field. On the horizon, the sun was at dusk. In the distance, there were a handful of farmers plowing their rice field. I felt uncertainty in my stomach. Having had so many mishaps in one day, I thought the worst. I thought we had entered the Khmer Rouge stronghold. We would soon be doomed and once again would be forced to relive the life under the Khmer Rouge regime.

In one very long day, I had encountered Thai bandits, had been shot at by

Vietnamese soldiers, had witnessed people stepping on landmines, and had been terrorized by Khmer Rouge guerrillas. Now what? Having journeyed a life full of tragedy, I would not have been surprised if the farmers were Khmer Rouge communists.

REFUGEE CAMPS

Having lost hope, I bent down to drink the water from the rice paddy. The water was fresh, cool, and clear. There were small crabs in the water. For the moment, my focus was utterly on catching a few crabs. Like everyone else, each time I caught a crab, I indiscriminately ate it alive.

Somewhat collected and fresh, we took a chance and approached the farmers. We were all relieved to hear the farmers speak Thai instead of Cambodian. I knew then that I had reached a safe haven.

I was also glad that my neighbors were still with us. They were our Thai speakers. One of the farmers took us to the nearby temporary military post, where a Thai soldier escorted us to his base.

At the base, there was a makeshift refugee camp in which there were many other Cambodian refugees. We were fed supper before being told to go to sleep.

The next morning, I was awakened by a whistle. The Thai soldiers told everyone to hurry up and get on a bus. There was a line of buses with engines running and doors open. Indifferent to the situation and the noise, Phon, Mealy, and I got on one of the buses and took our seats. Our neighbors were also on the bus. I did not know nor cared what had happened to the rest of the people who had crossed the border with us. There were just too many things happening, and they were all happening rather quickly.

Being on the bus was like heaven. The day before, I had been surprised by Thai bandits, shot at by Vietnamese soldiers, terrorized by Khmer Rouge guerrillas, and escorted to a military base by a Thai soldier. And the day before that, I had been an accomplice to killing and eating someone's dog. Today, I was on a bus.

Wow! The clean, cushioned seats, Thai music, glass windows, and painted pictures on the bus were surreal to me because I had not seen such things since the Khmer Rouge had taken over Cambodia in April 1975.

As the convoy of buses began to move forward, I was very excited. I was elated. I could not believe how my life had changed overnight. No one had told me where the bus was taking us, but it would have been irrelevant anyway. According to Mealy, we were not going to be sent back into Cambodia. So I was not a bit concerned about that. I simply entertained myself with the scenery as the bus took us through Thai villages and farms.

MAI RUT REFUGEE CAMP

When the buses dropped Phon, Mealy, me, and other Cambodians off at the Mai Rut refugee camp, the weather was miserable. It was cold and wet. The rain was relentless. The camp was nothing more than a stretch of beach bounded by barbed wire. There was no shelter of any kind. There was absolutely no sign of human habitat. The sandy ground was soaking wet from the tenacious rain. I could hear and feel the presence of an ocean, but I could not see it.

At first impression, I thought it was a prison for illegal immigrants from Cambodia. I felt anxiety from the adults. Nonetheless, I was excited. I had never been anywhere near an ocean before. So the oceanic rain and the sound of the ocean brought me an adventurous euphoria. The rainy land was peaceful, gloomy, and desolate, but the crowd was excited and active, like a gold rush.

For the first time in nearly five years, I felt like a normal Cambodian child. I had no responsibility other than going with the flow. Mealy had gradually emerged as the head of my new family, which consisted of Mealy, Phon, and me. I was oblivious to my present situation and future. Mealy and Phon were my new guardians, and they were fully responsible for my welfare and my future.

It was obvious that a budding romance between Mealy and Phon had developed over the course of our escape. From the start, Mealy had often rubbed me the wrong way. As Mealy and my sister grew closer, I felt like I was losing my sister. That created a friction between Mealy and me. He and I argued constantly, and I often felt like both he and Phon treated me like a child.

I was a teenager in an old handmade cotton shirt and pair of cotton shorts, and I had no shoes. I was among a herd of refugees escorted by Thai soldiers into the barbwire confinement. I was soaking wet from the cold rain. Yet, I was a jubilant child. I knew that I would be a free person inside the confinement. I knew that I would be able to roam free within the confinement. I knew I would not have to work thirteen hours a day, seven days a week, and 365 days a year without adequate food. I knew that I would remain in the custody of my new guardians, Mealy and Phon.

As I approached the barbwire fence and gate, I did not see a confinement or a gate to hell but a gate to my second chance in life, a gate to heaven. It was my chance to pick up where I had left off in 1975. Sadly, I had to redo my childhood without the guidance of my parents. Nonetheless, I knew that the spirits of my parents were with me at all times. I entered the gate with Mealy and Phon by my side and the spirits of my parents on my shoulders.

The first day inside the camp was miserable for the adults. Each family was given a spot on the drenched sandy ground to set up a tent. Plastic sheets and sticks were rationed to the families by western humanitarian workers for building tents. I had it easy. Mealy and Phon took care of the tent while I played with my fellow youths and little children. As Mealy was the only person who could speak English, he took on the responsibility of registering us. To ensure that we would stay together, Mealy registered himself as the head of the household, and Phon and me as his cousins—and dependants.

I do not remember how long I stayed in the Mai Rut camp, but I remember there was not much to do in the confinement. Nonetheless, it was heavenly to be a free child once again. I played all day with other children. The only times I came to the tent were at lunchtime, dinnertime, and bedtime. There was not much food, but there were enough rations, and I had nothing to worry about—I even got rations of Thai cigarettes to feed my smoking habit. My welfare and future were not mine to worry about. They were in the hands of fate, Mealy, and Phon. I was a young leaf at the mercy of the wind, but I was a happy and carefree leaf—life rocked.

The adults worried about Khmer Rouge raids, because the camp was right at the border of Cambodia and Thailand. At night, we could see battles between the Khmer Rouge and the Vietnamese at the top of the mountain inside the Cambodian border. I was oblivious to such concerns and felt safe within the confinement of the barbwire. I thought it was kind of cool to see bright bullets flying and rockets exploding on top of the mountain. My carefree life inside the barbwire camp was incredibly wonderful compared to the life I had just left behind in Cambodia.

During my stay in Mai Rut, my childhood friend Toeur and I redeveloped our friendship, which had been abruptly ended by the Khmer Rouge's evacuation of Battambang in 1975. During my escape into Thailand, there were other families that joined in the escape as the journey progressed. Among those families were my former neighbors whom I had not seen since the evacuation. Toeur was my former classmate and neighbor. Like my friend Trou, Toeur was more mature than I. Although Toeur and I joined other youths and played as children, Toeur usually came across as mature, reflective, and philosophical. To the contrary, I was immature, childish, and fundamentally carefree. Toeur had grown physically older and bigger than I had. I never understood Toeur's cerebral and philosophical approach to life. For that matter, I did not feel as close to Toeur as I had before our separation. We appeared as a young adult and a child. My friends had grown up, and I had remained a child physically and intellectually. My physical and intellectual growth hibernated during the reign of the Khmer Rouge.

Phon had asked me time and time again to quit smoking. I promised that I would quit after we got to a *piphob lok ti bey*—literally translated to a "third-world country," a term known by Cambodian refugees as a country of final destination. (Thailand was implicitly *piphob lok ti pi,* second-world.)

While I played all day, Mealy volunteered in the camp to help the World Vision staff with translation. That was when Mealy made friends with an American World Vision worker, Mr. Mike Carroll. Mr. Carroll would later be the one to tell Mealy that we had gotten permission to come to the U.S.

With the approval to come to America, we were told that we would be moved to a refugee holding camp in Bangkok. There, we would wait until a sponsor in the U.S. could be found by the refugee administration.

A few days before our departure to the holding camp in Bangkok, a group of new Cambodian refugees was brought into the camp. To my pleasant surprise, two of my cousins were among the newcomers. My younger cousin Vong and older cousin Vi were brothers. I had not seen either of my cousins since 1975. Only then did they learn of my losses. More fortunate than I, they had not lost any member of their family during the Khmer Rouge's rule. It was a good few days of reunion, but I was glad to be moved ahead into the holding camp in Bangkok.

Right before Mealy, Phon, and I got on the bus to Bangkok, Mr. Carroll gave us $20 USD and took a souvenir photograph with us. That day, I felt on top of the world because I was one of the few fortunate refugees selected to go to the Bangkok camp. I was one camp closer to heaven.

BUS RIDE TO BANGKOK HOLDING CAMP

I was still in the same cotton shirt and pair of cotton shorts, and still without shoes. (I don't remember ever washing those shorts or that shirt.) I was the poorest of the poor, but I was on top of the world; with Mealy and Phon by my side, and my parents on my shoulders, I stepped onto a bus. I was on my way to a world I had never known, one that would become the world of my second chance in life. Each step onto the bus was a step toward the world of opportunity and heaven. In such a world and heaven, I wanted nothing more than a clean shirt, a pair of "cowboy pants" (blue jeans), and a pair of shoes—of any kind. I had beaten the Khmer Rouge's idealism, and I was well on my way out of a living hell.

The bus ride to Bangkok was like a journey through paradise. Once out of the forest, rice fields, and farming communities with which I was familiar, the bus took us through a modernly paved highway and provincial cities. The bus passed schools, universities, markets, street vendors, tropical fruit stands, children in school uniforms, businesses, lampposts, automobiles, construction sites, electric and telephone cables, and all that was completely lacking during the Khmer Rouge. This made me realize that for nearly five years I had been like a frog seeing the vast sky from the bottom of a deep well.

The sentimental Thai music on the bus was beautiful and fresh, but it also brought me nostalgia for the era that predated the Khmer Rouge. Everything felt surreal. I felt as if I were in a movie. The bus ride gave me a lot of time to absorb the modern world and to dream of all the things I wanted in my future. I wanted nothing more than a clean shirt, a pair of cowboy pants, and a pair of shoes; now I realized there was more to it: *I had defeated the Khmer Rouge's idealism, and I was exiting the gates of hell.* I would be free to be materialistic and own nice things. I would have a clean shirt, a pair of cowboy pants, and a pair of shoes. I would have enough food, and I would be paid for my labor — instead of being starved and terrorized. At that moment, I was aware that I was now willing to kill anyone who would try to take away my freedom as the Khmer Rouge had.

A sight of children in their school uniforms alongside the highway brought me back to my childish dream. I wanted nothing more than a clean shirt, a pair of cowboy pants, and a pair of shoes.

As the bus passed more schoolchildren, my dream got bigger. *I wanted more than a clean shirt, a pair of cowboy pants, and a pair of shoes.* I forgot about the Khmer Rouge. I wanted to be in school. Oh, God, I missed walking to and from school with my youngest sister, Ali. I regretted not paying attention to my homework and teachers. I regretted not being a good student before the

Khmer Rouge. I yearned for my second chance in life. *I no longer wanted to waste my one shot at a second chance on a clean shirt, a pair of cowboy pants, and a pair of shoes; I wanted to be well educated.* At that moment, I truly understood why my parents had worked so hard to pay for their children's education. I daydreamed of attending school with American children and speaking "American." Oh, God, the thought of learning the American language and culture scared the living hell out of me. Nonetheless, I was actually excited.

BANGKOK HOLDING CAMP

Unlike the Mai Rut camp, the holding camp in Bangkok was boarded and could not be seen by the outside world. It was an isolated world inside of Bangkok. There was a poor but existing basic infrastructure that included communal sleeping quarters, electricity, a water basin, and showers. Rationed food was basic and adequate. There was a small noodle restaurant privately owned by a Thai peddler.

Like in the Khmer Rouge labor camp, the refugees slept tightly next to one another in two rows. The heads in one row were separated by about a foot of space from the heads in the other row. One refugee slept next to another; there was no privacy. Each family was given a mosquito net. Although the mosquito net was translucent, it marked our territory and gave us a modicum of privacy.

On the first day of our arrival, Mealy and Phon managed to sell my piece of gold to someone for 800 Thai bahts. Phon hid the money under her pillow that night, and someone stole it during our sleep.

When I found out that the money had been stolen, I cried my heart out. I boisterously cussed like a psychotic boy. I exploded in verbal violence. My cursing created a lot of attention in the camp, but I did not care, because I had lost more than 800 bahts that night. I had lost a priceless piece of gold. I had risked my life behind the enemy lines to earn it. During my escape to Thailand, I had discreetly carried it in my nostril through minefields, beneath the Vietnamese flying bullets and rockets, hidden from Thai bandits and Khmer

Rouge thugs, and across the treacherous border. Grrrrr, I hated the world. I really wanted to kill somebody.

Phon momentarily calmed me down; then, I walked away and spent most of the day by myself, hating the world and wanting to kill someone. That day, I wanted so much for someone to piss me off. I cast provoking looks at other boys, but no one dared to dignify my animalistic provocation.

In my anger, I impulsively went to the noodle restaurant and carelessly ordered a bowl of instant noodles. I had no money, and I had no intention of paying for it. The world had pushed me too far. It angered me. It owed me. This restaurant owed me. Looking for trouble, I came to the right place.

The hot and spicy noodles were delicious. The food diverted my anger and calmed me down. My focus was fully on the noodles. I enjoyed being served. It felt strange, but I appreciated the hospitality. The young man who served my table was polite. I took my time eating the noodles. The server's politeness and the scrumptious noodles brought me back to calmness. Peaceful, collected, and sensible, I now worried about how to get out of paying for my food.

My subsided anger shifted to anxiety, but then I noticed how the system of the restaurant worked. The servers who collected the cash were not the same servers who took the orders. In a busy time, a server who took an order had no clue nor paid too much attention to which customer had paid. When an opportunity came, I safely sneaked out without paying. From that day on, I ate a bowl of instant noodles in that restaurant almost every day without paying for it.

Some days later, Toeur and his family were also brought to Bangkok. As my only friend and confidant, Toeur joined me in my scheme to get free noodles. We played together and enrolled in an English class taught by the English-speaking volunteers from other countries. During my two-month stay at the Bangkok camp, I learned a limited set of English words and conversational phrases. My most memorable phrase was "Hello, Mister, how do you do?"

My view of Bangkok was defined by my experience in the crowded and dirty camp. Like a frog's view of the vast sky seen from the bottom of a deep well, my impression of Bangkok was not positive. The camp was crowded, and the weather was hot, humid, and mucky.

The rationed food in the refugee camp was absolutely basic. Nonetheless, life in the refugee camp to life in the Khmer Rouge killing fields was heaven to hell. There was no work, and I played all day. In the morning, when the noodle place was really busy, Toeur and I scored free breakfast. Before bed, I washed myself at the communal basin. There was plenty of water in the concrete basin, but I had to scoop the water into a large bowl to wash myself. This was the first time I had touched soap and shampoo in almost five years.

At the Bangkok camp, Mealy was registered as the head of the household, Phon as Mealy's dependant cousin, and I as Phon's dependant little brother. This was necessary because in order for us to stay together, we had to register as a family. For whatever reason, the romance between Mealy and Phon was discreet. So they did not register as husband and wife. There was a rumor that single people had a better chance of being brought to the U.S. The same rumor had it that families with school-age dependants would have a better chance of coming to the U.S. After all was said and done, I was registered as a dependant who was born in 1964.

One afternoon, Phon told me that World Vision had found a family in California to sponsor us to come to the U.S. Regarded as a child, I was given information on a need-to-know-only basis. I had no idea what kind of family sponsored us or when we would go to the U.S. I was not sure if we would travel by air or by sea. I had never been on an airplane, and I was scared of flying. I had heard exaggerated stories of turbulence, motion sickness, and plane crashes. I was excited and scared at the same time — mostly scared.

In preparation for our journey to the U.S., mugshots of Mealy, Phon, and me were taken as part of the travel and immigration documents. A camp official used white chalk and wrote Mealy's identity on a piece of wooden board: "TOUCH VANN MEALY METTA 1/3 T.31817." As directed by the official, Mealy held up his identity card (board) to his chest, and the photographer took the mugshot. At that moment, Mealy officially became the Cambodian refugee "TOUCH VANN MEALY METTA" and the head of household of a three-person family ("1/3 T.31817").

After the mugshot of "TOUCH VANN MEALY METTA 1/3 T.31817," the camp official wiped the chalk off the board and wrote "UNG SIV HENG 2/3 T.31817." Finally, I had my turn as the third and final member of the T.31817 family to get my mugshot. The world was in slow motion. The spotlight was on me. Jealous eyes of the other refugees were on me. I could virtually hear an ant crawling nearby. I could hear whispers among the refugees. I could hear the camp officials working on my travel and immigration documents.

"Min ey te. Kom prouy. Dak vea chnnam mouy pon pramboun roy hok seb boun tov," said a Cambodian camp official to Mealy and Phon. "Never mind. Don't worry. Just put down 1964 for his birth date" was what the official suggested to Mealy and Phon. At that moment, I officially became the fifteen-year-old "UNG KILONG 3/3 T.31817." Momentarily, I was a celebrity. Every refugee kid wanted to be in my shoes. I knew then that the sky was the limit. I had the labor skills and the perseverance to survive the new world. I was ready to come to the U.S. and work on a farm. I possessed the skills of a farmer. I knew how to handle oxen and water buffaloes. I knew how to raise chickens, ducks, and pigs.

I wondered if I were too old to pick up the American language. I remembered growing up making fun of the Chinese-Cambodians who had trouble speaking Cambodian. I feared being ridiculed by Americans for not being able to speak English. I was scared of the sky, the sea, and the big unknown: the future. I was deeply sad about the imminent reality of not ever seeing my sisters in Cambodia again. I was scared to be in a world I had never known. I thought about going back to rejoin my sisters in Cambodia. I thought a lot, but my life was no longer mine. I was the fifteen-year-old "UNG KILONG 3/3 T.31817," in the legal custody of Mealy and Phon. I was a leaf at the mercy of the wind.

Mealy, Phon, and I had our mugshots made, our documents prepared, and a sponsor in California. We were ready to come to the U.S., but first we had to pass the medical examination. So we were driven to a hospital in Bangkok to get our blood work, x-rays, and skin tests done.

In the hospital lobby and waiting room, I was acutely aware of all eyes on me. The children stared pointedly at me in my conspicuous refugee outfit, and the parents attempted (with little success) to divert the children's attention. The cleanliness was absolutely celestial and contrary to the sanitation of the hospital in which my mother had died. Live plants in the lobby seemed ridiculously unnecessary and out of place. The lighting was pleasantly foreign. A mechanical escalator and elevator were magical and mesmerizing. A patient in a wheelchair seemed sad, but I could not muster sympathy because she seemed sumptuously more fortunate than I.

People appeared extraordinarily beautiful and clean. Even the ugliest of the nurses, doctors, and patients were attractive. I felt drawn to the Thai language. It was soft, tender, seducing, and comforting. I was mesmerized by the people, their livelihood, and the surroundings. A shot of anger mixed with melancholy rose in my chest. Was this what the Khmer Rouge had tried to achieve, or was it what it had tried to prevent?

I felt out of place and insignificant. I wondered whether I would be able to adjust to this new world. I wondered whether it was too late for me to become like one of those clean and well-dressed people staring at me as they walked by. My mind wandered, but my anxiety was unmistaken. I worried about my medical examination. I worried about my potentially unhealthy lungs from years of tobacco smoking. I worried about my stomach after eating dog, rats, snakes, insects, and crude rice. I wondered what would happen if I did not pass the medical examination. Would Mealy and Phon go to the U.S. by themselves or stay with me?

A nurse called Mealy, Phon, and me into an examination room. I was given a small cup and told to urinate into it. I didn't have trouble producing the urine sample, but I could not understand how the doctor could determine my health from my urine. I also could not understand what drawing blood had to do with my medical examination. A nurse scratched my skin with a sharp metal object for a sample—that, too, was a mystery to me. The nurse told me to step forward and place my chest tightly against an x-ray machine. I understood the purpose of the x-ray machine because I had heard about it before the Khmer Rouge era. I understood that the x-ray would allow the doctor to see everything inside my body, but I worried about what the machine would do to my bones, heart, and lungs. I had heard rumors that x-ray machines could destroy bones and internal organs. I was nervous standing in front of the machine, and I was relieved when the procedure was done.

The examination went well, and we were driven back to the camp. The mysteries of the escalator, elevator, and automatic door occupied my thoughts as we rode back to the camp in a taxi. In my mental delineation, I concluded that there had to be hidden people pushing and pulling ropes to mechanically operate the escalator, elevator, and automatic door.

COMING TO AMERICA

Within days, the test results cleared Mealy, Phon, and me to enter the U.S. I kept my promise to Phon and smoked my last cigarette. Quitting smoking cold turkey was not an issue, as I was very excited about entering my *piphob lok ti bey*—America, my "third-world country." We were among a number of refugees bussed to an airport. By now, a bus ride was just a bus ride. The airport was interesting, but no more so than the hospital. The voice over the intercom inside the airport was somewhat new and fascinating, but not as mysterious and spectacular as the escalator, elevator, and automatic door. Before the Khmer Rouge, my family had a radio. I never understood how voices came over the radio, but I accepted the fact that the voices were somehow broadcast to the radio. I assumed an intercom worked the same way as a radio.

Each refugee was given a plastic bag with the World Vision logo printed on the outside. Inside my bag, there were documents written in English. Other than my name, my assumed birth date, my mugshot, and my legal identity of "UNG KILONG 3/3 T.31817," the document was absolutely cryptic and meaningless to me. I felt privileged to be holding the bag but also embarrassed by it. Next to the group of well-attired passengers, the bag advertised my nomadic stature. In my original pair of shorts and shirt and a new pair of cheap rubber flip-flops given to me at the Bangkok camp, I was a nobody among the regular passengers. I was glad I was not alone as a refugee. As out of place as I was, a number of other refugees were worse off. Some of my fellow refugees had never seen a light bulb before coming to Thailand.

I was embarrassed and wished that the entire plane had been dedicated to the refugees. There were at least a hundred refugees—perhaps 200 or 300 or more. I was surprised that the plane could carry so many people. I had never seen a plane this close before, nor had I seen any plane this size. It was huge. It was more like a building than an airplane. I wished my sisters and friends at home could see this enormous bird. I wondered if the Khmer Rouge knew of the existence of such advanced technology. I wondered if it would be able to carry its own weight, let alone the weight of the passengers.

The world seemed to be oblivious to what had happened in the Khmer Rouge killing fields, of what had just happened to my family and me. I was so lost in this new world. I was uncertain of my future. Where would I start? What would my new home look like? Would I ever see my sisters back in Cambodia again?

I boarded the plane with a large group of refugees from Cambodia, Vietnam, and Laos. I could sense the frustration from the flight attendants and the regular passengers. I did not like the way the regular passengers rolled their eyes. I was embarrassed but observant. I realized that I had to change: I had to be different in order to survive my new home. I watched the flight attendants, the regular passengers, and my fellow refugees. At that moment, I began to assimilate the new culture. One day, I would be a regular passenger.

During takeoff, my stomach tightened and my hands started to sweat. I totally forgot about the Khmer Rouge killing fields. I had no thought pertaining to my sisters left behind in Cambodia. I was oblivious to everything. I did not feel good. I shut out everything. I could not stop thinking about crashing.

Seatbelt tightly buckled, eyes shut, fists clenched, knees pressed, I was alone with my father. The long takeoff required a long conversation with my father. I asked him to carry the plane safely to America. My father and I discussed my future. I asked for forgiveness for my wrongs. He forgave me. I asked about my mother and my youngest sister, Ali. He assured me that he watched after them. He told me that my grandmother appreciated my effort to bury her body. She was proud of me and my courage. In return, I made a lot of promises that day: *Let me live, and I will be good. I will follow the family's tradition of giving back and helping the less fortunate. I will study hard. I will take care of my sisters. I will be the perfect son to my father.* I had a long conversation with my father. He assured me that I had nothing to worry about. He would watch my every step. He was talkative that day. He talked me to sleep.

I woke up when the flight attendants began to serve food. I had no idea how long I had slept. I had no sense of time or space. There was nothing beneath the airplane but clouds. Above the clouds, the sky was light, but I did not know whether it was day or night on the ground.

By now, there seemed to be more civility coming from the regular passengers and flight attendants. The flight attendants were extraordinarily beautiful in their short-dress uniforms. I had never seen any woman that exotic in my life, and I had a hard time hiding my coy stare. I felt self-conscious. The velvety, light-colored skin of a flight attendant reminded me of my own imperfect skin. I reached out with my hands and caressed the dry and cracked skin on my bare shins. I felt soiled and destitute. I felt out of place. I felt unworthy. Oh, God, I had eaten rats, mice, and dog. I had drunk my own urine. I had drunk from and bathed in a puddle in which human cadavers decomposed. In the midst of my self-reflection, the flight attendant caught my stare. As if she knew what was on my mind, she gave me a cordial smile. There was unmistakably a hint of compassion in her eyes. As much as I appreciated her comforting smile and kindness, I was embarrassed and consciously avoided any further eye contact with her for the rest of the flight.

Mealy, Phon, and I were hungry, but we could not eat the sandwiches that were served. They were bland and mushy. We joked about being able to eat rat and dog but not American sandwiches. We got by with juice, crackers, fruit, nuts, and other snacks.

The flight seemed to stretch for days. The plane stopped for refueling in Okinawa, Japan. We were not allowed to deplane, and it was too dark to see Japan. Once we were in the air again and above the thick clouds, I looked outside my window. I saw the atmosphere divided equally into dark and light. I cannot recall whether the light sky was ahead of me or behind me, but I remember the division of darkness and light. It was a remarkable sight. I had a vision of my future. I experienced a crossover from darkness into light, and I felt my father's presence heavily set on my shoulder.

After a long flight, the plane finally descended over the city of San Francisco. Looking out the window, I was enthralled by the magnificent city lights beneath. I had never seen anything like it. Looking down on San Francisco, I felt like I was gazing down upon the magnificent heaven densely filled with shining stars. The plane traveled at an unbelievably slow speed. I had my eyes fixed on a blinking light on the ground just slightly ahead of the slowly moving plane. It took the plane forever to pass the light. Life momentarily stood still as the plane moved so slowly that it appeared to be hovering instead of traveling.

City lights shined on buildings, bridges, waters, and sports fields. Many things were foreign to me. I did not recognize baseball fields and football fields. From the sky, I mistook a football field for a military base. The heaven beneath was magnificent, sparkling, mesmerizing, but absolutely foreign to me.

Although I was elated by the heaven beneath me, the vibrantly sparkling city was intimidating. Among millions of densely positioned lights, a single vibrant light seemed rather insignificant. I imagined myself as an unlit spot on the backdrop of this vast carpet of lights. I was bewildered. I felt insignificant. I doubted my future.

As the plane got closer to the ground, its speed appeared to be faster. In my mind, the plane would not be able to land safely at such acceleration. My ears were plugged. The pressure in my head was at its highest point. My head hurt. My eyes neared the point of popping out of their sockets. The cavity of my torso was vastly hollow, and my stomach performed somersaults. I gripped and squeezed my seatbelt. I was dizzy. I was sick. I could no longer look out the window and appreciate the approaching heaven. I closed my eyes, cupped my face with my hands, and leaned forward on my knees. In the midst of my nausea and fear of a plane crash, I made up my mind that I would never fly again. I was suddenly saddened by the absolute certainty that I would never again see my sisters who had stayed behind in Cambodia. The price of my heaven was inexplicably expensive.

The plane landed safely. The refugees were directed to a secured room where custom papers were processed. While waiting for the papers to be processed, I learned how our trip from Bangkok to the U.S. had been paid for. A financial institution in New York had made a loan in the amount of $3,000 USD under Mealy's name to pay for the airfares and other related expenses. The amount was daunting, and I had no idea how we would be able to repay it. I was grateful that Mealy and Phon were the responsible adults, because I had no idea how to get started in this vast heaven—the land of opportunity, the United States of America.

I was tired, hungry, and nauseated from jet lag. The refugees were seated in a secured waiting room while the custom agents and interpreters worked on the documents in the next room. Customs seemed to take forever. From time to time, the agents looked up and through the glass window toward the crowd of refugees. Every time an agent looked my way, my stomach turned in wonder about whether I would be returned or jailed. Stern faces, official uniforms, and badges reminded me of the Khmer Rouge officials. I wondered if the agents thought I was a member of the Khmer Rouge. I wondered if my documents had been lost. Processing a room full of refugees took forever. I was really tired and hungry.

Very late into the night, the documents were processed and the refugees were told to get on a bus. I had no clue what would come next, and I doubted Mealy and Phon knew, either.

Soft music was played on the bus. I had never heard such tunes, and I did not understand the lyrics. Through Mealy's interpretation, I was introduced to the voices of Anne Murray and James Taylor.

That night, I cried a tear, and Anne Murray wiped it dry. I was lost, and Anne Murray took me home. She gave me hope. She gave me strength to face the world again. Through her voice, I imagined that she was a white, blond, and blue-eyed American. She sounded soft, compassionate, and beautiful. I wanted to meet this white, blond, and blue-eyed American woman. She sang me to sleep as the bus took me home — somewhere.

The bus ride was long, and I had no idea where we were going. The cushioned seat was luxuriously comfortable, and I woke up to James Taylor's voice in "You've Got a Friend." Mealy again translated the lyrics. Out the windows, the sky above me was dark, and my heart called my father's name out loud. Thanks to James Taylor, that night, I was reminded that my father was on my shoulder. My world had been cold. The Khmer Rouge hurt me and tried to take my soul. Through the voice of James Taylor, my father came knocking upon my door. I was not an abandoned orphan.

After a long bus ride accompanied by the lyrics of Anne Murray and James Taylor and the conversations with my father, we arrived at a hotel. I still had no clue whether this was my new home. It was very late, and I was not fully functional. The United States of America was no longer exciting. Electricity, automobiles, and all other modern things no longer fascinated me. I needed food and sleep. I simply followed Mealy and Phon to a hotel room and crashed.

It was just past midnight when the television and room service woke me up. As much as I needed sleep, I happily welcomed the food and television. The food was foreign and bland but edible. The television was fascinating. I had seen television a few times before the Khmer Rouge era, but I had never seen anything other than the black and white "snow"—absolutely no recognizable image. This particular television was mounted from the ceiling. The images were clear and colorful. The sound was crisp, but I did not understand any of it. The only program I understood and appreciated was a cartoon. I was fascinated by the animations. The cartoon characters moved rapidly with lots of energy. The characters did not seem to know anything about the world from which I had just escaped. They hinted no reference to the Khmer Rouge killing fields, labor camps, and refugee camps. They were happy, energetic, feisty, and totally oblivious to my incredibly difficult journey. They temporarily erased my memory of my past and suppressed my apprehension about my uncertain future. They adopted me as an innocent child. They made me laugh. They were my friends and put me to sleep.

After a few hours of sleep, we were awakened and told to get on a bus. Through Mealy's translation, I understood that we were to be flown to San Diego, where our sponsor lived.

I had not washed since the day I had left Bangkok. I was still dressed in the same pair of cotton shorts, a shabby cotton shirt, and a donated pair of cheap flip-flops. Carrying the plastic handbag with the World Vision logo printed on it, I got on the bus with Mealy, Phon, and other refugees. Once again, I was a leaf carried by the wind. I neither knew my destination nor could influence the path of my journey. I was simply a leaf at the mercy of the wind—but I knew within my heart that the current wind was kind and that my father was directing it.

By the time we got to the airport, I was hungry again. Phon asked Mealy to help me get some food. With the $20 given to us by Mr. Mike Carroll before we left the Mai Rut camp, Mealy took me to a food stand near our waiting area. Mealy read and translated the menu for me. Neither of us recognized any food type except hot dog. We had just had a dog for dinner the night before we crossed the Thai border. Unable to eat the sandwich on the plane, we were skeptical about what we could eat from the menu, but "hot dog" was definitely our safe bet. Neither of us believed what we saw on the menu. Americans ate dog? Wow! Ironically, a familiarity from the world that we had escaped gave us some comfort—we could eat dog.

The line at the food stand was long. Mealy and I were oblivious to it because we did not know that we were supposed to stand at the end of the line. We went directly to the stand to look at the menu, and then we immediately ordered three "hot dogs" instead of going to the back of the line.

When the hot dogs were given to us along with the change from our $20 bill, we were shocked by how expensive the hot dogs were. I did not understand the value of $20, but I thought it was a lot of money. We were even more shocked by the looks of the Americans in line waiting to order their "hot dogs." At first, Mealy and I thought they did not like our refugee looks and smells. After a short observance, we realized that we had violated American social etiquette—we had cut in line. I learned my first hard lesson in American culture.

Phon, Mealy, and I unwrapped our hot dogs. We looked at one another, laughed, and decided not to eat the cooked dog penises wrapped in bread. Sure, we had eaten dog before, but dog penises? No, thanks. I concluded that American food was disgusting.

While the flight between Bangkok and San Francisco had seemed to take days, the flight from San Francisco to San Diego was a short hop and uneventful.

Deplaned into the arriving terminal, we expected our sponsor family to be waiting for us. Other refugees either reunited with their families who already lived in the U.S. or found their sponsors holding signs with their names. We scanned the welcoming crowd for signs with our names. We found none. After all the refugees had been picked up by their families or sponsors, we were left unclaimed. I was a lost leaf in the empty sky.

A Laotian social worker who had come to pick up a handful of the Laotian refugees noticed that we were lost. He came over and spoke to Mealy in English. The man worked with and knew our sponsor, Mr. Kung Chap. After a long wait with us, he invited us to his home, where we could eat, rest, and call Mr. Chap. At his house, his wife served elaborate Laotian food for an early lunch. She offered Mealy wine and beer. The food looked heavenly, but I was paranoid and did not trust the family; I did not eat.

I had barely set foot in the country. My life had gone through one mishap after another. I stood guard and would not take any chance of being poisoned by this Laotian family. I wanted to make sure that between Mealy and me, one of us stayed alert in case the man had a hidden motive. I really thought that he would get Mealy drunk, send me into slavery, and sell my sister to a brothel. I did not eat or drink, and I was annoyed by Mealy's excessive consumption of alcohol. Using jet lag as my excuse, I refused to eat and insisted on stepping outside for fresh air. Outside, I tried to memorize the house façade and location in case I needed to provide the information to the police. I stayed outside as long as I could until I felt sure that Mealy had not been poisoned by food or alcohol.

When I came inside, I was glad to see Mealy sober and well, and I learned that the social worker had been able to contact a Cambodian family that knew the Chap family well. I learned there had been a miscommunication between the refugee agency and Mr. Chap. Mr. Chap's family thought they did not have to pick us up for another day. Consequently, the family had gone camping and would not return until later in the day.

The Cambodian family came and took Mealy, Phon, and me to their house around noon to wait for Mr. Chap. At their house, I ate stir-fried beef with Chinese broccoli for the first time in what seemed like an eternity. The Cambodian food brought nostalgia for my mother's cooking.

The lady of the house brought me a homemade Cambodian-style pillow to rest my head on. I watched my first American Western movie on television in classic black and white. I was told that the cowboy was played by John Wayne. I did not understand the dialogue, but I understood the story: chasing on horseback, knocking out teeth, dipping heads in water, drawing guns, and shooting bows and arrows. John Wayne was ridiculously invincible but funny. Just before I fell into my nap, the thought that Bruce Lee could easily kick John Wayne's butt crossed my mind.

Later that day, Mr. Chap came and took us to his house. The house was in a fairly respectable neighborhood. I was impressed and intimidated at the same time. I was surprised to find a lime tree and a tangerine tree in his backyard. His backyard was exotic, tropical, and somewhat pleasantly out of place. The family was among the Cambodian noble class. My family was outclassed, but we were treated with respect and compassion. Mr. Chap helped us apply for welfare, school, jobs, and an apartment. His family housed us for about three weeks before we got out on our own.

On our own, we rented an apartment. We were introduced to other Cambodian families who could help us understand what we needed to do to survive in the new culture. Phon enrolled at a community college. I enrolled in ninth grade at Einstein Junior High. Mealy worked as a translator at my school. The government provided food stamps, rent money, and medical care. Mealy's income paid for the most basic necessities not covered by the government, such as bus fares, pay telephones, and shoes. I attended church with other refugees and brought home from church donated used clothes for Mealy, Phon, and me. After school and on weekends, I scavenged for cans and bottles. At night, Phon and I attended additional English classes together.

My first American experience in San Diego was both challenging and exciting. My learning curve for both the language and the culture was extremely steep. When I arrived at Mr. Chap's house on the first day, I did not know how to use the shower. I was too embarrassed to ask for help. So instead, I took at least fifteen minutes before I could figure out how to turn on the faucet, switch on the shower, and regulate the water temperature. For months, I thought I was supposed to squat on the toilet seat instead of sitting on it. I was taught by other Cambodians how to dial a telephone. Using a public phone was tricky. I had to know when to put the coin in and when to dial. Anytime I made a mistake, I was horrified by the voice of an operator—both human and machine. For months, I would not cross a street in front of a policeman because I did not know the traffic rules. I hated the school bus because the kids often made fun of me. When I needed to go to the welfare office or a doctor's office, someone would pick me up in a car. I hated car rides. They gave me motion sickness just like the flight from Bangkok had.

On the better side of the coin, life was looking up. I made new friends with other Cambodian refugees in my English as a second language (ESL) class. Kim Ang Tang (Ang), Horn Vinh Sov (Horn), and I became the three amigos among the Cambodian refugee students at Einstein Junior High. At the time, we were inseparable. We hung out together at school and on weekends when I was not busy collecting cans and bottles. The clique of the three amigos served as my security blanket at school. I picked up English quicker than my ESL classmates. I was a rising star in the ESL class. Although I was not generally comfortable in school, the ESL class became my home class. It gave me my first sense of belonging since setting foot in the U.S. Within a few months, I gained enough courage to try out my simple greeting on a few American students at school. I graduated from "Hello" to "Hi" and from "How ahyou?" to "Wassup?" I was afraid to interact socially with the American students much beyond that because I usually did not understand their hazy English. At any rate, I was no longer a leaf at the mercy of the wind, but a sapling with roots.

A few months after Phon, Mealy, and I arrived in San Diego in 1979, Mealy and his younger brother Van Chenda Touch (Sam) found each other. Sam had left Cambodia before the Khmer Rouge took over Cambodia. Sometime in the winter of 1979, Sam traveled from Portland, Oregon, to visit us in San Diego. That was the first time Mealy had seen his brother since before the Khmer Rouge. During his visit, Sam convinced Mealy to move to Portland.

When I was told about the moving plan, my heart sank. I was upset and sad.

I resented the fact that I had no vote in the matter. I already was accustomed to life in San Diego—vigorous traffic, sirens, and other characteristics of the big city. My friends and my ESL class were my security blanket—my roots. Now I had to leave all of that behind. Like a toddler's baby teeth, my roots fell off, and I was again a leaf at the mercy of the wind.

PORTLAND, OREGON

Very early one morning in February 1980, Mealy, Phon, and I took a Greyhound bus from San Diego to Portland. Along Interstate 5, the bus took me away from my recently established comfort zone. From 1975 up to that point, San Diego had been the only place that had given me stability and a glimpse of my future. So when the bus carried me away from the city of San Diego, I felt like a leaf being blown away from the forest. I once again felt uncertain about my future. I could not stand to look Mealy in the eyes. I was angry at my sister for going along with the plan.

I reminisced about moments with Ang and Horn, now left behind in San Diego. I dreamed of a future reunion of the three amigos. I ached over the thought that I might not see my friends again. The separation from my friends brought back sad memories of leaving my siblings behind in Cambodia. I recalled my bus ride from the Mai Rut refugee camp to Bangkok. I replayed my bus ride from the San Francisco airport to the hotel. My reminiscence of the tunes of Anne Murray and James Taylor gave me more pain than comfort. I was a boy full of anger. My chest was heavy as I watched the San Diego buildings drift farther and farther away from the back of the bus.

Coasting between my daydreaming and reality, before I knew it, the bus was in the middle of nowhere. There was nothing but I-5 and vast and lonely farmland. Farther and farther north, the bus passed patches of snow along the freeway. Sparse and isolated farmhouses spewed plumes of smoke out of their chimneys. Sheep and cattle reminded me of the Cambodian farms that were turned into Khmer Rouge labor camps and killing fields. The stark contrast between San Diego's metropolitan advancement and the farmland brought back the memory of how the Khmer Rouge had managed to turn the twentieth century into year zero and abolish currency, technology, and respect for human dignity.

The farther north the bus carried me, the colder the February weather became. At high elevations, mountains and farmland were covered with snow. Sometimes the bus went through falling snowflakes. Seeing snow for the first time in my life, I felt surreal and excited, but the anxiety of the unknown amplified. The thought that I might have to do farm labor in the snow undermined my hope for a reasonable future.

The weather in San Diego was colder than I was used to in Cambodia, but I had grown accustomed to it. Trees in San Diego were full of green leaves. To the contrary, trees along I-5 were either leafless or had sparse yellow and red leaves. The evergreen trees were fascinating. I could not believe that a tree could be vibrant in severe weather. My fascination with the evergreens did not last long. After a while, the evergreen forest appeared bleak, and every tree looked the same; my journey was depressing.

I do not remember how long my bus ride between San Diego and Portland was, but it was an all-day ride. Finally, the bus entered the city. Relative to San Diego, Portland in 1980 appeared more a town than a city. The buildings were shorter and older. The streets were less clean. I do not remember which part of Portland I first encountered, but I recall that the lawns — at that time — were not as pretty as those in San Diego. Traffic lights dangled primitively from electric cables as if they had been installed by amateurs. The majority of the trees were leafless and appeared dead. Within blocks of the bus station, there were homeless people in the cold along the city street.

Portland would have been a great city for me if I had not known San Diego. My heart was set on San Diego, the big city where my future was supposed to be seeded. Trading San Diego for Portland was like trading America for Cambodia. I felt that the promise of my future dwindled as the bus pulled into the Portland Greyhound bus station.

Mealy's brother Sam picked Mealy, Phon, and me up at the station and brought us to his rental house in Northeast Portland. At the time, Sam was married to an American woman who had a young daughter from a previous relationship. Sam's wife was nice to me and made me feel at home. She set up a room for Mealy and Phon on the main floor. I was given a nice private room in the attic, and her mother bought me a used ten-speed bicycle to ride to school. The attention given to me eased my void of San Diego and gave me courage to accept and explore my new life. Phon enrolled me in Washington-Monroe High School (WAMO). We stayed with Sam's family for just a very short while before we moved out to start our new life in Portland on our own.

With broken English, Mealy worked full time and took evening classes at Portland Community College. Phon worked part time and went to Portland Community College part time. I attended high school full time. We received a little bit of support from the state's welfare system to pay for a two-bedroom apartment. Mealy and Phon picked up side jobs cleaning offices and restrooms; when berries were in season, we picked them for extra cash.

The cold weather in Portland was difficult for me to get used to (especially when I had to ride my bike in the snow or strong wind), but eventually I adapted and learned to appreciate Portland for what it was. When Mount St. Helens erupted and covered Portland with its volcanic ash, I was excited and felt privileged to experience such an extraordinary event from nature. I came to like the Portland rain and snowy weather. Portland became more and more interesting as each day went by, and the fond memory of San Diego began to fade.

Coming into my freshman year at WAMO in the middle of the school year made me apprehensive. Without my Einstein Junior High amigos Ang and Horn, my ESL teachers, and my translator, I was unsure of myself. My confidence was at its lowest. I wished WAMO offered ESL classes. Besides me, there were three or four Cambodian students. Those students had come to the U.S. with their families before the Khmer Rouge turned Cambodia into the killing fields. They did not reach out to me, and I was scared to approach them for fear of rejection. They probably did not even know that I was a Cambodian. I admired their ability to speak English and to socialize, and I wished they had noticed me.

Classes were chosen for me either by my counselor or by my sister. Although I had had basic arithmetic by the time I left San Diego, basic algebra at WAMO was very difficult for me. Perhaps the difficulty was due to the fact that I came in the middle of the school year or that I did not have a translator in the class. I did not understand the majority of the lecture. Non-numeric symbols such as x, y, and z had no place in my mathematical world. After Phon helped me with my math homework and got me over the hurdle, I became known as a math whiz at school.

English class was my least favorite. I did not understand verbal instructions on homework. Written homework instructions were translated for me by Mealy and Phon at home. Mrs. McNamee and Mrs. Taggard were the two English teachers at WAMO who made a difference in my English learning. I would not have been able to excel in English if it had not been for my tutor Miss Jacobson. Each day, for a couple of long hours, Miss Jacobson and I read children's books. At the beginning, Miss Jacobson would read a sentence and I would struggle to read the same sentence. She explained each sentence using the English words that I already knew. For example, to explain the meaning of the word "swerve," she mimed a driver steering a car in a swerving motion and slowly said something like "I drive this way to miss hitting a man" and then repeated something like "I swerve to avoid hitting a man." I understood it after a few variations of her miming. We progressively moved up from a sentence at a time to a page at a time. Eventually, I was able to read by myself and only asked Miss Jacobson for help with words whose meanings were too difficult to derive from the reading context.

I discovered my artistic talents in Mrs. Buck's art class. I excelled in calligraphy, drawing, silkscreening, and pottery. My newly discovered talents caught the attention of Mrs. Buck. Her family took me camping, fishing, and hunting. For the most part, her family members and I did not really under-stand one other's English, but I learned a lot about the American outdoors from the family.

I was fascinated by my counselor Mrs. Wards' African-American accent. English was fascinating enough, but a hint of such accent captivated my attention. Mrs. Wards called me into her office practically every week as I finished my freshman year at WAMO. I had little clue of what she gener-ally said to me, but I knew she wanted to keep tabs on how I was doing. Our communication was limited — "Yes," "No," and "Okay" were about all I said, and the rest was up to her to read from my mind and body language.

Broken by the Khmer Rouge and unable to articulate well in English, I came across as obedient and respectful to the teachers, and I quickly became a model student. The teachers were eager to single me out as an example to other students. That made me feel uncomfortable, but I appreciated the praise and the attention. As I demonstrated my dedication to learning, the teachers reciprocated with their effort to see me succeed. A number of teachers stayed after class to help me with my English.

A few students were rude, mean, and sometimes outright racist, but most students were either nice to me or simply minded their own business. A handful of students took interest in me and my foreign demeanor. One of those students was Scott Easter, who was in my English class. Scott and I became the best of friends. That Scott talked nonstop, I rarely spoke, and I was eager to listen bonded me and Scott. Scott's friends adopted me as their friend. Together, we formed a small bunch that constituted the least popular clique at WAMO.

For whatever reason, my teachers were looking out for me. One day, Mrs. McNamee asked Scott to take me to a school basketball game — WAMO Bruins versus some high school team. That evening, I watched my first basketball game; I became a Bruin and took one step closer to being Americanized.

By the second semester of my sophomore year, I was the academic frontrunner among my friends and shared fewer classes with them. I became a member of the National Honor Society and enrolled in the talented and gifted (TAG) program. I was selected to participate in a citywide math competition with a handful of students. As English was still my Achilles heel, I did not win the individual category, but my WAMO team took fifth place—thanks to Andy Reed, the brain on the team.

Life began to show me its kinder side, and my academic lights began to shine. Additionally, my sister Pech and her family had come to live as refugees in Noranda, Canada. Although I wished my other four sisters had come with Pech, I was glad to know that Pech had escaped Cambodia.

Sometime during my second year at WAMO, Scott and I joined Junior Achievement, where we were taught about American enterprise and learned to make and sell trivets. Scott and I became very close through this common experience.

Scott introduced me to his parents, Connie and Kenneth Easter. Mr. and Mrs. Easter drove Scott and me on various outings, such as basketball games, movies, and skating. One day when Mrs. Easter picked Scott and me up after Junior Achievement, she asked if I would like to come and live with their family.

I was excited by the opportunity to become a part of an American family, but I did not know how to broach the subject with Phon. I did not know how to tell my sister that I was feeling like a third wheel between her and Mealy. I did not know how to tell her that I was resenting Mealy for moving me from San Diego. I did not want to offend her by trading her in for a new family. For all that I had lost during the Khmer Rouge regime, and all that she and I had gone through together, leaving her made me feel like a traitor.

Days turned into weeks, and Scott kept asking me to move in. When I visited Scott, his parents treated me like their son. They showed me which room would be mine. They told me their house rules—as if I were being given an orientation on being an Easter. After a while, the opportunity became too good to pass up. The thought of speaking English at home all the time was compelling. I thought this was an opportunity for me to gain a fast track to learning English and acclimating to being an American.

By the end of my sophomore year, the Portland Public School Board closed WAMO. One day that summer, while picking strawberries with my sister, I gathered enough courage to ask my sister whether I could move in with the Easters. My sister cried, knowing that she had to let me go. Deep down, I knew my sister was hurt by my choosing to move out, but I also knew she understood it was best for me.

Phon and I talked throughout the summer about the pros and cons of my moving in with the Easters. We reached an agreement by the end of the summer. I moved in with the Easters before starting my junior year and became a member of the Easter family.

At the time, the Easters fostered three other boys: Kevin Fox (American), Bin Lu (Chinese-Vietnamese), and Truc Guyen (Vietnamese). Kevin, Scott, and I were in the same grade at WAMO. Bin was one grade behind me, and Truc was two grades behind me.

In the fall of 1981, my four brothers and I went to Cleveland High School. A few of my teachers from WAMO were transferred to Cleveland. One of those teachers was Ms. Brenner. Ms. Brenner had heard of my studious and obedient reputation from my other teachers at WAMO. So when I landed in her English literature class, she paid close attention to my needs. She was known to be tough with students, but I felt she was especially tough on me. I made a personal commitment to succeed in her class, and I believed she was committed to seeing me succeed. Perhaps it was a fantasy on my part, but it did not matter, because my belief and hard work earned me an excellent grade in her class.

For the first two years in America, I experienced more than my fair share of ridicule from my fellow schoolmates for my English. I had been both embarrassed and angered by the experience. The embarrassment motivated me to work hard on my English. With the exception of a few outings with Scott and his friends, I had no social life for the first two years in high school. I spent practically all my free time perfecting my English. Often when alone in front of a mirror, I worked on my John Wayne imitation. I slept very little and studied a lot. I spent an incredible amount of time memorizing the dictionary.

Unlike WAMO, Cleveland had an ESL program that served a good number of Southeast Asian refugees, but by the time I got to Cleveland in the fall of 1981, I was too advanced to be in the ESL program. I excelled in regular English, history, math, physics, and arts. I was among the few students who could manage and maintain a modem connection from a classroom terminal to the Portland Public Schools mainframe—a big deal at the time. I was among the first few students at Cleveland High School who set up a computer lab and programmed in Basic. By my senior year, I was helping my fellow students (both Cambodian refugees and Americans) with their math, computer programming, typing, physics, and—believe it or not—American history.

Sometime during my junior year, my guidance counselor, Mr. Onishi, told me to participate in the Oregon Beavers Boys State, a one-week program held at the University of Oregon. Eleventh-graders were selected from Oregon high schools to participate in the program, where they formed a mock state to exercise elections, legislation, and law enforcement. I was scared to participate, but Mr. Onishi insisted and assured me that I would have a good time. With hesitation, I went ahead and took part. The participation boosted my self-confidence and seeded my leadership skills.

My junior year was the year I saw an American parade for the first time. During the Portland Rose Festival, my American family took me to see the Grand Floral Parade. I was enthralled by the incredible floats, costumes, and people in the parade. The marching bands were loud and full of energy. I had never seen anything like it. While I was digesting what I was watching, there came a group of distinguished gentlemen marching in white suits, white shoes, and straw hats. An announcer introduced the men. They took off their straw hats, held them above their heads with their right hands, and smiled with their conspicuously white teeth. The announcer continued speaking. The echo of the speakers and the loud crowd made it difficult for me to understand what the announcer said about the men in the white uniforms. The spectators went crazy. Some spectators stood up and placed their right hands on their hearts in salutation to the men. Others gave a military salute to the men. My eyes were completely fixed on the men. In the middle of this amazing parade, the men made an incredible impression on me. I stood up, mesmerized. I took notice of the U.S. flag carried by one of the men. I thought it would be so cool if one day I could be the flag carrier. I noticed the men's leader riding in a decorated car. The banner between the U.S. flag and the Oregon flag said "Royal Rosarians." I did not remember seeing the word "Rosarians" in the dictionary that I tried to memorize, but I knew the word "Royal," as in "Royal of Cambodia." It didn't matter what they really were. What mattered to me was that they were the symbols of peace and prosperity, and they commanded public respect and attention. At that moment, in my mind, they represented the ultimate American dream. My American parents tried to explain to me who these men were. I did not really understand, but I knew that they were special. While my eyes were still fixed on the men, I told my American parents in broken English that I would become one of those guys when I grew up. My parents giggled at my laughable dream, my American dream.

Sometime during my senior year, I applied to the only two universities I knew of: University of Oregon and Oregon State University. I was accepted to both but unable to afford the $100 acceptance fee. At the time, my American parents, Ken and Connie Easter, were making just enough to feed five high school boys and could not help me out. Someone suggested I go to the college coordinator at Cleveland High School, Mrs. Jean Frost, to ask for fee waivers. Mrs. Frost did not know me. She asked me to write down my name and my counselor's name—Mr. Onishi. She told me that she was busy and would get back to me in a few days.

Mrs. Frost would get back to me in a few days? Did she not realize that my dream was slipping away? What if the universities gave away my spots? I was not sure if I liked Mrs. Frost for stalling. I was troubled.

The following day, a note was given to me during Ms. Brenner's class. The note told me to see Mrs. Frost immediately. With angst, I grabbed my bag and headed straight to see Mrs. Frost. I walked into her office. She offered me a seat opposite from her at a table. I nervously and quietly sat down.

"I spoke to your counselor, Mr. Onishi, and reviewed your file," Mrs. Frost said, staring intensely at me through her thick glasses. She was official, serious, and unsmiling, and I was about to pee my pants.

She unexpectedly dropped the bomb. "And a man from the Reed College admission office wants to talk to you." What? What had happened to the fee waivers? College? Smart people don't go to college; they go to *universities*. From where I had come from —Cambodia, once a French colony— colleges were for flunkies. I wanted to attend a university, not a college. In my mind, Mrs. Frost was politely trying to let me down easy. I thought Mrs. Frost was trying to substitute University of Oregon and Oregon State University with Reed College. I felt that she was giving me Reed College as a consolation prize.

I was quiescent, unable to articulate my thoughts and feelings to Mrs. Frost. I resignedly accepted the reality of going to Reed College. Once again, I was a leaf at the mercy of the wind. No matter how hard I tried, the wind had its way. Come to think of it, I felt intimidated by Mrs. Frost's stern and official tone. I did not understand most of what she told me about Reed College. I didn't even know that Reed College was only a couple of miles from Cleveland High School. I wished Mrs. Frost would just be kind and give me the fee waivers that I had requested. Mrs. Frost made the world way too complicated for me. I had already been accepted to the two most prestigious universities— of course, the only two I knew. Mrs. Frost was in the way of my dream.

The next day, I was called back to Mrs. Frost's office. She introduced me to a man from the Reed College admission office. Oh, boy ... my chance of going to a university was definitely slipping away. The man came to interview me.

Disappointed, I no longer cared. The interview meant nothing to me. I did not want college; I wanted university. I was ready to face this man. Whatever!

The man started with lots of small talk. Perhaps it was his kind attempt to put me at ease, but what would I know about baseball and other American-oriented stuff? He asked about my classes. I spoke passionately about my math and my physics classes. He was impressed by my "A" in American history, my participation in the Oregon Beavers Boys State, my ability to survive the Khmer Rouge genocide, and my endeavor to assimilate the American culture. He seemed to have a little bit of trouble understanding my English. I had to repeat myself often for him. Then the interview homed in on what I had read in my English class.

"What books have you read for your English class?" My interviewer went in for the kill.

"Lots," I responded proudly.

I didn't care; I wanted university and not college. Perhaps failing this interview might convince Mrs. Frost to give me the waivers. Yeah, lots … I read lots.

"Can you tell me which books you read?" the man continued more intensely.

"*The Chocolate War*," I confidently replied. I gave him my review of the book. I told him that the book was not bad. It was okay.

"What else have you read?" he continued asking.

"There was *Fahrenheit 451*, but it was about the same. It could be better written." I gave him a piece of my mind. He didn't seem impressed by my assessment. I didn't care; I wanted university and not college.

"What else?" the man asked.

"*1984*, by George Orwell," I responded. I pronounced George Orwell as "Chorch Owev." I told him my opinion of the book. The story was plausible because, in some regards, it was kind of like the Khmer Rouge era. The book could have been written better, though—a good book should be written using simple words and phrases. There were lots of unnecessarily big words—too sesquipedalian.

"Are you saying that George Orwell is not a good author?" the man asked.

Oh, boy ... I hated confrontation ... I wished I were more articulate.

"No ... not really ..." was all I could articulate. "There is one book by him that I really like," I nervously added.

"Which one?" the man continued.

"*Animal Farm*," I responded.

"Can you tell me about it?" the man asked.

The man did not know he had touched my hot button and tapped into my intimate experience with the Khmer Rouge. Having survived the Khmer Rouge genocide, I told him, I had just come out of an animal farm. I passionately gave him my verbal dissertation on *Animal Farm*. I spoke of *Animal Farm* in the context of my own personal experience in the Khmer Rouge labor camps. The man leaned back in his chair, crossed his hands behind his head, and gave me his full attention. His eyes were intensely fixed on me as I highlighted the metaphors and drew parallels between the Khmer Rouge labor camps and *Animal Farm*.

The man had no more questions, and I had nothing more to say. I didn't care; I wanted university, but I was being interviewed for a college. I would have liked to have had control over my own destiny for once.

"Wow!" said the man.

"Wow" was an understatement. Deep down, I wanted to say: *Yeah, "Wow" is right. You have no idea how disappointed I am in my life. A university would have been an end that might have justified the means — the means that took away everything I had (including my parents, grandmother, and youngest sister). You and Mrs. Frost are standing in the way of my dream to attend a university.*

Instead, I was my typical self: polite and acquiescent. I thanked him for his time and consideration. It didn't matter; I had no chance of going to a university. I filled out the Reed application and waited. I was a leaf in a dead wind.

For days, I kept the prospect of my going to Reed College to myself. I was embarrassed to tell my American parents, my sister, and my friends for fear that they might think less of me. I lost sleep over it. I didn't know how to broach the subject with my American parents. I stayed up late at night with a stomachache and pondered how to relay the bad news. I felt like a failure. I disliked myself for not standing up to Mrs. Frost and explaining to her the essence of my dream to attend a university. I felt small and helpless.

When I finally told my American father, Ken Easter, he laughed. I was somewhat baffled and a bit offended by his insensitivity. He called out to my mother, Connie Easter, to come downstairs. With a big, insensitive grin on his face, he told Mom that I had something to tell her. Totally embarrassed — and a bit annoyed by Dad's insensitivity — I told Dad, "You tell her." Dad pushed it back on me to tell Mom. Dad and I went back and forth while Mom kept annoying me with her tenacious "What?"

American parents can be very annoying sometimes. Everything has to be spoken and spelled out. That was the hardest part of my adjustment to living with an American family. I paid attention to body language and expected my family to read my mind and my body language. My American family, in contrast, expected me to spell out everything.

When Dad realized that I was not going to tell Mom, he told her what I had told him. They both broke out laughing. I did not like the way they were laughing at me. I did not like my American parents' lack of sensitivity. I did not like their low expectations of me. I felt totally disconnected from them. My Cambodian parents would have had higher expectations of me. They would have been disappointed to know that I ended up in college instead of at a university. More irritating was my American parents' laughter at my disappointment over the prospect of going to Reed College instead of University of Oregon or Oregon State University.

Mom and Dad had their laugh. Then came Mom's serious face.

"Oh, sweetheart," said Mom, reaching out to hug me.

Baffled and doubting Mom's sincerity, I allowed myself to be hugged. With his inconsiderate grin on his face, Dad sat down in an armchair in the living room.

"Kilong, you have no idea," continued Mom. Darn right, I had no idea. That day, Mom and Dad spoke a lot. I understood most of what they said, but not all, because they used lots of unusually big words in their attempt to explain Reed College to me. One thing I came to clearly understand was that Reed College was one of the most prestigious schools in the country. I understood that Reed College was a private school with a hefty price tag on its tuition. I was told that I should be flattered.

Wow! Mom was right: I had no idea. I was once again embarrassed. I felt naïve. Nonetheless, I felt relieved and proud. I could not believe that Mrs. Frost thought I was worthy of Reed College. I realized that behind Mrs. Frost's stern and official tone, there was a kind woman.

I lost another night of sleep…tossing…and turning…waiting for the sluggish morning to send me back to school. I could not wait to thank Mrs. Frost.

When I saw Mrs. Frost that morning, I noticed for the first time that she was a warm person. She had a smile on her face. She was not the person I had pictured earlier. I was so wrapped up in my problem that I hadn't noticed any smile on her face. Until now, Mrs. Frost had been no more than a stern and official voice that stood in my way of attending a university.

Mrs. Frost seemed excited to see me.

"Good morning, Kilong," greeted Mrs. Frost.

"Hi," was all I could muster in response.

Expressing my gratitude to Mrs. Frost became an impossible task. Although I was now less intimidated by her firm voice, I still had a hard time articulating all the things I had composed in my head overnight.

Mrs. Frost and I had a one-way conversation in her office that morning: She talked, and I nodded. Mrs. Frost told me that I had made quite an impression on the Reed College admissions counselor. I smiled bashfully and nodded nervously. She went on to tell me that she had arranged for me to interview with the YWCA for a summer position as a camp counselor at Camp Westwind. I smiled and nodded. I wanted to thank her, but I was afraid to interrupt. She told me that the American Legion Club had invited me to receive an award presented at its luncheon. I smiled and nodded. I did not know how to truly express my gratitude in "American." Mrs. Frost continued to talk, and I continued to nod and to fight back my overwhelming, emotional gratitude.

I could not believe how quickly Mrs. Frost had opened doors for me. She was an agent who negotiated a better future for me. That was Mrs. Frost—the kind wind that blew me in the right direction. Thanks to Mrs. Frost's intervention, I got a summer job as a camp counselor and enrolled at Reed College after my high school graduation.

HIGHER EDUCATION

Thanks to Mr. George Orwell (for writing *Animal Farm*), University of Oregon and Oregon State University (for requiring the acceptance fees that I could not afford), Mrs. Jean Frost, a Reed College grant, student loans, and work study, I ended up at Reed College.

Reed College was not just one of the most prestigious colleges in the country; it was also one of the most difficult colleges for any student. Armed with four years of rudimentary English, I spent four hours for every hour spent by the average Reed student on his or her homework. Unlike most colleges, Reed did not have English reading and writing courses. Instead, reading and writing were incorporated into the mandatory freshman humanities curriculum. The course was based on Greek mythology. Although reading Homer's *Iliad* and writing humanities papers were not a cakewalk for other Reed students, the work was absolutely Greek to me. I miserably flunked the course.

In collaboration with Lewis & Clark College, Dr. David Groff from Reed College Student Affairs managed to enroll me in an English writing class at Lewis & Clark. Due to my difficult commute between Reed and Lewis & Clark, I never finished the course, but what I got out of the class helped me significantly in passing my repeated humanities course.

Although I had been a math genius in high school, I was humbled by math courses at Reed. My classmates and I were given just two or three problems to complete within a week or two. One problem could result in as few as a couple of pages or as many as ten pages. I could do math in my sleep before entering Reed. However, my freshman math course (calculus in vector space) deprived me of much of my sleep.

Likewise, physics at Reed was not that easy for me. I had had no trouble with physics at Cleveland High School, but physics at Reed was different. While the humanities course was more Greek than English, the physics course was more English than science—which definitely was not in my favor.

Halfway through my freshman year, I doubted if the liberal arts college was right for me. I just wanted a math degree, but there seemed to be a lot of unnecessary courses. There was a reason why I had chosen math. There were supposed to be more symbols than words. I did not care about learning to interpret dreams—my dreams were usually nightmares. It was interesting to see female human anatomy in the human sexuality class, but I thought my precious time was being wasted on useless information. I did not understand why I needed to know about the Oedipus complex in order to earn my math degree. What did the relationship between Zeus and humans have to do with my dream of becoming a scientist? I was more interested in disproving Einstein's $E=mc^2$ than the explicit pictures of female anatomy in the psychology class or the odyssey of Odysseus in the humanities class.

Reed was very difficult for me, and I had to study a lot—much more than an average English speaker—so I found myself less and less able to function as a part of the Easter family. I went to the Reed financial office and met with the head officer. I explained my situation to the officer. My financial assistance for the following year was adjusted to include room, board, and additional work study. I moved to campus in the fall of 1984 with my new roommate Seth Reames.

For the entire time at Reed, I had a few secondhand clothes (purchased from Goodwill), one dictionary (a gift from Mrs. Taggard), one thesaurus (a gift from Ms. Brenner), one small trunk (a gift from Mrs. Buck), one pair of stinky tennis shoes, one small television (purchased with earnings from a summer job), one cassette player, and a couple of Kenny Rogers tapes (gifts from my tutor, Miss Suzan Jacobson).

I worked at the Lloyd Center Red Lion as a porter earning minimum wage. On the weekends, I collected cans and bottles left by students during parties on the Reed campus. Once, Seth invested a couple hundred dollars in my T-shirt silkscreening business. Seth and I made a few bucks selling the silkscreened T-shirts on campus. It was my first true lesson in American small enterprise. The best job during my time at Reed was tutoring a high school student in math. I got paid $10 an hour.

By the end of the year, I became a U.S. citizen.

I began dating a high school friend, Elizabeth Roe. Like any relationship, Elizabeth's and mine had its ups and downs. I grew up in a liberal home, and she grew up in a conservative home. I was raised in Buddhism, and she was raised in Christianity. We were day and night religiously, culturally, and politically. Elizabeth was my unwanted distraction but also my pillar and confidant. When she graduated from Cleveland High School after my first year at Reed, she left Portland to attend LIFE Bible College in Los Angeles. Our long-distance relationship became impossible and we split up. Her absence gave me more time to focus on my schoolwork but also created a void in my life. I experienced romantic pain for the first time in my life. I set her free and made up my mind that if she came back, I would marry her.

During my relationship with Elizabeth, I got to know her parents, who were ballroom dance teachers. Her father, Martin Roe, became my primary dance teacher. Her mother, Freida Patrizio, and her stepmother, Meredith Roe, were my secondary teachers. During Elizabeth's absence, I continued to take ballroom lessons from her father. I also maintained my friendship with her mother and her stepfather, Jack Patrizio.

The dance lessons played a significant role in developing my social confidence. Without my ballroom dancing skills, I would have had a difficult time fitting in at Reed's social events — I did not drink and I had a hard time keeping up with the intellectual chit-chat. It didn't matter whether I was the best dancer on the floor; I was confident that I could dance. Reed women might not have liked my refugee looks, but they liked my dancing. I gave dance lessons to a handful of women. I made enough friends to give me a feeling of belonging.

My third year at Reed was my most difficult year thus far. While my English had gotten much better, the classes had become more difficult. I also had to study for the junior qualification two-part exam — written and oral. (Without passing the junior qualification, I would not be allowed to declare the topic of my senior thesis and would have to repeat my junior year.)

As if the academic pressure was not enough, I got news from Cambodia that one of my nieces had died from an epileptic seizure. She had drowned in a mud puddle during a seizure. I had always had symptoms of post-traumatic stress disorder, but somehow I managed to keep myself above it. This news, however, put me into my worst depression. I no longer cared about my future. I no longer wanted to overcome my stupid English handicap. Whoever had invented the junior qualification was stupid. The whole world was stupid. Nothing made sense. What was the fucking point? Even the brightest of the brightest was not able to stop the devastating Vietnam War before millions of people died. I attended one of the most prestigious colleges in the United States of America, yet I was unable to help my family in Cambodia. All my sisters changed their names and ages numerous times to avoid persecution. The entire country of Cambodia was occupied by Vietnam. I lost all hope of returning to Cambodia. Who cared about the stupid junior qualification? I could not seem to catch a break. The more ground I gained on English, the more foreign English was.

For weeks at a time, I was unable to stay focused in class. The quality of my papers was slipping. My fellow students annoyed me. I was angry at my fellow students who had the audacity to ask me to join them in fasting against the injustice in Africa and the Middle East. No one seemed to care about what happened in Cambodia. No one seemed to care about what happened to me. I had self-pity. Why not? No one understood me, and I deserved it. I pitied me.

Everything came crashing down on me: the stupid junior qualification exam, English that kept turning into Greek, lack of money, nightmares, bad news, and fear of failure.

At my wit's end, I called the Red Cross for help. I have no idea why I called the Red Cross. Perhaps it was the only crisis organization I knew at the time. Crying over the public telephone at my dorm, I told someone at Red Cross that I wanted to commit suicide. I needed help. I needed to talk to someone.

The next day, I met with a caseworker at the Red Cross in North Portland. I was disappointed to see a Cambodian-American counselor sitting across from the caseworker in the meeting. I did not want my personal stuff leaked to the Cambodian community. The entire community looked up to my sister for having a brother attending Reed College. I was supposed to be an example to other Cambodian refugees my age. I did not want people to know that I was losing my mind. I did not want people to know that I was incapable of controlling my depression. I was ashamed and disappointed that I had not been informed of the counselor's participation. Or perhaps I had been informed, but I was too wrapped up with my self-pity.

"What's going on?" the Red Cross caseworker asked.

The caseworker could barely finish her question before I came loose. I sobbed like a toddler who had had his most precious toy unjustly taken. For the first time, I let out the pressure that had built up in me for years. For the first time, I was able to tell my story the way I wanted to. I totally forgot that another Cambodian was in the room. I did not care. Wait ... I did care ... but words and sobs were now involuntary. I was on a roll, and it felt right to tell my story. I cried hard. I let out my anger, frustration, and fear. I clenched my fists. I pounded the table. Tears were pouring uncontrollably. I cried out for my parents like a little boy. I wanted my mother to cuddle me. I wanted my father to tell me to tough it up. My heart hurt. Pressure mounted be-hind my eyes. My head was heavy. My sinuses were plugged. My hands were shaking. I felt small.

No one uttered a word. All eyes were on me. Two compassionate and sad faces were helplessly staring at me. That was all I needed, someone to hear me. There was nothing either of them could say or do other than sit quietly and let me humiliate myself. Deep down, I knew what I needed to do to solve my problem, but the pressure had built up too much. My outpouring decom-pressed me. After I had said all I had to say, I regained my composure as a strong survivor and a Reed student. I thanked both people for their time and moral support and returned to my dormitory.

About a week later, the caseworker called me at my dormitory for a follow-up. I told her that I was now fine. She left me her number in case I ever needed someone to listen to my problems again.

I had put the death of my niece in Cambodia in an acceptable perspective. I no longer wanted to commit suicide. However, the pressure of keeping up with Reed academics was still tremendous. I contemplated dropping out of Reed. I completely lost my confidence. I decided to take a day off from Reed to go visit Cleveland High School, a place where I had been on top of the world. I was on a hunt for reassurance.

By this time, all my American friends had already gone off to college, but a few of my Cambodian friends were still around. The ESL teachers, Mr. Dick-erson and Mrs. Klug, were still at Cleveland. Being a Reed student, I was quite welcomed by my friends and teachers. I visited all my teachers. I visited my counselor, Mr. Onishi, and (of course) Mrs. Frost. Everyone praised me for my achievement of making it to Reed. The compliments flattered me but did little to restore my confidence in my ability to complete my Reed education.

In privacy, I confided to Mrs. Klug that I might not be able to finish my schooling at Reed. I told her that the pressure had become unbearable.

"Kilong, you have come so far. You are so far ahead now. Even if you quit now, you would still be ahead," Mrs. Klug stated simply and with heartfelt expression. "Everyone thinks the world of you. I think the world of you," she continued.

I sought out reassurance, and I got it from Mrs. Klug. That did it. It no longer mattered whether or not I completed my schooling at Reed. I had already won in life. I had done all that was required of me. The pressure was off. The cloud was lifted, and I saw the light. It did not matter whether I graduated from Reed or not. All I needed to do was to keep going as long as I could and quit should the time come.

After that day, I did my best and was happy with my best. At each crossroad in life, I stopped and looked both ways. Each day, I took time to smell the roses. I slept an average of two hours a night to keep up with my studies, but I was happy doing it. Pressure at Reed never let up, but I dealt with it by putting it in perspective. I kept reminding myself that the Khmer Rouge had forced me to work thirteen hours a day, seven days a week, 365 days a year. Reed became relatively easier. I passed both the written and oral parts of my junior examination and declared my senior thesis. Additionally, Elizabeth and I got back together and resumed our relationship as boyfriend and girlfriend.

During my last year at Reed, I lived in the Foster Shultz dormitory, where I met Julian Kilker. Julian was the dorm advisor. He was interested in my past, and I was interested in his worldly experience. His parents worked for the United Nations, and he had lived outside of the U.S. and gone to an international school. I had the impression that he wanted to make the world a better place. He applied to the Peace Corps. Encouraged by Julian, I also applied for the Peace Corps. My American parents helped me fill out the Peace Corps application. My interview went extremely well—so I thought. I wholeheartedly believed that I would be joining the Peace Corps after Reed College. Pursuing the Peace Corps became my absolute plan A.

My plan B was to become an actuary after graduation. I had no knowledge of what an actuary was truly supposed to do, but my friend Clyde Cutting, who had graduated the previous year, had gotten a position as an actuarial consultant with a local firm and suggested that I consider applying for a position with the firm. I told Clyde that I wanted to focus on getting into the Peace Corps.

Julian got accepted to the Peace Corps, so I had high confidence that the Peace Corps would soon accept me, too—Julian had put in a good word for me at the Peace Corps. I had my second interview shortly after Julian got accepted. The interviewer was impressed by my past, resilience, intelligence, and compassion. She had a concern about my verbal and written communication. Since I had tutored math and physics, I was confident that I would be a very effective math teacher; unfortunately, the Peace Corps did not see it my way and sent me an amicable rejection letter.

My plan A was now gone, and the end of my senior year was approaching fast. Falling back on my plan B, I contacted Clyde and asked if I could get a tour of his office. Clyde graciously gave me a tour and introduced me to his colleagues and boss. Clyde also invited me to the company party. His colleagues were very friendly and showed high regard for my Reed education. However, in my secondhand clothes, I was not comfortable in the corporate environment. I felt intimidated. Furthermore, I realized that an actuary was not what I wanted to be.

Now both plan A and plan B were gone, and I had no plan C. I was completely lost. I was not sure what I could do with my liberal arts education. Pressure was mounting to get my senior thesis completed as part of the requirements for graduation. Once again, I hit my bottom. I had to dig deep and remind myself what Mrs. Klug had said:

"Kilong, you have come so far. You are so far ahead now. Even if you quit now, you would still be ahead."

One warm afternoon, Professor Albyn Jones decided to take the probability class outside on the Reed front lawn. The class was made up of fewer than ten students—mostly seniors. Like most professors at Reed, Professor Jones was passionate about the subject he taught. That afternoon, he was distinctively passionate about explaining combinatorial analysis in the context of computing a probability. The green lawn, small-group discussion, Professor Jones' vivid energy, and the warm sun lifted my spirit.

After class, I shared my situation with Professor Jones; I flat out told him that I was lost and not sure of what I would do after Reed. Professor Jones pointed out my passion for math and suggested that I go to graduate school. I was not surprised when he recommended a statistics major for my graduate study. When I asked him to endorse a graduate school, he recommended Carnegie Mellon.

By this time, many graduate schools had already stopped accepting applications. My chance of going to a graduate school was not too favorable. On top of finishing my senior thesis, I now had to study for a college exam to get into graduate school. When I took the exam, I checked a box on the form to allow graduate school admission offices to pursue me. I passed the exam.

I applied to and got accepted by Carnegie Mellon. However, I was told that the institution had already given out all the budgeted grants and fellowships. I would be financially on my own for the year.

Not fully understanding and appreciating the economic value of higher education (especially from an institution such as Carnegie Mellon), I was concerned by my $10,000 student loan debt at Reed. I decided not to pursue graduate studies. Once again, I was a man with no future in sight. I was a leaf at the mercy of the wind, and there was no apparent wind that would carry me to a better world.

Like inclement weather to a leaf, my senior thesis added pressure to my uncertain world. My nightmares from the Khmer Rouge killing fields caught up with me once again. My former roommate and friend Seth Reames provided a little wind in my chaotic world. Seth stayed up a number of nights correcting and typing up my thesis on his Macintosh. His altruism served as a token of confidence in my otherwise uncertain future. To a poor leaf, Seth was a fresh breeze.

One very early morning, on April 1, 1987, there came a rude, loud knock on my dorm-room door. In those days, each floor in the dormitory shared a public phone at the end of the hall. When the phone rang, someone would answer it and go fetch the intended recipient. I was the recipient of a phone call that morning. The voice outside my door told me that I had an important phone call waiting. I immediately thought it was my American mother, who never failed to call me on April Fools' Day. Writing my thesis had kept me up practically all night. So I was not in the mood for her prank. I asked my dorm mate to take a message. My dorm mate took the message and slipped it under my door. The message instructed me to urgently return the call to Dr. Ralph St. John at Bowling Green State University (BGSU). I thought my mother was getting very creative with her pranks, and I ignored the message.

After a week had gone by, Dr. St. John called me again. Once I realized it was not my mother's usual pranks, I took the call. Dr. St. John introduced himself and told me that he wanted to recruit me to do my graduate studies at BGSU. As soon as I understood the purpose of his call, I felt embarrassed for ignoring his previous call.

Since I had already given up on the idea of going to a graduate school that year, I did not care much whether I got into BGSU or not. In fact, I knew nothing about the university. Carelessly, I drove a hard bargain. I boldly told Dr. St. John that I had a lot of student loan debt and did not want to incur any additional debt. To my pleasant surprise, Dr. St. John told me that he was way ahead of me. The school was already prepared to give me a grant that would pay for my tuition and basic living expenses. In return, I would have to be a teacher's assistant. Still feeling like I had nothing to lose, I haggled for more. I demanded that I be given the opportunity to develop my English. Without hesitation, Dr. St. John told me that there would be proper English courses as a vehicle for me to further my English. The deal of my life was made. I was a leaf, and Dr. St. John was the wind that carried me to Bowling Green, Ohio.

Mrs. Buck gave me enough money to purchase a one-way plane ticket to

Detroit, about an hour and a half from BGSU. Dr. St. John arranged for me to be picked up in Detroit by one of his graduate students. The student let me stay at his place for a couple of days before I found a place of my own.

I found a very cheap studio. The room was about half the size of my dormitory room at Reed College. It was furnished with an old sofa, a lamp, a barely functional refrigerator, an old stove, and dull carpet. There was one small window to the parking lot in front of the studio. The furnished white curtain was too transparent to keep out the car headlights. The wall was not well insulated, and even the weakest sound could easily penetrate it. The bathroom could barely fit a tiny sink, toilet, and shower stall. The front door was not well insulated. The Ohio blistering wind in winter blew chills into the room. The studio was practically a dump, but I was proud of it because it was my own place.

I struggled to make ends meet before receiving my first stipend check. The small amount of money I had brought with me from Portland ran out by the end of the first week. I had not factored in the studio's security deposit or first and last months' rents. I stretched my money by eating only Top Ramen noodles. In those days, I paid $1 for ten packages of noodles. When I ran out of money, I made a collect call to my American parents for help. My parents were generous people, but at the time they did not have any disposable income. My mother contacted her Seventh-day Adventist church in Portland and got me a contact at a Seventh-day Adventist church in Bowling Green.

A few Seventh-day Adventist Christian fellows in Bowling Green brought me food and invited me to their potluck. I was very grateful for the assistance. However, I was turned off by the religious aspect of our relationship. I was not ready to accept faith as the supreme solution to my life. For years in the Khmer Rouge labor camps, I had prayed for liberation. None of my prayers were answered. The lack of an answer to my prayers eradicated my faith in a higher power. At the time, I needed food but not spiritual comfort (and certainly not religious philosophy). My parents' friends wanted to kindly give me more than what I needed, but I was not ready to accept anything more than food. So I stopped asking for help.

My stipend from being a teacher's assistant was barely enough to pay for rent and food. There was no Asian grocery store in Bowling Green (if there had been, I couldn't have afforded to shop there, anyway). The nearest grocery store was at least two miles from my studio, and there was no public transportation. Carrying groceries on foot in the deep Ohio snow often reminded me of the labor camps in Cambodia. All I could afford were Top Ramen noodles (ten packages for a dollar), turkey hot dogs (65 cents per package), and fresh broccoli. Fresh garlic was a necessary ingredient, but it was not cost-effective. So I always sneaked it out without paying for it. I went to McDonald's and stole packages of sugar, salt, pepper, and ketchup (fresh tomato was too expensive) to include in the Top Ramen recipe. I never paid for any unnecessary items. There were plenty of free napkins and plastic forks, knives, and spoons at McDonald's. I rarely ever ate breakfast. I ate the same food for lunch and dinner. Consequently, I perfected the art of cooking Top Ramen noodles.

As recommended by Dr. St. John, I joined the BGSU Graduate Student Senate. During the last year of graduate school, I was elected to serve as the senate's treasurer. The position taught me a lot about being an executive and a leader. Under the leadership of Graduate Student Senate President Teresa Tancre, I learned about executive responsibility, accountability, and ethics. I was involved in humanitarian projects such as giving out turkeys to needy families during Thanksgiving and collecting food supplies for people in South America.

My studies at BGSU were more focused and thus easier than my undergrad studies at Reed. My graduate studies concentrated on math, statistics, and operations research. Consequently, graduate school required significantly less study time. PTSD gave me insomnia. Between less study time and more insomnia, I had lots of time to party practically every night. The constant partying and clubbing enabled me to develop my much-needed American social skills.

CORPORATE CULTURE

Just before my graduation from BGSU, Dr. St. John contacted his former student Bob Sloan at Andersen Consulting and got me an interview with the company. The screening interview was on the BGSU campus. Before the interview, I went down to a secondhand store in Bowling Green and bought myself a pair of dark gray slacks, an old dark blue sports jacket, a white shirt, and a tie — all for less than $30. I had a pair of old, unfashionable dress shoes to go with them. In the waiting area, I felt inferior to my competing interviewees, who were well-dressed in business attire. I had had interviews in the past, but they all were for work study jobs that paid minimum wage. This interview was an interview for my career, the first of its kind thus far in my life. I entered a new world. Although I had somewhat assimilated the American culture, I was beyond inexperienced in the corporate culture. I was absolutely ignorant. I was the only interviewee with unfit attire and Reed College hippie long hair. Nonetheless, I was invited to a second interview in Cleveland, Ohio, and got hired by Andersen Consulting right after my graduation from BGSU.

Andersen Consulting in Cleveland offered me a $29,000 annual salary plus its usual benefits. Additionally, the firm offered to pay for my moving from Bowling Green to Cleveland, apartment start-up costs, and an advance for business suits, coat, shoes, and ties. Pushing my luck, I asked to be started in the Portland office. That did not go well, because the Cleveland office needed a statistician on one of its consulting teams. Full of idealism, I held my ground and asked to be transferred at the end of the initial project. A deal was made, and my starting salary was reduced to $26,000, which was in line with the rate in Portland — so I was told. I accepted the offer as a member of the Portland office working out of town in Cleveland. Andersen Consulting agreed to pay for my moving to Portland at the end of the initial project.

I was alone during my commencement at BGSU. I had reached a height that was rarely possible for many refugees in my situation. Yet, at my graduation, I had no one with whom to celebrate my success. During the ceremony reception, I had my BGSU friends to share my triumph, but afterward I was completely alone in my studio. The majority of my friends left Bowling Green and returned home with their families. I spent all afternoon in my studio crying and laughing alone like a madman. I celebrated my success alone in the confinement of my tiny studio — two packs of Top Ramen noodles, two eggs, three turkey hot dogs, broccoli, a pack of sugar, a pack of black pepper, four packs of ketchup, and a can of Coke. I had no place to go and no one to visit. I had no means of transportation to get out of Bowling Green. I walked alone from one end of town to another and back. I walked all over the campus, realizing that this was my last walk on campus. Besides anthills, Bowling Green was flat like a piece of paper; the town that once was my party town was now lackluster. I felt alone. I could not wait to move to Cleveland.

An apartment in downtown Cleveland next to the office was arranged for me by the human resources manager. After I arrived in Cleveland, I invited Elizabeth to move in with me. She accepted my invitation, and we began living together. I started my new chapter with an American girlfriend, a fancy apartment in the middle of downtown Cleveland, and a dream job with one of the world's biggest consulting firms.

The project in Cleveland ended after nine months, and Andersen moved Elizabeth and me to Portland. In Portland, my sister Phon and her Cambodian friends noticed how good my English had become. At the same time, I realized that I had trouble speaking Cambodian. During my four years at Reed, I spoke very little with my sister, and when we spoke we often spoke in English. During the two years at BGSU and nine months with Andersen Consulting in Cleveland, I did not come in contact with any Cambodian speaker.

I began to get involved with the Cambodian-American Community of Oregon. As one of the better-educated refugees in the community, I was elected to serve as the organization's president. Unfortunately, the community was not ready for my Americanized ideas and dreams of taking the community to the next level. After some months, I resigned. However, I kept in contact with the community, and my Cambodian continued to improve.

While working as a consultant at Andersen Consulting in Portland, I was sent out of town weekly and came home on weekends. My professional travel included U.S. and Canadian cities. My clients included Boeing, Boise Cascade, James River, EB Eddy, MacMillan Bloedel, Pope & Talbot, and the State of Washington.

Although I made strides to assimilate the corporate culture, my heavy accent and looks remained my biggest handicaps at Andersen Consulting.

Given my cultural handicaps, it was a miracle that I managed to stay on schedule with my promotions. I was promoted from staff consultant to senior consultant. At the end of my fourth year, I was supposed to be promoted to manager. I felt ready, but the company thought otherwise. So I was passed up for my promotion to manager.

My senior manager and his boss, a partner at Andersen, tried to be helpful. They helped prepare me for my promotion the following year by sending me to a Dale Carnegie public speaking course to improve my communication skills. Between missing my promotion and my bruised pride, I doubted their sincerity. Reluctantly, and with little choice, I enrolled in the Dale Carnegie course. The course was a revelation that changed my life forever. I learned to speak confidently in front of people. I learned techniques for how to win friends and influence people. Additionally, I learned how to manage my stress. The Dale Carnegie training elevated me from my hellish nightmare into a life full of hopes and dreams. My friends, colleagues, and boss noticed the positive changes in me. More and more people wanted to be my friend. My confidence soared.

Unfortunately, the Dale Carnegie training came too late in my career to undo the accumulated perception of my professionalism. I was passed up for another round of promotions. My manager delivered the bad news while his boss was out of town. Knowing that there was a strong chance that I might quit, my manager and his boss wanted to meet face to face with me before I decided what to do with my career. I was hurt, and I was not about to give my manager and his boss that satisfaction; I immediately began looking for a new job, hoping to find one before my manager's boss returned to the office — I had to keep my dignity. Before the week was over, I accepted a job at United Data Processing (UDP), which nearly doubled my salary and benefits. I regained my dignity, held my head up, and turned in my resignation.

My manager tried to talk me into reconsidering my position, but I was too mad and too proud to appreciate his sincerity. I forgot all the kindness that he had shown in helping me advance my career. I forgot all the times he had gone to bat for me, including lobbying for the company to pay for my Dale Carnegie training.

When my manager's boss met with me, I felt that he was sincere when he asked me to reconsider my resignation. Unfortunately, I was too mad to believe it. He went out of his way to ask me to put aside my pride and give Andersen another shot. He even offered a small increase in salary — not a promotion. He told me that he believed in me and my ability to rise above adversity. He pointed out my noticeable improvement as a result of the Dale Carnegie training. He wanted me to consider the long term. His sincerity and sound advice did not get past my bruised ego. In the culture of up or out, I felt that the company wanted me out by not moving me up. I felt that there was no way I could be respected by my peers in that culture. Hence, I felt that there was absolutely no chance for me to advance my career at Andersen Consulting.

The Dale Carnegie training was too late for me at Andersen Consulting, but it gave me the needed confidence and courage to move on. To the disappointment of my manager and his boss, I stood my ground and gave up on climbing Andersen's corporate ladder.

For my more than four years of dedicated service to the company, Andersen Consulting threw me an expensive farewell party at Alexis Hotel, located on the Portland waterfront. The party room setting was nearly enough to make me regret my resignation. It was extravagant, prestigious, and seducing. There were balloons and farewell signs in a big, fancy room that could easily accommodate fifty colleagues. To my disappointment and embarrassment, only a handful of people showed up. I knew then that it was right for me to move on, because in the culture of up or out, no colleague wanted to be associated with an unsuccessful colleague. Andersen was not the place for me to put down roots.

ROOTS

During the summer of 1991, while still working for Andersen Consulting, I was assigned to a project at Boeing in Issaquah, Washington. Andersen provided an apartment in Redmond for me to stay in during the week.

At the time, Elizabeth and I were steady boyfriend and girlfriend and lived together in an apartment in Portland. Between my constant out-of-town projects and Elizabeth's undergraduate studies at Portland State University, I only got to see Elizabeth on the weekends. Occasionally, she came up to visit me in Redmond. During one of her visits, I took her to Seattle, which was only about a half an hour away from the apartment.

Elizabeth and I had dated each other for about eight years by this point. During those eight years, family members and friends had repeatedly wondered out loud why I had not asked Elizabeth to marry me.

"Not ready," I abruptly replied whenever I was asked.

I had thought often about marrying Elizabeth. I knew deep down that I loved her and wanted to spend my life with her. When we broke up after her graduation from Cleveland High School, I promised myself I would marry her if she came back (which she did). However, having had everything taken away by the Khmer Rouge, I felt inadequate in more ways than one. I knew I could not get back what I had lost. My home was gone. My parents were gone. My grandmother was gone. Ali was gone. My freedom to return to Cambodia was gone. Having come to the U.S. with nothing but an old handmade cotton shirt on my back and a pair of shorts, I had a lot of ground to cover. I felt that I had to work harder than most of my colleagues — just to catch up. Living from one paycheck to another, I felt like I had almost no control over my life. Being sent on projects all over the country and to parts of Canada, I was too busy for a marriage. I was still somewhat a leaf at the mercy of the wind. However, on this one particular weekend, I was a leaf with a soft heart.

One Sunday afternoon in Seattle, near Pike Place Market, Elizabeth and I were on a municipal light rail train. We sat on a bench seat with our backs against the window. The train was going south from Pike Place Market through the touristy waterfront. Piers, shops, and restaurants passed by outside the windows. Elizabeth had no clue that I had been thinking all week long about asking her to marry me. Looking out the windows, Elizabeth pointed out a few tourist attractions, but I was in my own world. I wanted to commit to sharing my life with Elizabeth, but I was not sure if I was really ready to give up my past or the possibility of going back to Cambodia to help my sisters.

One of us obliviously had a great time, and the other was in his own world, with sweaty palms and butterflies in his stomach. A couple of times, Elizabeth noticed my absent mind, but she thought I was preoccupied with work. She comforted me and annoyingly apologized that I had to work so hard. Hiding my nerves, I played along and let myself be comforted.

Sitting next to Elizabeth, I reached out and held her hand. Inside the train was noisy. Elizabeth was awed by the tourist attractions.

"Lisa, would you marry me?" I asked timidly, using her nickname.

I felt a modicum of comfort for having the courage to blurt out the question. Unfortunately, my question was buried by the buzzing noise from the train and other passengers. I could not tell whether Elizabeth had not heard my proposition or she was ignoring me.

Now I was really nervous. I thought about dropping the whole thing. I let go of her hand, looked out the windows, and tried to recollect my composure. Elizabeth looked diagonally forward out a window. I stared briefly at the left side of her neck. It was white and exquisite. I looked at her brunette ponytail. I reconsidered my proposition. I ran my eyes downward to her left arm. It was slightly tanned by the summer sun but unmistakably white. I took another look at the side of her neck, and then quickly fixed my eyes on her left hand, laid peacefully prone on her left knee.

I regained my composure and courage. Again, I reached out and held her hand. I squeezed her hand gently to get her attention. She turned slightly toward me. I leaned forward and whispered in her ear.

"Would you marry me?" I proposed nervously. I jumped off the cliff and counted on the wind to carry me. This was it. I had done my part. The rest was up to Elizabeth. She was the wind.

The nearby passengers had heard and understood me. Everyone stared at us with obvious smiles. Elizabeth showed no emotion. She looked me in the eyes. She had heard me. She had understood my English; her eyes said so.

I had miscalculated her. I knew she had always wanted to marry me. In fact, without a doubt, she wanted it more than I did. I really thought she would be overjoyed. I thought she would be jumping up and down. I was thrown off balance by her composed face. I felt like a fool.

"Yes?" I encouraged her response and tried to regain my composure. The same disinterested look was on her face.

I did not let go of her hand; I eased the grip but held on. We broke our eye contact and looked out the windows across from us. We rode in silence. I had butterflies in my stomach. I hoped she would say yes. I hoped she would say no. I hoped she would say, "Sure, why not?" I hoped she would say no.

The train carried us past restaurants and shops on the waterfront avenue. After a couple of transit stops, Elizabeth leaned over and lightly kissed my cheek.

"Say that again!" she demanded quietly.

"You know," I responded timidly. It was hard enough to propose the first time; I was not about to repeat myself.

"I know, but say it again!" she insisted.

I let go of her hand and turned to look outside the window across from my seat. I was silent. I felt Elizabeth's hand grab mine. We sat in silence. I felt Elizabeth smile. I felt good.

Elizabeth and I got off the train and crossed the busy street that separated the rail line and the boardwalk. Off the busy street and onto the curb, Elizabeth stopped and grabbed my hands. She looked straight into my eyes.

"Say what you said to me on the train!" Elizabeth demanded.

"Do you want to marry me?" I asked.

"No, that's not what you said. Say what you said on the train." She continued to demand.

With confidence, I got down on my knee and proposed. "Would you marry me?"

Still no response, but Elizabeth's big grin was reassuring. We spent the rest of the day like two teenagers on a date away from home. Elizabeth never gave me an explicit answer that day. But her mood, smile, and laughter gave me all the answer I needed; I became engaged that day.

On August 7, 1993, just before I left Andersen Consulting, and a week before my ten-year high school reunion, Elizabeth and I got married. Elizabeth Roe officially became Mrs. Lisa Ung, and I got myself a family of my own. I was a golden leaf with roots.

A TREE WITH A NEW LEAF

After I left Andersen, I started immediately at UDP as an account manager. I earned enough to take out a mortgage to purchase my first home and a rental duplex, as well as trade in my very old car for a brand-new one. As my career advanced, I left UDP and accepted a position at Step Technology as a senior consultant. Financially better off, Lisa and I managed to help my friends and relatives. For a period of four years, we took into our home two little boys and two teenagers.

I had come a long way. For a very long time, I was a leaf at the mercy of the wind. My perseverance had made me a golden leaf. Then later, I put down roots. Now I had become a tree. I provided shade for those who needed it.

In 1997, Lisa and I had our first baby, a boy. We named our son after my father, Kilin. Having once lost everything at the atrocious hands of the Khmer Rouge, baby Kilin brought the world back to me and drooled on me a new life. Lisa was sick from giving birth, and I took care of baby Kilin in the first three weeks of his life. Every moment that I spent with baby Kilin brought me a new experience. The more children's books I read to him, the better my English pronunciation became. The more I gave to him, the stronger I became. I was on top of the world. I was no longer a leaf at the mercy of the wind but a tree that gave life to a new leaf named Kilin.

I was exhausted, but baby Kilin's cry energized me. More than the salary I earned, more than the house I owned, more than the brand-new car I had just purchased, more than my love for Lisa, more than my own life, I loved rocking and holding baby Kilin. After calming him down, I held him tightly against my chest. I felt him drool over my shoulder and down the top of my back. I felt his low and calm heartbeat. I felt my father's heartbeat. I savored Kilin's baby odor. I smelled my father.

Standing up and holding Kilin, I swayed in a rocking motion. With Kilin breathing heavily in deep sleep, I drifted back into my past while staring blankly out the window. Up to this point, I had suppressed the memories of

my past — for a journey down my memory lane would be emotionally painful. Somehow, Kilin gave me courage to face my past head on. I wondered
how I would one day tell him my story, his grandparents' stories, his aunts'
stories, and the stories of the other Khmer Rouge victims. I wondered how to
make him proud of his Cambodian heritage given that the heritage is forever
stained by the atrocious acts of the Khmer Rouge. I wiped my tears, clenched
my jaw, swallowed my deep pain, and forced a thought that I was holding a
baby descended from a race that had built Angkor Wat, the famous Cambodian
monumental temple built in the twelfth century.

In my private moments with baby Kilin, I thought a lot about my past and
his future. Unbeknownst to him, I made him promises. I will always love him
no matter what. It was my choice to bring him into this world, and, as long
as I am able, I am forever his guardian. I promised to write down my story
for him to read. I promised to expect no wealth, power, or fame from him,
only his happiness. I promised to do all I could to ensure that he would not
be a leaf at the mercy of the wind. I held him tightly, tenderly took his baby
ear into my mouth, and sobbed in disbelief that I had come out of the Khmer
Rouge labor camps to hold this most precious being. I wiped my tears, inhaled
deeply through my wide-open mouth, looked up into the ceiling, and felt the
presence of my parents. I closed my eyes, squeezed out my tears, and thanked
my parents for watching over me.

One afternoon, I held tiny baby Kilin on my left arm while trying to smack
a fly buzzing over our heads with my right hand. I accidentally smacked
Kilin's forehead. He cried at the top of his baby lungs. All my emotional pain
incurred during the Khmer Rouge and throughout my journey burst inside
my heart. Hitting Kilin hurt me more than it hurt him. I gathered him in
my arms but was unable to calm him down. Lisa took him from me. I went to
the bathroom, calmed myself down, and washed off my tears. Lisa and I took
Kilin to the emergency clinic and had his head checked.

While waiting for the registered nurse to take Kilin into the examination room, I reflected on how my parents must have felt watching me labor and starve during the Khmer Rouge. I recalled my mother secretly sharing her food ration with me and my youngest sister. I recalled the look in my mother's eyes that said "I would die for you." Right there and then, I knew that I would have died for Kilin. The fresh bruise on Kilin's forehead made me feel horrible. I felt absolutely stupid for hurting my baby over a fly. Fortunately, Kilin's examination revealed that he was okay, and we went home.

Lisa and I sold our house and duplex to build a new house in an affluent neighborhood. The house was big. As a former Cambodian refugee, I thought it was more like a mansion than a house. It was an unbelievable realization of the American dream.

RETURNING TO CAMBODIA

When I escaped Cambodia, I did not look for a better world; I simply escaped hell. Deep in my heart, I always hoped that hell would one day change back into a peaceful Cambodia, and then I would return home.

As soon as the relationship between the U.S. and Cambodia improved, and I was allowed to contact my family, I began sending small amounts of money to help my sisters. Each time I sent money, my sisters sent back letters detailing their poor living conditions. Their letters kept me up many nights in depression and frustration for not being able to do more for them and their poor families.

In the late '90s, Cambodia advanced in technology, and I was able to hear my sisters over the telephone with poor reception. After years of losing hope of reuniting with my sisters, my first phone conversation with them brought me deep emotional pain. At one end of the phone conversation, my sister Phon and I were on two separate cordless phones of a single landline. At the other end, all my sisters in Cambodia took turns talking to me and Phon. I was in tears, but I was able to speak to all of my sisters except Peak. When Peak got on the phone, she nervously giggled and called out my name.

"Dong?" Peak repeatedly called out my name on the other end of the line.

My tears gushed, my lips quivered, my heart pounded, my sinuses congested; I was silent. In disbelief that I could talk to Peak a world away, I wanted to reach out and gather her in my arms. My heart hurt, I clenched my jaw, and I forced myself to hold back tears; I was silent. My past caught up with me, and I was consumed by it.

"Dong, answer Peak," intervened Phon in her effort to ease my pain.

"Dong, talk to Peak," Phon continued to urge.

Phon understood my pain. She understood the special bond that Peak and I had forged through our suffering inflicted by the Khmer Rouge.

"Vea niyeay min chenh te (He cannot speak)," said Phon into the phone. Peak giggled uneasily and let out a few sniffles. I felt her tears and her held-back sobs.

"Dong, oan ah (Dong, my darling baby brother)," Peak repeatedly tried to calm me down.

I was embarrassed and unable to control my emotions. I felt like a child in the presence of my sisters. I missed my mother. I felt a tremendous void. I wanted back my time with my mother, father, and sisters. I wondered if Peak knew that I had fully grown into a fine man. I wondered if she had changed. Her voice was unmistakably the same as always. She did not sound a day older.

"Beur niyeay min chenh chhob niyeay tov." Peak urged me to hang up if I could not speak.

I could no longer control myself. I broke into uncontrollable sobs. My body shook, I felt like a little boy, and I hung up the phone. I rushed upstairs, through my master bedroom and into the master bathroom. I locked the bathroom door, turned on the shower, and stepped into it—fully clothed. I cried in the shower. I repeatedly beat my clenched right fist into the left side of my chest, trying to remove the pain that was wrapped around my heart like a giant leech. I drummed my fists into the shower wall. I could not feel the temperature of the shower. I hated the world. I felt like a helpless leaf.

A long shower finally calmed me down. I turned off the water, took off and hung up my wet clothes, stepped out, dried myself off with a towel, went to the master bedroom, and put on a fresh pair of jeans and a T-shirt. When I got downstairs, Phon had already left for her own home. At that moment, I knew that I had to start planning a visit to Cambodia.

By the late '90s, Cambodia was still a dangerous place, but my sister Phon and I decided to go back anyway and visit Cambodia for the first time since we had left it in 1979. The decision was extremely difficult, because Kilin depended on me to read and rock him to bed practically every night and Lisa was pregnant with our second child. Having heard the hellish stories coming out of Cambodia and knowing that Cambodia was still a dangerous place, Lisa worried about my safety and had a hard time supporting and accepting my decision. However, she understood the essence of my visit to Cambodia after twenty years.

Just days before my trip, Lisa made a videotape of me reading stories to Kilin so she could replay it for Kilin in my absence. I was torn between two worlds. In one world, my past, heritage, sisters, and the spirits of my parents awaited my return. In another world, I was about to leave behind the best things that had ever happened to me (my pregnant wife and baby). Elation, anticipation, anxiety, fear, and guilt rolled into a single boiling emotion in my aching heart. Phon was on the phone with me every night trying to ease my guilt. Regardless of constant and reasonable justifications, when I tried to explain to my fifteen-month-old baby why his papa had to leave him for three weeks, something ripped in my heart. I worried about my own safety solely in the context of my family's welfare — Kilin was a baby, Lisa was pregnant, I was the only source of income that made ends meet, and we didn't have enough savings to cover the family should something happen to me in Cambodia.

My anticipation ran high after waiting for twenty years to return to Cambodia. I expected to get on the plane, make one stop in Taipei, Taiwan, and arrive in Cambodia within twenty-four hours. Far from my expectation, with multiple flight delays, it took me a few days to reach Cambodia. In some ways, the long trip was a blessing in disguise. It gave me a golden opportunity to give Phon detailed accounts of my family life during the Khmer Rouge and in her absence. Phon had many questions about what had happened to our family during the rough time, and I had all the answers. Answering Phon's questions about my family's life under the Khmer Rouge was therapeutic.

Whenever unrestricted by the flight attendants, I lifted the armrest separating my seat and Phon's and sat tightly next to her. I was a grown man, but sitting next to my sister, I regressed and became the boy I once was.

Cuddling with each other, my sister and I shared the memories of our past. We recalled good and bad times. We recalled our struggles in the refugee camps, San Diego, and Portland. We shared the memory of our picking strawberries to make ends meet while living in a cheap apartment in Southeast Portland. We speculated about what could and would have been if our other sisters had joined our escape in 1979. We congratulated ourselves for having come so far through our shared and respective difficult journeys. We shared our excitement and disbelief of returning to Cambodia as well as our fear of facing danger in Cambodia. We were unsure whether we could adapt to Cambodia's third-world conditions.

When tired, I put my head on my sister's lap and fell asleep. I dreamed of good times and had nightmares of horrible times.

Awake, head on my sister's lap, I felt boyish and safe. I smiled and was glad my sister was with me on this first return trip to Cambodia. I looked around and was reminded of the stark difference between this trip and the trip that took me from the refugee camp to California. I felt big. I felt triumphant.

During my flight from the Bangkok refugee camp to California in 1979, I felt conspicuous in my refugee outfit and flip-flops. On that flight, I was embarrassed to be so noticeable. To the contrary, on this flight back to Cambodia, the other passengers were oblivious of the fact that I was a former refugee returning to Cambodia. I felt invisible. I wanted to stand up, walk to the cockpit, and ask the pilot to announce my twenty-year return to Cambodia.

When I was hungry, I buzzed a flight attendant. A young and beautiful

Chinese flight attendant made me a hot bowl of instant Chinese noodle soup. Unlike the American flight attendants, the Chinese flight attendants looked more like girls than women. This one particular flight attendant reminded me of my beautiful youngest sister, Ali. More significant, I was reminded of how far I had come. I remembered feeling hunger during the flight in 1979 but being incapable of asking a flight attendant for food.

Between each bite, I looked into the plastic-foam bowl of noodles and reflected on the time when I only had a ration of rice porridge consisting of mostly water and two tablespoons of white rice. Tears welled up, and I was not sure whether I was sad or happy. I drifted off to sleep shortly after eating.

Awakened by the voice of the pilot over the plane's intercom, I was unsure of my whereabouts. I found myself reorienting and coming to the realization that I was returning to Cambodia. I experienced disbelief and surrealism multiple times during the trip. I imagined what it would be like in Cambodia. I could not deny the thought that the Khmer Rouge was still around along the Thai border. I could not refute the possibility that I could be stuck in Cambodia like a number of Cambodian expatriates during their visit to Cambodia in 1975 when the Khmer Rouge took over.

As Cambodia got closer, my recollection that Cambodians were capable of heinous brutality made my stomach sick. I popped an antacid in my mouth and downed it with half a bottle of water. My symptoms of PTSD surfaced; I felt claustrophobic and angry. My hands sweated and slightly trembled. I got up and out of my seat. I walked up and down the narrow aisle. I stretched and then proceeded to do forty pushups in the aisle space between the two restrooms in the back of the airplane. I went to the restroom and returned to my seat.

"Are you okay?" Phon asked.

"I'm fine," I responded. What else could I say? There was nothing else I wanted to say. I sat down, put on the headphones, and watched a movie. I knew my sister knew how I felt, and I knew I was not alone with anxiety.

We arrived at Bangkok International Airport in Thailand quite late at night. After a few hours of light sleep in the terminal chairs, we went to the transfer desk to check in for the flight to Phnom Penh. A handful of western passengers gave me some degree of comfort, but the large number of Cambodian passengers made me uneasy. A few Cambodian passengers appeared official, and a few others could have been representatives of the communist party, the former Khmer Rouge.

All of a sudden, I felt conspicuously out of place in my liberal American outfit. I was in a pair of shorts (with more pockets than necessary), Nike golf T-shirt, Nike golf cap, ankle socks, and Timberland leather boots. I was accessorized by a leather belt with a heavy stainless-steel buckle that would never fail to set off the airport security scanner. My Fossil watch and my white-gold wedding ring pronounced my western image.

I felt eyes on me the same way I had on the flight from Bangkok to America in 1979. I felt foreign then, and I felt foreign now. I wished I had saved my old cotton shirt, shorts, and flip-flops for this trip.

My sister Phon constantly reminded me about my posture and mannerisms. She was concerned that I stood out too much. My American confidence could be misinterpreted as arrogance and put both of us in danger when we arrived in Cambodia. Although I had trouble articulating my true feelings in Cambodian, I made a serious effort to avoid speaking English with Phon. I kept my tone low, and I avoided direct eye contact with other Cambodian passengers.

Each step toward boarding the Cambodian plane was excruciatingly slow. My stomach churned, and my imagination ran wild. I took each step with disbelief that I was about to be in Cambodia. The palms of my hands perspired, and I had butterflies in my stomach. The rhythms of my heart accelerated. The Cambodian language over the intercom was beautiful but simultaneously brought me both comfort and anxiety; I was about to re-enter Cambodia—hell, heaven, foreign land, and home.

The mucky atmosphere and relatively unclean looks of other passengers reminded me of a gate to hell. Doubts about my decision to visit Cambodia crept into my mind. Suddenly I was angry, and I was ready to kill anyone standing in the way of my homecoming. Cambodia was my home, and twenty years in waiting was a long time.

I fought to hold back my tears when I entered the Cambodian plane and faced the female Cambodian flight attendants. The Cambodia—hell—that I remembered from the Khmer Rouge era had been transformed. The flight attendants were dressed in elaborate Cambodian outfits and showed signs of peace and tranquility. There were no indications of Khmer Rouge roughness instilled in the flight attendants. The attendants were as traditional as Cambodian women had been for centuries.

"Chumreab sour, Lok!" a beautiful flight attendant greeted me after I stepped onto the plane. She uttered a few more words, but I only understood "Greetings, Sir." It was enough for me to momentarily convince myself that I was home again. It was enough to briefly divert my anxiety.

My palms continued to sweat profusely during the flight, and my mind wandered from present to past and back to present again. I had lots of conversations with my parents on the flight. I missed my family in the U.S. I worried about Lisa's pregnancy. I worried about my safety in Cambodia. I had a lot on my mind.

The plane flew at low altitude, and I had a clear view of rice fields and villages. Cambodia was quiet and peaceful through the narrow view of the plane window. From time to time, looking out the window over the vast open Cambodian farmland, my mind superimposed an image of the Khmer Rouge labor camps on the quiescent scenery of the provincial parts of Cambodia. As if I had died and gone to heaven, I looked down at myself working in a Khmer Rouge labor camp. I saw myself toil in the sun and in heavy rain thirteen hours a day, seven days a week, 365 days a year in the Khmer Rouge hellish labor camp. An image of my mother's emaciated body flashed before my eyes. Looking down on the superimposed Khmer Rouge killing fields, I saw my brother-in-law clubbed to death. I watched my father at his last breath waiting for me to show up. I watched my father's disappointed eyes close as he gave up on waiting for me. I watched myself tiredly dig a grave and bury the body of my grandmother. I turned my head away from Phon, pretended to be asleep, and sorted out my emotions.

The plane set its wheels on the landing strip and decelerated forward on the runway. Through the windows, I watched tall palm trees pass by. The plane came to a full stop about a hundred yards outside the terminal.

Looking out my window, it felt odd that there lacked the familiar mortars and rockets that were regularly launched at landing planes during wartime. It felt even odder not seeing the Khmer Rouge, with their evil black uniforms and AK-47 rifles. My mind oscillated between my past and my present. I had trouble reconciling the memory of my horrible past with my peaceful present.

I did not know what to expect. I was unsure whether I would be welcomed back or escorted to jail for being a traitor. I was not ready to step out of the plane. I was ready. I was scared. I was courageous. I was happy. I was angry. I was sad. I wanted to hold someone affectionately close. I wanted to punch someone in the face. I missed Lisa and Kilin. I wanted to scream. I wanted to bend someone's fingers backward until they snapped off. I wanted to take an AK-47 rifle and shove its barrel down someone's throat. I wanted to stab a bayonet into someone's stomach. I wanted to kick someone into blood, bruises, and urine. I wanted to kill someone. I became bold and wanted someone to piss me off. I stood up, took down my backpack from the overhead compartment, and forced my way through the crowd. I wanted someone to fuck with me and piss me off. I was ready to step off the plane onto the Cambodian soil, my goddamned fucking soil.

I stepped out of the plane and onto the top of the stairs. I took my time descending the stairs. Contrary to the mixed emotions somersaulting in my stomach, the air was ignorantly peaceful. The atmosphere appeared oblivious of the Khmer Rouge's heinous crime against humanity. I felt alone. I wanted to scream and make the world aware that the Khmer Rouge genocide had killed two million Cambodians and starved my parents to death.

My hands trembled and my legs wobbled as I took steps toward the ground. I paused at the bottom of the stairs, took a deep breath, exhaled through my mouth, and languorously took my first step onto Cambodian soil—for the first time since I had left Cambodia twenty years ago.

Once both my feet were securely placed on the ground, my knees buckled. I went down on my hands and knees. I broke down in public, sobbed uncontrollably, lowered my face, and kissed the ground. To my disbelief, I had returned.

People watched. I lifted my head, clasped my hands, and pictured my parents' smiles. I cried. I cried hard. I sobbed. I held up the line. People watched.

I stood up, better composed and slightly embarrassed; I wiped my nose and tears with the sleeves of my shirt.

Outside of the terminal, a man in an official outfit approached me and Phon. It was odd that he smiled directly at me and my sister. He was taller and bigger than an average Cambodian. The man's ruggedly tough appearance made it clear that he had fought in war battles and was a ranking officer. He approached with commanding confidence. I had butterflies in my stomach.

The man stopped just a few feet away from me. He put his hands together and lifted them up above his chest to greet me and Phon.

"Ming, Pou, chumreab sour!" the man pronounced his greeting. He addressed Phon and me as "Aunt" and "Uncle" rather than "Madam" and "Sir." From his intimate greeting, it was clear to me that the man knew us, and he knew us well.

I was puzzled, but before I uttered a word, the man introduced himself.

"Khgnom bat Tonat," said the man, my nephew. In disbelief, I was speechless. When I had left him in 1979, he was a little boy. My memory of Tonat was of a little boy with a runny nose, shirtless and in shorts herding oxen with me. Now he was an officer in the Cambodian military police. I did not know what to say to him. I threw myself at him, grabbed his big frame, held it tight, buried my face in his strong shoulder, and let out a humongous burst of sobs. Phon joined in the sobs. Tonat gently giggled, and a few tears welled up in his eyes. I broke up the sobbing huddle, stepped back, and took an admiring look at my nephew Tonat. I was proud of him and could not believe what he had done for himself.

Tonat directed my attention toward a thin woman behind him coming toward me. I recognized her. I could not move. I wanted to run to the woman, grab her, and hold her tight. I could not move. My legs were virtually detached from my body. My tears welled up, my lips quivered, my jaw clenched, and my teary eyes fixed on the woman running toward me. I froze. My hands trembled. I could not move. The woman was Tonat's mother and my sister Dy. I opened my arms and wrapped Dy tightly against my chest.

Now that I was older, taller, and stronger, Dy's thin frame in my arms seemed fragile. The tough life she endured in Cambodia made her look ten years older.

Tonat stood by while Phon, Dy, and I were locked in an airtight hug. No words were uttered. No words could express what we felt in that moment. We just cried. We sobbed. We avoided one another's eyes. We were oblivious to public curiosity. We avoided admitting to one another our timeless sorrow and loss. We cried. We sobbed. We held one another tight. We could not let go of one another. We did not want to let go. The twenty-year hug deficit melted our skins into one.

My sister's smell was the same as it had been when I was a little boy. The smell took me back to my boyhood. With seven beautiful sisters, I was the boy to whom every man in the village wanted to suck up. Men such as my sisters' schoolmates and young naughty Buddhist monks paid me special attention, hoping to get closer to my sisters. A couple of the monks gave me things and money in exchange for trivial information about my sisters, such as their names and what schools they attended.

I held Phon and Dy for a long time while other passengers passed us by. Finally, Dy broke the hug, stepped back, wiped off her tears, and smiled.

"Aphon (Dear Phon), Dong (Kilong) thom nass nah (is very big)," Dy said to Phon. Phon agreed. In Dy's memory from 1979, I was at the height of Phon's shoulder. Thanks to my American diet, active life, and meditation, I had grown taller than Phon and Dy. I was a man, but in the company of my sisters, I felt like a little boy. I wanted to be a little boy. I wanted to reclaim the childhood that I had been deprived of. I took advantage of the moment and allowed myself to be weak, emotional, and boyish. I felt safe.

Once the emotions cleared the air, I felt even safer knowing that my nephew was an officer of the Cambodian military police. In those days, Cambodia was still somewhat lawless, and having a close relative in the military helped keep one out of danger.

Walking through the airport, I could not believe how far Cambodia had come since the day of my escape. Having lived in the dark ages for nearly five years during the Khmer Rouge, I could not believe that Cambodia had survived and had the potential of becoming a renascent nation.

Outside the airport terminal building, my other relatives and family friends waited for me. My oldest sister, Sim, awaited me with tears welled in her eyes. I charged forward like a bull and threw myself at Sim. My chest against hers, our hearts interlocked, and our souls momentarily became one. The twenty-year absence seemed like an eternity. The two decades of yearning for this moment glued me tightly in my sister's arms. I dug my chin into her shoulder and let my tears pour down the top of her back. I was in my own world for a long time and was not aware of who joined in the reuniting hug.

My sisters Phorn, Pech, and Peak were not there. For whatever reason, Phorn had decided not to meet me at the airport and waited for me at Tonat's guesthouse in Phnom Penh. Pech was in Montreal, Canada, and could not make the trip to this reunion. Peak could not leave her house and her children unattended in Battambang. It would have been better if all my sisters had been there, but I was just as happy at that moment.

In her absence, Peak sent her second-born daughter, Apol, to welcome me at the airport. Apol was thirteen years old and looked every bit her mother. Apol's stark resemblance to Peak triggered another emotional outburst. I took her in my arms. I tightened my hold. Apol reciprocated. I felt her mother's body. I smelled her mother's hair. Reminiscence of the misery that I had shared with her mother flashed before my teary eyes. My uncontrollable sobs shook my body. Other passengers and their families and friends turned into spectators. I held onto a niece whom I had never met, but I felt as if I had known her all my life. Her emotional reciprocity pronounced her profound kinship toward me. I held her tight and wondered to what degree she had learned about the history between me and her mother. I took in a deep breath, exhaled, and freed Apol from my prolonged hug.

I was introduced to Tonat's wife, his two baby daughters, and his in-laws. I was overwhelmed by introductions to family friends, distant relatives, nieces, and nephews—most of whom I was meeting for the first time.

In front of the airport terminal, Tonat pulled up his Toyota Land Cruiser and loaded the luggage in the back. Tonat's wife and his children took the shotgun seat. I took the back seat between my two sisters Dy and Sim. Apol sat on Sim's lap, and Phon sat between Sim and the back window.

At the exit gate of Po Chen Tong Airport, a military policeman stood at attention and saluted Tonat. A civilian policeman leaned out of the fare booth window, greeted Tonat, and took the parking fee from Tonat's hand. I sat speechless watching a system contrary to what I had pictured. I had not expected modern technology, civilized protocols, or freedom. From reading print and Internet news, I knew that Cambodia had become a free country, but seeing it firsthand mesmerized me. I sat speechless and in amazement, with my eyes watching out the back seat window as Tonat pulled the Land Cruiser into the busy paved boulevard.

For twenty years, I had imagined Cambodia without electricity, running water, markets, or any form of technology. Now I struggled to reconcile my imagination with reality. The boulevard was heavily trafficked by cars, trucks, motorcycles, and bicycles. Alongside the boulevard, street vendors densely set up stands to sell fruit, clothes, electronics, watches, cell phone cards, and food. Restaurants were everywhere. Contrary to my horrific memories and misguided imagination, Phnom Penh was a vibrant city.

I smiled in awe, for Cambodia had come a long way from what I remembered. Yet my heart sank when I noticed people living in poverty. Amputees and beggars were rampant. The disparaging legacy of the Khmer Rouge was manifested in poverty. Smiles on the new generation's faces were indicative of the country's peace and relative prosperity, but sorrow and lingering agony in the older generation's faces took me back to the suffering inflicted by the Khmer Rouge.

The heavy traffic was mostly created by bicycles. Looking out the windshield, I watched a mass of bicycles part in front of the Land Cruiser like heavy snowflakes. I held my sisters' hands tightly. My sisters watched me with attentive curiosity and admiration. My emotion alternated among happiness, sadness, and anger. I was happy to see my sisters. I was sad for the poor. I was angry at the Khmer Rouge for killing my parents and youngest sister. I experienced overwhelming joy and deep depression at the same time. I could not share my feelings with my sisters. I felt alone.

My mind wandered involuntarily and relentlessly. I was present. I was absent. Conflicting emotions battled within me. I hated the world for standing by while the Khmer Rouge had committed such a heinous crime against humanity. I was angry at Vietnam for creating the Khmer Rouge in the first place. I was angry at China for backing the Khmer Rouge. I was angry about the American bombing that had weakened Cambodia's stance against the Khmer Rouge. I was angry at Thailand for mistreating the refugees. I was angry at Buddha for his disinterest while my life went to hell during the Khmer Rouge. I had no evidence regarding which nations were partly responsible for the Khmer Rouge's atrocious crime against humanity (nor whether Buddha had anything to do with anything), but it didn't matter because I momentarily had no control over my embattled emotions. I simply hated the world and wished I could push a button that would make the world extinct.

So much had come to me that day, and I could not process it. I could not reconcile my imagination and the reality of modern Cambodia. I looked on, dazed, bedazzled, stupefied, joyous, sad, and angry. I could not believe the plethora of fruit, food, and clothes put up for sale alongside the boulevard. The reminder of Cambodia's abundance made me very angry at the Khmer Rouge. Cambodia had so much natural resource, yet people were starved during the Khmer Rouge regime. For the first time in my life, I felt the true degree of cruelty by the hands of the Khmer Rouge thugs. I covered my face with my hands and placed it on my knees. I broke down into sobs. My sisters rubbed my back. No words were spoken.

Attempting to end the melancholy, Tonat asked me what I wanted to do or see. I told him I had waited twenty years to eat a fresh coconut. Tonat pulled over in front of a fruit stand. I was happy and excited—until I stepped out of the Land Cruiser and onto the curb. Suddenly, I was surrounded by beggars. Little boys and girls with dark skin and runny noses, some as young as four years old, pulled the bottom of my shirt begging for money. There were women of all ages begging that day. Some women and older girls carried naked and soiled babies. Amputees were among the male beggars. In total, there were at least thirty beggars flocking me.

My relatives attempted to drive the beggars away, but I adamantly told them to leave the beggars be. I pulled out my wallet and handed out my U.S. $1 bills. At the time, $20 per month was regarded as high earnings in Cambodia. To the beggars, getting $1 was an unbelievable fortune. Before I knew it, the number of beggars doubled. I was overwhelmed, but I didn't mind. I continued to hand out my dollar bills. When I ran out of $1 bills, I bought more from Tonat and continued to hand them out. Before I knew it, an overwhelming number of beggars became an uncontrollable mob. Some beggars wanted second or third handouts from me. The begging mob became aggressive and demanding. It became dangerous to continue handing out money as the mob grew. A handful of civilian and military policemen approached the scene. Tonat corralled me into his Land Cruiser and drove away while the mob momentarily chased the vehicle. I looked back at the mob and watched the beggars fade into the distance. Sadness and anger battled inside me.

Once composed, I realized how good I had it back in the United States. Before this visit to Cambodia, I had gotten too caught up in the rat race and in making ends meet. Like many Americans, I worried about my finances. I wanted beyond my needs. I saw greener grass on the other side of my fence. On occasion, I envied the Joneses. And here, poor people had no fair means and were willing to stampede any golden goose for a chance at a golden egg, a lousy U.S. dollar. I fought back my tears. I missed my family in Portland and appreciated my life as an American.

Tonat drove all over Phnom Penh to give Phon and me a tour of the city. I had never been to Phnom Penh and could not draw a contrast between its past and present, but I was awed by its relative freedom and vibrant capitalism. Even in my wildest imagination, I never thought Cambodia could reach this state of modernization. There were movie theaters, shops, restaurants, printing companies, schools, universities, embassies, military bases, police stations, car dealers, motorcycle shops, and more. Buddhist temples, mosques, and churches were renovated and occupied. Buddhism was resurrected and thriving. The city at face value showed no evidence of Khmer Rouge history. On the surface, life in Cambodia appeared as if the Khmer Rouge's crime against humanity had never taken place. The renascence of Phnom Penh made me momentarily forget my horrible past. I was mesmerized and took in more than I could process.

Deep into the city and along Tonle Basak (Basak River), Tonat drove past the Royal Palace and pulled into a parking lot of a restaurant. As soon as I stepped out of the car, a handful of panhandlers surrounded me and begged for money. I handed out my dollar bills again. A couple of well-dressed restaurant hosts immediately ushered me into the restaurant before I attracted too many beggars to their establishment.

I took a look at the menu and choked up in disbelief at how much Cambodia had developed in my twenty-year absence. It seemed like yesterday that I had survived daily on a rationed bowl of rice porridge made solely from a tiny amount of white rice and a disproportionate amount of water.

Luxury decorations, fancy tables and chairs, and clean dishes in the restaurant took me back to the time when I had only one cotton handmade shirt and one pair of shorts, slept on dirt in the rain, and had no personal belongings.

Modern music in the restaurant stirred up a painful remembrance of the time when all music and songs created before 1975 were banned by the Khmer Rouge. I remembered attending kindergarten, following orders like a sheep, and reciting communistic lyrics full of jingoism.

After a waiter greeted me and took my order, my memory took me back to the barbaric era during which civility was interdicted by the Khmer Rouge. A shot of pain and guilt penetrated my chest as I remembered the time when I was forced to treat my parents as my equals—my comrades instead of my parents.

Having my relatives at a round table reminded me of the times when I crouched in a circle of ten going at a shared pot of rice porridge.

When the table was filled with food, I recalled the time when a Khmer Rouge commander fed me his food. I lowered my face, tipped down my Nike golf cap to hide my eyes, and fought back my tears. My chest was tight. I clenched my jaw, trying to get hold of myself. I really missed my parents.

Tonat made jokes, cheering everyone up and disrupting my train of thought.

I missed the jokes, but I was brought back by the laughter. I emerged from my own emotional trap and joined everyone for a delightful brunch.

After brunch, we left the restaurant and went straight to Tonat's house. As Tonat pulled up in front of his house, my sister Sim pointed to a middle-aged woman standing in front of the house.

"Dong," Sim addressed me by my nickname, "nous, neang Phorn." I looked in the direction of Sim's pointing and barely recognized my adopted sister, Phorn. Twenty years of separation was a long time, and all my sisters had aged quite a bit.

I jumped out of the car and ran toward Phorn. I threw myself at her. She held me, and we both cried like little children. Besides Peak, Pech, and Sim, Phorn was another sister who had suffered my family's losses together with me.

In her arms, I sobbed at the memory of when the Khmer Rouge arrested her and my family lost hope of seeing her alive again. We held each other. No instrument could measure the pain and joy that Phorn and I tearfully shared at that moment. Bystanders knew we relived our suffering, but none truly understood the full meaning of our reunion.

Phorn and I shared our lives beyond the Khmer Rouge era. When the Vietnamese invaded Cambodia and drove the Khmer Rouge out of power in 1979, she and I sometimes went behind the lines of scrimmage between the Vietnamese and Khmer Rouge soldiers to loot for food supplies. On multiple occasions, we were chased by the Khmer Rouge and had to elude the spraying AK-47 bullets. We slept under the dark sky waiting for battles to subside before we could look for food.

I eased my grip and let her go. She held onto me. I relocked my arms around her body. She sobbed uncontrollably. I regained myself and tried to comfort her. Our roles reversed. She became the child, and I became the big brother. After a short reaffirming bear hug, I pushed her out to arm's length. I looked her straight in the eyes. I took a good look at her for the first time. Life in Cambodia had taken a hefty toll on my sister.

"Chhop yum tov!" I told her. Stop crying!

I teased her and made fun of her crying. She laughed. She slapped my face. She smiled childishly, pointed her finger about an inch away from my face, gritted her front teeth, and asserted her big-sister authority over me.

"Apov, kom mok banhchea bong nah!" Addressing me as "youngest darling," Phorn jokingly told me not to give her orders.

The moment was precious. Fond memories of the good past permeated the atmosphere. It was evident that my sisters and elders were no longer my equal comrades. It was a clear reminder that the Khmer Rouge era was over. Now I had to take my place as the youngest sibling at the bottom of the inverted pyramid among my surviving siblings.

That day, I was introduced to my nieces and nephews and in-laws whom I had never met. Dy's children besides Tonat were Toneang, Anine, Anet, and Aponlok. Phorn had one and only one daughter, Aheanh. Peak's children were Apine, Apol, Alo, and Ali. I learned that I also had grandnieces. Dy's daughter Anine had a baby daughter, and Tonat had two daughters. I suddenly felt old thinking of the missing years in the making of my family clan.

That night, many people came to visit me in my room. My sisters and my niece Apol shared a single room with me. The time difference and the excitement created by the twenty-year reunion kept me up late into the night and long after everyone else had fallen asleep. Unable to sleep, I sat up and turned on a small lamp by my bed. In silence, I watched my sisters in their deep sleep. I missed my own family in Portland. I was in disbelief and tried to process what had transpired earlier that day.

My eyes fixed and rested on Apol, who was deep in her sleep and covered with a thick bed sheet to her neck. I could not believe the stark resemblance between her and her mother. I had an epiphany that brought me back to the time when Apol's mom and I were young growing up under the Khmer Rouge. I remembered a time when Peak and I were allowed to visit my mother. Then, like now, I could not sleep. Then, I stayed up watching Peak like I was watching Apol now. Unable to hold back, I let tears flow freely down my cheeks. I turned off the light, lay down, pulled the covers over my head, and quietly sobbed myself to sleep.

Roosters outside woke me up just before the sun rose. I woke up to the stare of my sister Dy. Dy lay on her side, fully awake, resting her head peacefully on a pillow. She smiled at me, and I reciprocated with my smile. I got up and went over to her. I lay down behind her, grabbed her body from behind, and tucked it tightly against mine. No words were exchanged. We shed tears in silence, trying not to disturb others in the room.

Everyone was up at sunrise. Like the good old days in Cambodia, there was no clock in the room; we simply woke up early in the morning.

The bathroom at Tonat's house was not fancy, but it was far beyond my imagination. I took a hot shower, brushed my teeth, and got dressed. When I came out of the bathroom, a big cup of Cambodian coffee with a touch of sweetened condensed milk awaited me. Next to the coffee cup was a large bowl of tropical fruit. For two decades, I had dreamed of the day when I could once again smell and taste the fresh fruit of Cambodia. All eyes were fixed on me and Phon, and I humbly treasured the attention.

BATTAMBANG

After breakfast, Tonat called a family meeting to discuss my itinerary. Given the fact that I had missed twenty years of Cambodia's development, Tonat wanted the best time for me and insisted that I visit his in-laws, who own an ocean-view hotel in Kompong Som (aka Sihanouk Ville). There, I would be spoiled and enjoy the best that Cambodia could offer me. Tonat's proposition was intriguing, but I was more anxious to see Peak in Battambang. The primary target of my visit was Battambang—my home that had turned into hell.

Tonat's good intentions turned into pressure, but I stood my ground and insisted that I be taken to Battambang. With a bit of friction, I was able to have it my way.

At that time, a trip between Phnom Penh and Battambang was still relatively dangerous. Corrupted civilian and military policemen and village chiefs put up random barricades and imposed unlawful tolls. American-Cambodians were viewed as wealthy people and could be kidnapped for ransom. As a military police officer, Tonat was armed. However, by himself, he could be overpowered by the armed thugs in the countryside. So we invited my cousin Vuth, who was a military officer, to come along to Battambang. Vuth and Tonat once had been in the same combat unit. They both had fought against the Khmer Rouge in the '80s and early '90s.

Before midmorning, we had our luggage tied on the top of Tonat's Land Cruiser. Since it was summertime, the luggage was not covered. Like a group of circus clowns in a tiny Volkswagen Bug, most of my family cramped inside the Land Cruiser. Tonat was in the driver's seat, and Vuth rode shotgun with his son on his lap. Vuth's wife sat with my sisters, Phorn's husband, my nieces, and me in the back seats.

The highway became unpaved and full of potholes as soon as we got out of Phnom Penh's city limits. Provincial bridges were in treacherously poor condition, and many had to be circumvented. The precariously bumpy and dusty ride ultimately pronounced the true third-world condition of Cambodia.

For lunch, we stopped at a restaurant in the middle of nowhere. For $1.50, I had a bowl of noodles with two large freshwater lobsters, but not before a group of beggars closed in on me and my sister Phon. The more money we gave, the more beggars showed up. The abundance of fruits and beverages on the table signified the depressing economic chasm between me and the poor. The beggars reminded me of my starving days. They reminded me of my inhumane hardship during the Khmer Rouge. They also reminded me of how fortunate I was. Unfortunately, I could not fully enjoy my fortune, because no matter how much money I gave away, the beggars would not leave me to enjoy my lunch. The restaurant owner stepped in, yelled at the beggars, and told them to leave. Reluctantly, the beggars left me. I forced myself to shut off my bad feelings toward the beggars, but it was hard.

The cool breeze of the countryside, the sound of the rattling leaves, and the scenery of the open rice field reminded me of my own past and diverted my thoughts away from the beggars. My mind drifted into the open field and rested on a receded lake full of lotus. Vacillating between my horrible past and peaceful present, I struggled to understand how the Khmer Rouge's crime against me, my family, and humanity could have taken place.

It had been more than twenty-five years since I had had a taste of freshwater lobster. I savored every bite. Each bite took me back to the time before the Khmer Rouge had taken over. Each bite reminded me of the time when my family would sit on a rice mat in a circle for our family dinners.

After lunch, my family and I pushed our way through a band of beggars and into the Land Cruiser. As we pulled out, poor children without shirts chased the vehicle, begging for change. I rolled down the window and threw out a handful of $1 bills. Watching the children shoving one another for the bills, I was reminded of my own childhood before the Khmer Rouge.

The road was bumpy and dusty. On occasions, deep potholes caused the vehicle to toss me upward until my head banged against the ceiling of the vehicle. I was tossed upward, sideways, backward, and forward. Whenever the Land Cruiser pulled up behind another vehicle, a thick cloud of red dust completely erased the front visibility. Traveling by automobile was dangerous, but it was even more dangerous for provincial bicyclists, moped drivers, pedestrians, schoolchildren, and farm animals. For the life of me, I could not imagine how I had survived Cambodia before I escaped to Thailand and came to America.

Rice-farming children as young as five or six years old peddled food alongside the highway. My sisters bought me young lotus fruit, fresh ripe cashews, young palm nuts, and young coconuts—all of which I had yearned for over the past twenty years.

We crossed the border of Posut Province and Battambang Province by late afternoon. Shortly after that, we entered the area where I had labored, starved, and suffered during the Khmer Rouge. While major cities like Phnom Penh had developed and advanced, the countryside had not changed much in my absence. I immediately recognized the area, as if I had never left the place. Of all the people traveling with me that day, only Sim and Phorn had lived with me in that area during the Khmer Rouge. If anyone could truly understand how I felt at that moment, it would be Sim and Phorn. The three of us took turns pointing out the history of the area in the context of our horrible experiences in the labor camp.

Far off to the right of the highway was a village barely seen by the naked eye, Phoum Khsouy. It was the village that served as my family home during the Khmer Rouge. For the first time, Dy and Phon had an idea of where I had buried my grandmother. I told them all the things that happened to my family in that village.

Within minutes, as we continued to head west toward the provincial city of Battambang, we came upon an old and abandoned hut just off to the right of the highway. I immediately recognized the place. I recounted for everyone in the vehicle the horrible life I endured in this place. This was one of my harshest labor camps. Here, I worked thirteen hours a day, seven days a week, 365 days a year. Here, I watched a man tortured to near death. I watched his face while he was suffocated by a plastic bag that covered his head. Here, I ate rats, termites, bats, snakes, snails, leaves, and roots to keep myself alive. Here, I pulled leeches off my skin.

Beyond the hut that marked my memory of a harsh labor camp stood a village farther off the highway. As the vehicle passed the entrance of the village, I told the story about the village in the context of my family's experience. The village was called Kbal Khnol (head of the road). It was the place from where my brother-in-law Chip was purged and executed. It was the place where my sister Pech labored and suffered.

Immediately to the right, there stood a monumental manmade water reservoir. Unable to hold back, I broke down and sobbed. I had been part of the slave labor that had manually constructed the reservoir. Phorn also broke down, because she and Peak had also been part of it. I reached over, grabbed Phorn's hand, and squeezed hard.

It was not long before we came upon a Buddhist temple, Wat Kompong

Preah, where my mother was hospitalized and died. I spiritually reflected on my parents. In my own private thoughts, I told my parents that I missed them. I asked my parents to spiritually hold me. I made a spiritual apology to my parents for not being able to be with them during their final moments. I told everyone in the vehicle about the death of my mother.

The temple's perimeter was clearly marked by a tall and conspicuous fence. At the moment before the vehicle came square with the east perimeter of the temple, the sun was shining, the temperature was typically hot, there was no cloud in sight, the sky was crisp blue, and there was absolutely no indication of raindrops.

At the very moment when the front of the Land Cruiser passed the east perimeter, the sky was suddenly covered by a dark cloud and unexpected rain violently poured down on the Land Cruiser. Everyone in the vehicle was startled. There was commotion inside the vehicle. I looked back, and found no rain behind the vehicle. Everyone was baffled.

Within seconds, the vehicle passed the entire perimeter. My hands shook, and my heart was pounding. My brain shut off. Someone in the vehicle said it was a miraculous sign made by my late parents. With bewilderment, everyone looked back and was confused by the clear sky. We all looked out the windows, trying to spot a rain cloud, and found none. Within about three minutes, the mysterious rain disappeared without a trace of it in the entire sky.

Everyone looked at one another in search of reassurance that the miracle had happened. We looked at the absolutely clear sky, raindrops on the windows and windshield, and wet highway behind us.

"Yeung trov te nimon lok srouch teuk dak bai ouy ov yeung me yeung," said Sim. A Buddhist nun, Sim told us to invite Buddhist monks to perform a memorial ceremony for my parents as soon as possible. According to Buddhism, the spirits of my parents suffered and roamed aimlessly because a religious memorial ceremony was never done for them. Sim said the miraculous rain was a desperate sign from my parents.

The rest of the way to the city of Battambang was a ride down my memory lane. Sim, Phorn, and I told everyone in the vehicle about our family's extraordinary experience during the evacuation. We pointed out specific locations along the highway and detailed what had happened during the evacuation. Dy and Phon cried. I knew they felt guilty for not being with the family during the most difficult times. I felt deep love and a sharp pain in my chest.

It was near dinnertime when we arrived in Battambang. I generally recognized the city, but much had changed. The city was more crowded. Technological advancement (even for the third world) made Battambang a different city from what I remembered. I felt both at home and out of place. I was angry and nostalgic for all that was taken from me. I was sad and angry about being a stranger in my own town. Once mine by my birthright, this place now made me a foreigner.

I was mesmerized by the city's normalcy. Defying the idealism of the heinous and dogmatic Khmer Rouge, Battambang thrived. There were automobiles, electricity, running water, theaters, and coffee shops. Signs of the free market were everywhere.

Memories surfaced as Tonat drove around the city. The governor's mansion was newly renovated and well-kept. City streets were paved. The temple Wat Domrei Sor seemed smaller than its image in my memory. Everything seemed smaller and shorter than what I remembered.

Finally, we arrived in front of Hotel Teo. The hotel was built on the land where my home stood until the Khmer Rouge demolished it after the 1975 evacuation. Reality began to set in. The land was no longer mine. My parents were dead. My youngest sister was dead. Everything that belonged to me by my birthright was gone. My heart sank. I felt empty. My stomach trembled, and I felt as if I were levitating. I was light.

Tonat drove past Hotel Teo. I didn't recognize a few things, but I generally remembered the neighborhood very well. I remembered where I played hide and seek with my friends before the Khmer Rouge. I remembered where I played war. I remembered practically everything. I noticed missing homes, and I saw new homes. I recognized my aunt's house, still standing and occupied by my aunt and my cousins. I recognized the homes of my neighbors, now occupied by strangers.

Tonat took the immediate left turn onto a narrow dirt pathway. Huts of poor people were situated tightly next to one another on both sides of the narrow path. Little children were dirty and naked. The poor people living in the huts had no electricity and no running water. They collected and stored rain for water use. It was obvious that some families made ends meet by means of prostitution. Others scraped by with their roadside peddling and begging. The poor reminded me of my own past during the Khmer Rouge regime. I felt fortunate but guilty about my better fortune. My heart went out to the poor, and I momentarily forgot about my own horrible past.

I felt out of place riding inside the Land Cruiser. A runny-nosed child standing naked reminded me of my own son, Kilin. Momentarily, I wanted to return to Portland and hold my son tightly against my chest. My mind spanned my past, present, and future. My heart broke into pieces. My feelings of anger, melancholy, helplessness, fortune, and guilt rolled into one frustrating emotion. I fought to keep my emotions inside, but I was depressed and angry. I regretted coming back to Cambodia. I wished I were with my family in Portland.

A poor and wrinkled old lady, almost topless, sitting in front of a makeshift shelter reminded me of my starved mother and grandmother. A shot of pain sharply burst inside my stomach as I recalled the time when I buried the body of my grandmother.

The Land Cruiser moved slowly through the tight pathway to avoid hitting the pedestrians, moped drivers, and bicyclists, but my eyes stubbornly fixed on the old lady, and my memory persistently kept me next to the grave of my grandmother.

Tonat took the immediate right turn and then immediate left turn through the ghetto and then out into a slightly better neighborhood where houses were moderately middle-class.

Tonat pulled the Land Cruiser off the dirt road and through a residential gate. I immediately recognized the house perched on big stilts. It belonged to the family of Tonat's father before the Khmer Rouge and was reclaimed by Tonat's father after the Khmer Rouge.

Next to the house, there was a tiny wooden hut with just a single room. It belonged to my sister Peak, who was now a single mother with four kids.

Tonat pulled the Land Cruiser slowly forward and parked it squarely beneath his father's house. My mind returned to the present, and I got excited. I stepped out of the vehicle and found myself involuntarily catching a small woman who threw herself at me. At first, I didn't know who it was. But once my arms wrapped around her body, my chest felt her heart, and my right cheek felt her left cheek, I knew the woman. I recognized the sob and immediately shared an overwhelming grief, a grief that could not be understood by anyone else. This woman was my sister Peak.

While everyone stood by watching, I tightened my arms around Peak's body and silently pressed my cheek against hers. I was without words. Peak continued to burst into sobs in my arms. I clenched my jaw, fighting back tears. My tightened lips quivered. I shut my eyes and lost control of myself. I buried my face and let out the flood of my dammed emotion. I emptied myself. A gush of tears flushed out all that I had inside my body. I had nothing left inside of me ... no blood ... no flesh ... no bones ... nothing. All that I had inside my body was completely emptied. My twenty-year dammed emotion burst like a volcano.

SPIRITUAL REDISCOVERY

Familiar sounds of roosters, hens, and ducks woke me up to a pleasantly warm morning. I had not slept well. I stayed up most of the night catching up and crying with my sisters. I had mosquito bites. I was tired, but my adrenaline was high.

One of my nieces made me coffee and brought me fruit. My sister Peak made me breakfast. A fresh day put me in a better mood. The sky was clear.

The air was fresh and warm. Trees and birdsongs were intimately familiar. I felt at home.

I was in the same clothes that I had worn the day before because all of my clothes were still wet from the miraculous and unexpected rain. I was bombarded by close and distant relatives, old family friends, and neighbors. I felt idolized and adored and out of place. Visitors came and went. Some visitors stayed all day chit-chatting.

Midmorning, my father's only sister, Chheang, dropped in to visit. Her resemblance to my father brought me nostalgic tears. Likewise, the fact that I was the spitting image of my father brought my aunt to tears. We cried together.

Many people came to visit me. I did not remember many of them until my sisters pointed them out one by one. The visitors shared one sad story after another. Living in poverty was the common theme of their depressing stories. They were consumed by their personal tragedies during and after the Khmer Rouge regime. I was emotionally drained by lunchtime and needed to be left alone. I took a walk by myself.

My sisters sent a man to tail and protect me from kidnapping and robbery, because Cambodia was still a dangerous place at that time. I knew that the man followed me, but I didn't care and pretended not to know. In fact, I was kind of glad that someone watched my back.

I walked alone. I cried alone. I replayed my childhood with every step I took. I went to the temple, stood in the middle of it, and cried in memory of my Buddhist master, Dekun Dul.

I went to my elementary school and reflected on my Buddhist upbringing. I went to my middle school and recalled my academic struggle. I stood in disbelief that I had come from this poor and provincial school and graduated from Reed College. I wondered if anyone would believe the true story of my extraordinary journey through the Khmer Rouge killing fields, Reed College, and Andersen Consulting. I wondered whether I could put pencil to paper and write a book about my misery, struggle, and triumph.

I walked alone. I cried alone. I was aware of the man tailing me. I felt safe. I kept walking with no destination in mind.

I arrived at the Songke River, in which I had bathed daily before the Khmer Rouge regime. The river seemed much smaller than I remembered. I thought about my childhood friends. We played. We wrestled. We fought. We threw clay in one another's eyes. We raced across the river. We dove off tall trees and bridges. We lived in a dream world. The thought made me smile, but then I looked downstream and remembered damming the river. A fresh image of the Khmer Rouge labor camp abruptly brought me back to reality.

I went to the municipal radio station, where my friends and I used to loiter outside listening to its broadcasted programs. The facility was defunct and abandoned.

My next stop was the stadium where my family once contracted to park thousands of bicycles during kickboxing events. Looking inside, I noticed the stadium was ruined and occupied by makeshift homeless shelters. I turned and walked away with a fond memory of when I used to sneak inside to watch the boxing.

The man who tailed me pulled up his moped alongside me and encouraged me to return home. I knew the man well; he was my neighbor before we were separated by the Khmer Rouge's evacuation. I got on his aged moped, straddled the rugged seat behind him, and let him chauffeur me home. When we got home, I handed him a $10 tip. He refused to accept the tip. My sister Sim yelled at him to take it. He subserviently took the money, put his trembling hands together in a praying position, bowed his head to me as if I were a re-vered king, fought back tears with his fake smile, and overly thanked me. I was embarrassed.

Later that day, Sim told me that the man did not earn much more than $10 a month driving his moped. I was humbled by the experience and reflected on my own financial situation. I felt fortunate. All my financial worries and ambitions ended that day. A mountain was lifted off me, and I thought that if

I achieved no more than making ends meet throughout the remainder of my life then I would humbly regard myself as fortunate.

The experience took me out of my anger and depression and into exhilaration. I enjoyed the authentic Cambodian lunch especially prepared to my personal taste by my sisters. I was happy. I was high. Nothing could bring me down. Nothing until a man who grew up with me in the Khmer Rouge labor camp approached me. He knew the whereabouts of a Khmer Rouge leader named Mok, and he offered to murder Mok for $800. Mok was an evil man among the Khmer Rouge leaders. He was a village chief who put my family through hell.

While $800 was not that much to me as an American, to my poor friend (who earned about $10 a month), it was a lot of money. He could have bought a modest home for $800.

I had frequently fantasized about vengeance for all that the Khmer Rouge had done to my family. But I never thought there would be a chance in hell or heaven to take out my revenge on those who committed crimes against my family, and this golden opportunity was incredibly surprising. A curveball was thrown at me at lightning speed, and I was not ready to catch it. Indecisive, I told the man that I would let him know what I had decided in a couple of days.

I handed out $5, $10, and $20 bills to those who came to visit me. I gave away as much as $100 at a time to those whom I considered special friends of my family prior to the Khmer Rouge. After a while, I could not tell whether people came to visit me or to get my handouts. Shortly after lunch, a woman past her middle age came for a visit. Her presence stoked my anger. Her family was dirt poor before the Khmer Rouge regime. My family rented to her a small shack and a food stand. More than half of the rent was never collected. Furthermore, my parents helped her family with extra cash and food. Then, during the Khmer Rouge regime, she informed the Khmer Rouge that my family was filthy rich and my brother-in-law Chip was a member of the military police who escaped the mass execution in April 1975. Her description of my family put us in even harsher conditions during the Khmer Rouge regime.

All my sisters went on chit-chatting with the woman as if the woman had done nothing wrong. I did not understand and was irritated by that. When the woman tried to have a dialogue with me, I was terse and unwelcoming. I held back my anger and rudeness, but I did not give her any money like I did the other visitors. I tried hard to maintain my civility, but as a generally nice guy, I did not fool anyone — especially my sisters.

My sister Sim asked me to help her with something in the restroom.

"Ah-eng kom twer enh cheung. Yeung chea kon mean pouch," Sim told me not to behave in such a cold manner, and she reminded me that I belonged to a good family. She said past was past, and nothing good would come out of my resentment. She pleaded with me to let go of my bitterness.

Sure, it was easy for Sim to say all of that to me; she was a Buddhist nun, and she had lived in Cambodia for the past twenty years, healing her emotional wounds and making peace with what had happened to us. I, on the other hand, had twenty years of bottled-up anger. I was disappointed that my own sister sided with the woman who was partly responsible for putting my family through hell. I showed my disappointment by walking out of the restroom. I walked past everyone and exited the gate. I took off on my own.

Once again, I walked alone. I cried alone. My hands clenched into iron fists. I wanted to punch someone's lights out. I walked through the ghetto. The poor people reminded me of life during the Khmer Rouge era. The naked children along the dirt pathway reminded me how an innocent child could grow up to become a vicious murderer. I thought about luring those children to a place where I could end their lives before they had a chance to become killers. Whatever degree of sympathy I had for the poor before, I now had none. My tears dried up, and my anger was replaced by arrogance. I walked tall with my chest out and chin high. I had no smile. With a dry face, I gave long eye contact to practically everyone I came across. My eyes invited trouble. My iron fists could not have been harder, and I was ready to come loose.

I went through the entire ghetto without any trouble. I was absentminded until I arrived in front of Wat Domrei Sor. The ruined temple reminded me of the time when I ran away from home and went to live with Dekun Dul. I remembered my Buddhist upbringing. I came to my senses, and I was ashamed of myself for my behavior. I could not believe that I had wanted to kill those poor children. I could not believe that I was capable of hatred. I could not believe that I was an American. I could not believe that I was a Reed College graduate. I could not believe that I had been willing to lose everything I had built in the U.S. I felt unworthy of being my parents' son. More important, I felt unworthy of being my son's father. I did not like myself.

I spent a little bit of time roaming inside the temple, and then I stopped by a coconut stand just outside the temple. I sat down and ordered a fresh coconut. I sipped the young coconut juice ever so slowly through a plastic straw while my mind meandered aimlessly through my past, present, and future. Occasionally, I was aware of curious eyes on me. My American look stood out.

A Land Cruiser pulled up alongside the curb. Tonat rolled down the passenger side window and asked me if everything was okay. He wanted me to get in the car and come home. I assured him that I was okay and wanted to walk home by myself. Tonat left. I paid the vendor $2 for the 10-cent coconut. I felt strangely good about being a big spender. I smiled and started to walk back through the ghetto.

I walked through the ghetto with apologetic eyes, compassion, and sincere empathy. I was calm and reflective. I was spiritual. I wanted to help the poor. I forced out my smiles and waved at the naked children. I nodded with reverence to the wrinkled old women.

When I got home, the woman who had angered me was gone. My sisters expressed concern for my emotional well-being. I reassured them that I was okay. My aunt Chheang, Tonat, my sisters, and I gathered and discussed a plan to have a Buddhist memorial ceremony for my parents and other family members who had died during the Khmer Rouge regime. We decided to do the ceremony the next day.

That night, I went to bed with a heavy thought on my mind. In the next couple of days, I had to decide whether to end a man's life at the cost of $800 or set personal precedence and forgive the Khmer Rouge for its atrocious crime against my family. I tossed and I turned. In darkness, I cried alone. I pondered alone. For twenty years, I had dreamed of my cruel revenge. I thought of killing the man myself. I thought of torturing him first before killing him. I conscientiously weighed the prospect of my own act against the prospect of hiring someone else to act. I thought about what had transpired that day during my walk through the ghetto and the temple. I questioned my true identity. I questioned what I had to gain and lose. I tossed and I turned. I sweated. I sat up. I lay down. I got up and went to the restroom in the dark. I listened to giant bats outside. I heard crickets and tree frogs. I heard geckos. I heard mosquitoes. I heard snoring. I heard my sisters turning in their sleep. I felt my restless heart. I struggled to fall asleep. Finally, I wondered how I would face my son if I went through with the deal to murder Mok. Late past midnight, I cried myself to sleep. I had reached no conclusion.

A new morning arrived and went. I slept through it until someone woke me up for lunch. A strong cup of coffee was made especially for me, and I downed it to get rid of my headache. I took a very short shower, dressed quickly, and joined my family for lunch. To my liking, Dy made me my favorite dishes using my mother's own recipes. All attention was on me and Phon during lunch. I especially enjoyed the attention. I felt at home and like I was on top of the world.

After lunch, Tonat drove my sisters, my aunt Chheang, and me to the market. We purchased candles, incense, and other trinkets for the ceremonial offering. Walking through the market reminded me of multiple occasions when I was a little boy accompanying my mother to the market. I fought back tears when my sisters and I walked past a stand that sold freshwater turtles. It reminded me of a time when my mother bought a few turtles to prepare for dinner and gave me one for a pet. We walked past a fresh fish stand. It reminded me of the Khmer Rouge era when I had to catch fish in secrecy in order to survive. My good and bad memories surfaced as I walked through the market, and I struggled to hold back my emotions.

Once we had purchased all we needed for the ceremony, Tonat drove us to a Buddhist temple named Wat Kompheng. Before the Khmer Rouge regime, I spent a lot of time playing inside Wat Kompheng because my elementary school was located across the street from it. So, like Wat Domrei Sor, Wat Kompheng meant a lot to me. I could not have been more pleased when my aunt Chheang insisted on having the ceremony at Wat Kompheng.

The ceremony took place in the backyard of Wat Kompheng. Rice mats were laid down for the monks and guests to sit on. The temple's elder led the ceremony. He took out a piece of blank paper and a pencil, and he wrote down the names of those to whom the ceremony was dedicated. The list included the names of my grandmother, my father, my mother, Ali, Chip, Hok, Hok's mother, Hok and Sim's son, and over fifty other dead relatives, including those who were not with my family during the Khmer Rouge time:

The monks chanted. My relatives and I sat facing the monks. I sat flat on a rice mat next to my sisters. Throughout the chant, I had my eyes closed, hands clasped in front of my forehead, and head bowed down close to the ground. In my entire life, I had never been more spiritual than at that moment. Although the Khmer Rouge failed to completely eradicate my faith in humanity, it had managed to eradicate my religious faith. During the Khmer Rouge, I had called out to Buddha every day for help, but I received none. What little of my religious faith was left in me was completely gone the day I buried the emaciated body of my starved grandmother—a wholly dedicated Buddhist nun—in the eerie field. Now, however, the monks and their chanting slowly made me become spiritual again. With my eyes closed, I asked Buddha to take care of my parents' and youngest sister's spirits. I whispered thanks to my father for watching over me throughout my life. I let my spirit drift and connect with my parents'. The chanting was comforting and mesmerizing. I smiled and fought back my tears. Suddenly, I thought about my friend who had offered to kill a Khmer Rouge chief on my behalf for $800. I could no longer hold back my tears. I sobbed and decided what to do with my $800.

After the memorial, Tonat drove me and my sisters all over the place. Before long, I began to feel at home again. I thought about returning to live in Battambang. The thought tore me up, and I felt divided between my birthplace and my home in Oregon. I missed Lisa and Kilin. I missed Portland. I missed Portland at that moment as much as I had missed Battambang when I was in Portland. I realized that I would never be fully happy in one home or the other. I knew then that I would always be equally torn between Portland and Battambang. My heart was saddened.

My friend who had offered to kill Mok came to visit me after dinner. My relatives, other friends, and neighbors hung around, making it difficult for my friend and me to talk about what to do with Mok. Away from the crowd for a brief moment, I managed to let him know that I had decided not to go through with it. I told him that the cycle of killing must stop. I did not have to explain my decision; he grew up with me, and he knew my family values. He was not surprised that I turned down his offer. His family always respected mine, he respected me … he respected my decision not to kill another human being. He stayed a bit afterward, but we had no more words to speak to each other. When it was time for him to leave, I walked him to the front gate, and then inconspicuously slipped $50 into his hand before we said goodbye.

Although I knew I had done the right thing, I wavered in my decision for days afterward. I questioned my own courage to face a killer. I wondered if I could punish a bad guy. I doubted whether I had what it took to kill a person. I was unsure of myself for quite some time. In the end, however, I decided that I had picked the right choice. I knew that my being a father had a lot to do with my course of action. I also realized that I had become a civilized individual. I no longer doubted my courage. I did not forgive Mok, but I moved on. I gave the $800 to Sim and Peak to help them purchase a new home.

In all, I visited Cambodia for approximately three weeks. For the duration of my visit, I experienced sadness, anger, and happiness. I realized my inner strength, and I found myself; I was a tree.

SECOND NEW LEAF

Two years after Kilin was born, Lisa gave birth to our baby girl, Kila, who was named after my late brother, Kila Ung. As profound as Kilin's birth was, Kila's brought me a new dimension. Since my utter loss at the hands of the Khmer Rouge regime, Kila's birth was the first event that caused me to feel that my life was being truly rebuilt. Kila completed me. With Lisa, Kilin, and Kila by my side, I became a full-fledged tree with vibrant roots and leaves.

Kila was born at Good Samaritan Hospital. Watching Kilin cuddle with his newborn baby sister in the hospital bed reminded me of the physical void of my sister Ali in my life. Kilin's instant love for baby Kila brought me both joy and sadness. I was happy to see the bond between my sister Ali and me reincarnated between my two children. As I watched Kilin lovingly kiss and languorously caress Kila's baby skin, my heart wandered off seeking my past affection for Ali. My sinuses swelled, my jaw involuntarily clenched, and I held back my tears. My heart hurt.

I took time off from work to be with my family during the entire stay at the hospital, and we did not allow any visitors. Much like after Kilin's birth, Lisa was sick, and I took care of both children at the hospital. Both children never left my sight, not even during baby Kila's routine examinations. When Lisa needed her rest, I let Kilin sit next to Kila, on top of the diaper changing cart; I pushed the cart through the hall, around and around, passing the nurses' station numerous times. Kilin had the time of his life. I had the time of my life. I was on top of the world. I felt the eyes of the nurses, doctors, patients, and other guests on us. We were the three "KUs" (Kilong, Kilin, and Kila Ung). Not a soul at the hospital detected the hidden fact that I had an incredibly horrific past, and I completely forgot I had such a past.

LEVERAGING THE PAST

My family and I had a lot of fun living in my dream home, but keeping up with the Joneses was beyond my means. The house turned me into a slave of my own dreams. My family did not get enough of my quality time because the house demanded so much of me. I worked all day and took care of the yard in the evening and on weekends. My quality time with my family diminished further when I started my own consulting business — Knowledge Unlimited (KU) Consulting. Although KU Consulting brought me more money and freedom, it destroyed the balance of my life. Influenced by my Dale Carnegie training, I had promised myself to live a balanced life, which includes self, family, community, and career. To the contrary, however, I weighed my priorities most heavily on my career and the house.

Kilin began to display his natural talent in golf, and I wanted to help him foster that talent. Unfortunately, I had very little time.

I went into a depression. I felt trapped and unworthy of my heritage and self. I had trouble accepting the fact that I descended from the people who built the twelfth-century Angkor Wat. I struggled with my identity. I wanted freedom and happiness, but I pursued wealth and materialism. I wanted freedom and happiness, but I lived in a self-imposed slavery and depression. My tolerance for humanity was at its lowest. I no longer cared about the world. I was a ticking bomb. I contemplated suicide. I thought of starting a revolution to reform Cambodia — and the world.

Unable to get myself out of my depression on my own, I began a nightly dialogue with the spirit of my father and occasionally with the spirit of my mother. I asked my father for guidance. The dialogue gave me comfort and eventually led me to humbly open a conversation with Lisa about a journey to find a better life for me and the family. It was the first time I opened up to Lisa about my emotional weakness and my depression. Before that, I spent hours alone crying. Before that, I drove alone crying. Before that, I walked alone crying. I had spent lots of time alone searching for myself.

With Lisa's full support, I decided to never again be a slave to my materialistic world. Lisa and I decided together to live moderately and manageably. Together, we decided to find me a balance that would include self, family, career, and community. Consequently, we sold our luxury home, gave away eighty percent of our belongings, moved into a two-bedroom apartment across from Reed College, and became more financially prudent. Additionally, I got a well-paid position as a senior software engineer at Corillian, a leading online banking software company in Hillsboro, Oregon.

The apartment was part of the much-needed foundation for me to regain my balance. My only obligation was my job that provided for my family and empowered me to give back to the community. I did not have to take care of the apartment. When something broke, Lisa just called the front office to get it taken care of. I was not even allowed to change a light bulb. The apartment had a swimming pool, hot tub, gym, parking, and a big yard. It was located only a short walk away from Eastmoreland Golf Course. A block away from it was Reed College, adorned with a soccer field, bike path, hiking path, trees, stream, swings, and more. As a Reed alumnus, I had full access to the sport center, library, computer lab, and more. The apartment was close to Lisa's parents, and the children were able to visit their grandparents more often.

After work, I had nothing to do but spend time with my family. Lisa was able to take evening breaks from the children. I took the kids to the Reed College soccer field, where they could run around, play tag, and throw balls. My children's childish spirits slowly mitigated my depression. As I desired, I was able to help Kilin develop his golfing. I took Kilin to the open field behind Reed College and let him hit golf ball after golf ball. We had our poor-man version of an Earl-and-Tiger golf lesson. We rocked.

Each weekend, I went to Eastmoreland Golf Course just before sunrise, played a round of nine holes, and returned to the apartment before the family even knew I was gone. I was a super dad and hardly missed a beat. I played silly with Kila, and I taught Kilin to throw and catch a football. I put my children to bed practically every evening except on weekends. I read them books and told them bedtime stories. With the children, I discovered the joys of the zoo, airport, air shows, flight museum, and more. I was a dad and a child at the same time. I learned to see and appreciate life through the eyes of my children.

Golfing, my job, and family time gave me three parts of my sought-after four-part balance—self, career, family, and community. Although I was very much out of the depression and relatively happy, I still felt somewhat empty. I still had so much energy and great ideas left, and I wanted to do more. I clearly did not want more material things, as I had just gotten rid of over eighty percent of my possessions; I just wanted to do more. I wanted to make a difference. I wanted to channel my energy for a higher purpose. I wanted to leverage my horrible past to make the world a better place.

I decided to get more involved in the Cambodian community. When the Cambodian Dance Troupe of Oregon needed someone to teach Cambodian to the young dancers between dance practices, I volunteered. I committed myself to seeking opportunities to serve others in the community. I wanted the new generation of Cambodians to be better than their predecessors, including me. I thought that by improving the future generations, the world might be able to prevent future genocide. Whenever a Cambodian youth needed a mentor, I volunteered. Whenever a member of the Cambodian community got into trouble, I stepped in. I sincerely wanted every youth to achieve higher education. I shared what I knew in the hope that everyone in my community would do better than I.

My sincere desire to give and share with others caught the attention of the Cambodian-American Community of Oregon (CACO), which was in serious need of a strong leader. CACO Chairman Mony Mao confided to me that no one wanted to take on the responsibility of being the president of the organization, and he proposed dissolving its 501(c)(3) charter. I captured the opportunity and volunteered to serve as president. I asked Mony for his full support and dedication to help me rebuild the community. With his strong support, along with the support of other volunteers, I led CACO to redefine itself and rebuild its foundation. The community had all the necessary elements for success, and all I needed to do was to inspire people to believe in themselves. I constantly reminded myself and the community members where we had come from. We survived the Khmer Rouge genocide. We journeyed through minefields, rockets, and bullets. We struggled to learn English and assimilate the American culture. We picked berries, cans, bottles, and apples to make ends meet. We graduated from welfare. We traded our nightmares for dreams. We had our worst days behind us. We had taken the impossible journey. There should be little that we as a community could not do.

As the organization's president, I expected a lot from myself and my community. I brought to the community my relentless encouragement, mentoring, servant leadership, and service above self. I worked hard serving and leading the community, and I pushed the community hard to develop its credibility and visibility among the mainstream communities.

Under my leadership, the volunteers managed to attract Portland Mayor Tom Potter to the community's annual events. With the help of Lillian Tsai, president of TsaiComms LLC, CACO managed to bring in Governor Barbara Roberts to its Khmer Heritage Night as a keynote speaker. It hosted a public forum at Portland State University to discuss the Khmer Rouge tribunal. It managed to land Sichan Siv, retired U.S. ambassador to the U.N., as the keynote speaker at the forum. CACO expanded itself to include an annual summer camping trip, golf tournament, heritage banquet, and more. For the first time, the community implemented a youth program, a women's support group, and an elderly support group. CACO collaborated with the Boy Scouts of America to provide access to a camping facility and activities for the entire Cambodian community. It collaborated with the Portland Youth Golf Association (PYGA) to enroll Cambodian-American youths in the First Tee of Portland—PYGA's program aiming to impact the lives of young people by providing learning facilities and educational programs that promote character development and life-enhancing values through the game of golf. I introduced Dale Carnegie leadership training programs to the community. I mentored a number of youths in their preparation for college. I leveraged Cambodia's horrible past to inspire the community to stay united and give back to the world—especially Cambodia. The way the community came together helped restore my own faith in Cambodians, the faith that was nearly eradicated by the Khmer Rouge.

As Mahatma Gandhi said, the best way to find yourself is to lose yourself in the service of others. I found myself in my service of others. I stopped believing that my insomnia was a curse. I began to believe that my insomnia was meant for me as a means to serve others. For example, my insomnia afforded me the time to serve CACO without compromising my personal time, family time, and professional time too much. I found my balance, and I found myself. I am a tree.

Shortly after I found myself, other people discovered me. One of those people was Rotarian Michael Cottam. Michael was my engineering manager when we both worked for Step Technology. He left Step to start TheBigDay.com. We ran into each other one day in 2005, and he invited me to a Thai restaurant. Over lunch, we exchanged our updates. Michael learned about my newly discovered self as a tree and was captivated by my service to others. He invited me to join the Rotary Club of Portland, where I could further commit to service above self. I became a Rotarian in 2006.

The other person among those who discovered me was Portland Mayor Tom Potter. His interest in my service to others gave me an opportunity to tell the stories of my community, heritage, past, nightmares, and dreams. He enabled me to serve on a couple of civic committees. He recognized my service to others in his State of the City speech and his speech at the Rotary Club of Portland. After his wife, Karin Hansen, learned about my lifetime dream of becoming a Royal Rosarian, he introduced me to Minister of the Foreign Affairs of the Royal Rosarians Sir Knight Ray Hanson. Sponsored by Sir Knight Ray Hanson, I was knighted by Rose Festival Queen Grace Neal on the evening of April 7, 2007, and became Sir Knight Kilong Ung. As a member of the Royal Rosarians, I serve as an official goodwill ambassador of the city of Portland, the City of Roses. Once inspired by the Royal Rosarians to have a lifetime dream, I now have joined the ranks of those who inspire hopes and dreams and promote goodwill and peace. Within my first year as a goodwill ambassador, I had the honor of greeting and shaking hands with high-profile dignitaries, including Liberian President Ellen Johnson Sirleaf and Chinese Ambassador Zhou Wenzhong during their visits to Portland. Whenever I marched in a parade, I volunteered to carry the American flag in honor of someone or a cause. My first two flags were dedicated to the two million Cambodians killed by the Khmer Rouge genocide and the 9/11 victims and heroes.

The list of people who contributed to my success and helped me regain my faith in humanity is too long to be recounted in this book, but like a leaf at the mercy of the wind, I would not have made it here without these people. My extraordinary thanks must be wholeheartedly given to those who saved my life:

- My sister Sivheng Ung (Phon)
- My brother-in-law Vann Mealy Metta Touch (Mealy)
- My sponsor, Kung Chap, and his wife, Sophalla
- The World Vision folks who made it possible for me to come to America

Last but not least, I want to unapologetically and publicly express my sincere gratitude to those who militarily drove out the Khmer Rouge and liberated me from the killing fields, because without their courageous sacrifice, I might not be alive to tell my story today. My life is filled with love, forgiveness, understanding, humility, support, and friendship. My success and wonderful life may fool you into believing that the end has justified the means. Make no mistake about it; no end can ever justify the means that I experienced. I am a tree, but I forever remain a:

- Khmer Rouge genocide survivor
- Former refugee

- Legacy of the Vietnam War
- Child who lost his parents to starvation
- Case of post-traumatic stress disorder

Although my difficult journey has led me to a wonderful life that includes a loving wife and two very adorable children, I would not wish it on anyone, including my worst enemy. The suffering and hardship that came with it were incredibly sadistic, and no one should ever endure them, not even the most resilient golden leaf.

I was a leaf at the mercy of the wind. The wind carried me from one remote part of the world to another. It blew me through turbulence and catastrophic weather. It took me to a Khmer Rouge labor camp and lingered for an eternity. It dehydrated me and nearly starved me to death. I helplessly watched the most devilish mother of all winds ruthlessly crush my tree into lifeless pulp. Like an almighty Olympian god, when the wind wanted to toy with me, it blew me through minefields, rockets, and bullets. While two million leaves disintegrated, I persevered. Through an extraordinary journey, I discovered myself. I am fortunate, and I don't easily perish. I was a golden leaf. Against all odds, I survived, laid down roots, and became a tree.

I am a tree.

THE END

UPBRINGING

Ali, just before the Khmer Rouge took over Cambodia in 1975.

Before the Khmer Rouge took over Cambodia in 1975. Front row, from left to right: Ali, me, and Peak. Back row, from left to right: Phon, Phorn, and Pech.

AT LEFT: Dy in my family home's master bedroom, getting ready for her wedding in the early '70s.

BELOW: My mother and father at Dy's wedding. My father is seated directly in front of the microphone; my mother is seated next to it.

OPPOSITE PAGE, TOP: At Dy's wedding reception, from left to right: Hai (cousin), Ahear (Phon's boyfriend), my father, my mother, Phon, and Vouch (cousin).

OPPOSITE PAGE, BOTTOM: Grandmother Touch at Dy's wedding (woman behind Dy).

BUILDING A DAM

OPPOSITE PAGE, TOP: Courtesy of Documentation Center of Cambodia (DC-Cam). This picture is an accurate representation of my typical day, working to build a dam or water reservoir, during the Khmer Rouge rule.

OPPOSITE PAGE, BOTTOM: The broken dam that nearly killed me. I took this picture during my first return visit to Cambodia, in 1999.

BELOW: From left to right: Sim, Phorn, and I visited Sras Keo water reservoir in 2009. We are standing on the dike. Phorn and I (and also Peak, who is not in this picture) were part of the slave labor camp that built this huge reservoir.

REFUGEE CAMPS

TOP: Refugee camp in Mai Rut, Thailand, in 1979. From left to right: Mealy, me, Mike Carroll, and Phon.

BOTTOM: Mugshots taken at refugee camp for travel and U.S. immigration documents. From left to right: Mealy, Phon, and me.

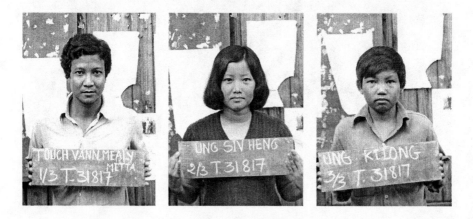

COMING TO AMERICA

ESL (English as a second language) class at Einstein Junior High in San Diego, California. From left to right: Ang, me, Horn, and my fellow Cambodian refugees.

PORTLAND, OREGON

AT LEFT: Behind Washington-Monroe High School in Portland, Oregon. From left to right: Gilda (exchange student from Brazil), me, Scott, Ed, and another student in the back.

ABOVE: Mrs. Buck's family took me fishing and camping at Wallowa Lake, Oregon.

AT LEFT: Mrs. Buck's family.

AT FAR RIGHT: Miss Suzan Jacobson, my tutor at Washington-Monroe High School.

AT RIGHT: My English teacher Mrs. Taggard.

BELOW: Practicing my Bruce Lee moves while living with the Easters.

ABOVE: Scott and me at the Pendleton (Oregon) Round-Up.

AT LEFT: Posing with Tina, a classmate, before my Cleveland High School commencement.

ABOVE: Giving away the bride: Phon and Ken Easter (my American father).

AT LEFT: At Phon and Mealy's wedding in Portland, Oregon. From left to right: Mrs. Buck, me (in a secondhand suit from a Goodwill store), Phon, and Mealy.

HIGHER EDUCATION

The Trustees of

REED COLLEGE

In pursuance of the authority vested in them by law and on recommendation of the faculty hereby confer upon

Kilong Ung

the degree of

BACHELOR OF ARTS

In witness whereof this diploma is granted in the city of Portland in the state of Oregon on the twenty-fourth of May nineteen hundred eighty seven.

PRESIDENT OF THE COLLEGE   CHAIRMAN, BOARD OF TRUSTEES

Bowling Green State University

Graduate College

hereby confers upon

Kilong Ung

the degree

Master of Science

together with all rights, privileges and honors appertaining thereto.

Witness the seal of the university and the signatures of its officers.

Given at Bowling Green in the State of Ohio, this sixth day of May, 1989.

Paul J. Olscamp
President

Chairman, Board of Trustees

Louis L. Katzner
Dean

AT LEFT: Toeur (right) and I reunited for a weekend at my cousin Vi's wedding in Long Beach, California.

BELOW: Partying with my fellow Bowling Green State University graduate students.

ABOVE: Jamaica food relief volunteers, from left to right: a fellow graduate student, me, and Teresa Tancre.

AT RIGHT: Posing with Dr. Ralph St. John at my graduation from BGSU.

ROOTS

BELOW, AT LEFT: Lisa's graduation from Portland State University.

BELOW, AT RIGHT: Family friend Ratana's and my nephew Amrin's graduation from Cleveland High School. From left to right: Lisa, baby Kilin, me, Ratana, and Amrin.

BOTTOM: My wedding, from left to right: Greg, Khai, Lisa, me, and Mark. Photo courtesy of Greg Layman.

TOP: Visiting with the Easters. From left to right, front row: Truc's son Kavan, wife My-Hoang, daughter Eva, Truc, Lisa, and me. From left to right, back row: Grandpa Easter, Ken, Connie, my distant nephew Jon, Amrin, and Scott.

BOTTOM: Buddhist blessing at my new home.

NEW LEAVES

BELOW: Kilin, me, Lisa, and Kila.

OPPOSITE PAGE, TOP: Kila, me, and Kilin.

OPPOSITE PAGE, BOTTOM: At the Oregon coast, left to right: Kilin, me, and Kila.

RETURNING TO CAMBODIA

ABOVE: First return visit to Cambodia, in 1999, twenty years after my escape. The boys reminded me of my own childhood.

BELOW: Climbing Peak's coconut tree during my visit to Battambang, Cambodia, in 2009. This picture reminds me of the time when the Khmer Rouge soldiers arrested me for attempting to steal a coconut.

ABOVE: I took this picture during my visit to Cambodia in 2009 because it reminded me of my time with Dekun Dul.

TOP: Peak and Sim's hut in 1999.

BOTTOM: Peak and Sim's new home in 2006.

THIS PAGE AND OPPOSITE PAGE: Photos from the Buddhist memorial ceremony for the more than fifty members of my family who did not survive the Khmer Rouge genocide. The names of my grandmother, father, mother, sister, and other relatives were ceremonially listed for the blessing.

OPPOSITE PAGE, TOP: Coming back from my visit to Cambodia in 2009. Looking out the window of the plane, over the wingtip, I remembered the crossing from darkness into light—as if from hell into heaven—during my flight to the U.S. in 1979. What is so incredible about this picture is the fact that I was deeply asleep on the plane and all of the window shades were shut, but I miraculously woke up at the moment of the crossing, opened the window shade, and took this picture.

OPPOSITE PAGE, BOTTOM: Visiting with my sisters in Battambang in 2009. From left to right: Sim, Dy, Phorn, Peak, and me.

BELOW: In 2009, visiting Wat Kompong Preah, the temple that was converted into the hellish hospital where my mother died.

LEVERAGING THE PAST

Photo courtesy of Mony Mao. September 15, 2007, carrying the U.S. flag in the
50th Annual Beaverton Celebration Parade. I dedicated my honor to the
two million Cambodians who died as the result of the Khmer Rouge genocide
and in memory of the 9/11 victims and heroes.

Ḥear ye !
Ḥear ye !!
Ḥear ye !!!

Be it known to all Rosaria, river and wood, field and hill, that in true accord with our custom we have this day exalted a certain worthy squire, who in his own province hight

Kilong Ung

of the fair town of _Portland_

Shire of _Oregon_

And be it further known that this most worthy one, learned in the lore of the Rose, and of high and happy heart, is hereby honored and accepted as a member of the

Royal Rosarians

subject to the Rose and the ordinances of Rosaria, and pledged to the performance of deeds befitting the Knighthood of the Royal Flower.

Wherefore, we summon the royal heralds to proclaim his high degree, to publish both near and far our comrade's royal investiture with the seemly and right honorable title of

Sir Knight Kilong Ung

and his election to the fellowship of the **Royal Rosarians** of the Rose City, ofttimes hight Portland, of the Shire of Oregon, by the great river, Wallamet.

And that now and hereafter his privilege shall be the guardianship and culture of that most fragrant, beauteous and felicitous flower the said rose called

Mt. Hood

whose name and fame he shall spread, whose presence he shall wait upon, until its bloom blesses many folk, in youth and age.

Signed and Sealed in the Royal Council of Rosaria, met for this purpose and none other, on this _7th_ _day of the Month of_ _April_ _, Anno Domini,_ _2007_

_____
Prime Minister

_____
Lord High Chancellor

_____
Secretary of State

ACKNOWLEDGMENTS

I owe my gratitude to the many people who directly and indirectly helped me become who I am today—especially my Cambodian family, my American family, and those from Washington-Monroe High School, Cleveland High School, Reed College, Bowling Green State University, Cambodian-American Community of Oregon, Rotary Club, and Royal Rosarians.

Since a complete listing of these people would not fit inside this book, I would like to mention just a few here:

Al Jubitz—Al provided constant encouragement and helped me to stay focused on my writing. Whatever support I needed, Al let me know that I could count on him.

Angelo S. Carella—Angelo read the second draft of the manuscript, was impressed by the story, gave me valuable feedback, and enlisted Al Jubitz to convince me that I needed a professional editor. Angelo—in collaboration with Darin Honn and Al Jubitz—played a significant role in getting me the right editor.

Cambodian-American Community of Oregon—CACO is my community, home, family, and foundation. The members of CACO have always been there to support my endeavors—whether writing my book, or making the world a better place.

Chanrithy Him—Chanrithy shared a number of valuable lessons learned from the publishing of her book, *When Broken Glass Floats*. She gave me advice on how to choose an editor and on the publishing process. As a fellow Cleveland High School alumna and genocide survivor, Chanrithy gave me inspiration and encouragement to write my own story.

Chris Brooks—When I interviewed for a software engineer position at Corillian, an online banking software company, Chris was the company's CTO. While each of my interviewers, one after another, homed in on my technical skills, Chris only had one question for me: "What is your aspiration?" At the time, I did not have an answer to the question, because I had never thought about my true aspiration. The question played an important role in driving *Golden Leaf* to its completion; Chris inadvertently reminded me that I aspire to tell my story.

Christine Chin Ryan—Christine provided constant support and encouragement. When I needed a friend, she was there as a mentor and supporter. Working with her, to help other people achieve their dreams, gave me the idea that my story can serve as a tool to make the world a better place.

Cory Jubitz—Cory was the perfect copy editor and proofreader for *Golden Leaf*. She stayed up many nights to make sure that she met my aggressive publication schedule. I am grateful for her professionalism, directness, dedication, and sensitivity.

Dale Canfield—Dale urged me to work toward realizing my dream to become a motivational speaker. Dale introduced me to Dr. Tom Morris' audio CD titled *What if Plato Were My Mentor? The Greatest Success Ideas of All Time, From Aristotle to Zeno*. The self-help audio CD furthered my motivational speaking ability and improved my writing skills.

Doug Mendenhall—Doug shared technical advice, the invaluable contact of a print broker, and lessons learned from the publication of his book, *Spark!*

Emily Harris—Emily interviewed me live on OPB Radio's *Think Out Loud* about my experience with post-traumatic stress disorder. While on the air, Emily read an excerpt of *Golden Leaf* posted on my blog; listeners sent me praising emails, and they encouraged me to finish my writing.

Jigme Topgyal—Jigme wrote a letter on my behalf to the office of His Holiness the Dalai Lama in order for me to request His Holiness' foreword for *Golden Leaf*. Jigme's endorsement of my work gave me strength and encouragement needed to reach the difficult finish line.

Julian Kilker—I am grateful for Julian's wise influence in unblocking my writing by simply pointing out that the golden leaf had done the impossible, in real life: survived the Khmer Rouge, learned English, assimilated into the American culture, graduated from Reed College, and was serving others; I modified the manuscript to demonstrate that the leaf had put down roots and had become a tree.

Kilin and Kila Ung—For the entire year in 2008, I had to cut back on my time with my two children in order to complete my manuscript. I am grateful for Kilin and Kila's understanding and sacrifice.

Lisa Ung—My wife, Lisa, made it possible for me to write and publish *Golden Leaf* while maintaining my busy life as a husband, father of two children, volunteer, community leader, Rotarian, Royal Rosarian, and software engineer. Additionally, she was the first to edit the first draft of the *Golden Leaf* manuscript.

Maileen Hamto—Maileen was the first to write about my story, in the newspaper *Asian Reporter*. Her interview helped me heal some of my emotional wounds inflicted by the Khmer Rouge, and her article provided me the necessary inspiration to continue writing *Golden Leaf*.

Marri-Beth Serritella—Marri-Beth designed the book, including the cover, and provided technical and moral support. Special thanks also go to her husband, Stephen Bachara, and their son, Monk, so that she could assist me with the publication of *Golden Leaf*.

"Reed Magazine"—I would like to express my gratitude toward the entire staff of "Reed Magazine," and special thanks to Associate Editor Aimée Sisco and writer Rebecca Koffman. Aimée contacted me about my story; Rebecca interviewed me. Through her interview, Rebecca gave me the impression that I had a publishable memoir.

Rodney Mazour—Until I met Rodney, a fellow Royal Rosarian, my thought of publishing a book was just a dream. On a bus traveling on an out-of-town parade trip, Rodney looked me in the eye, gripped my right hand with his, and offered to help me make my dream real. His unquestionable confidence in me gave me the courage to keep writing weekend after weekend. Rodney expected me to finish the book and held me to a very high standard. He gave me little choice but to finish the book.

Ronault (Polo) L.S. Catalani—Polo was always there to encourage me. When I needed an answer, Polo was my go-to guy. The publication of his book, *Counter Culture*, showed me that ordinary people like me can write and publish a book.

Ronnie Yimsut—Ronnie shared lessons learned from his effort to publish his book, *Journey Into Light*. A fellow genocide survivor and a friend, Ronnie gave me the inspiration to write my own story.

"The Rotarian"—I would like to express my gratitude toward the entire staff of "The Rotarian," official magazine of Rotary International, especially Features Editor Barbara Nellis, Deputy Senior Editor Janice S. Chambers, and Senior Designer Ken Ovryn. Barbara contacted me with the idea of putting my story in "The Rotarian." Janice reviewed the unedited manuscript of *Golden Leaf* and interviewed me. Her interview helped me edit the manuscript to improve its clarity. Ken worked hard selecting the right pictures for the layout. It took a few iterations of Ken's effort to get all the right photographs shipped and scanned. Ken's photo selection triggered additional details of my past.

Skye Fitzgerald—During the shooting of his documentary film *Bombhunters* in Cambodia, Skye met me for breakfast in Siem Reap, Cambodia. He convinced me to publish my memoir.

Sophorn Cheang—I am grateful for Sophorn's speedy help in translating the *Golden Leaf* section headers to Khmer and for typesetting them in a Khmer font.

Tiara Delgado—A documentary-film maker and journalist, Tiara tried to get draft copies of my manuscript to actor Matt Dillon and actress Angelina Jolie. She was not successful, but her effort demonstrated her absolute faith in my work.

Tom Cook—In the first draft of the manuscript, I painted myself simply as a leaf at the mercy of the wind. Tom would not accept that description of me and drove me to transition the helpless leaf in the story into a golden leaf. A golden leaf was still not good enough for Tom; consequently, I turned the golden leaf into a tree. Tom and his wife, Viki Schwab, later helped edit the manuscript and provided helpful feedback.

Truleen Maria Delgado—Truleen was the second to edit the first draft of the manuscript and provided outstanding grammatical feedback.

Van M. Touch (aka "Mealy")—Van offered lessons learned from the publishing of his two books, *Angkor Culinaire* and *Behind the Cambodian Killing Fields*. Van has not had an easy time with the English language after coming to the U.S. as an adult; yet, he managed to publish two books. His aspiration, endeavors, and success inspired me to publish my own story.

Last but not least, I want to give my gratitude to **Starbucks and its staff**. *Golden Leaf* is personal, and it was emotionally extremely difficult to write. I attempted to write the story in my home office, but when I got too emotional, I became weak and stopped writing. I realized I needed to write my story in a public place, a place where I had to control my emotion and keep going. I tried writing in a number of public places, including parks and libraries, but somehow, Starbucks seemed to fit my needs the best. The stores provided power outlets, soft music, and restrooms. Every time I cried, I paused my writing, went to the restroom, rinsed my face with cold water, went to the cashier counter, treated myself to a cup of Americano, and returned to hitting my keyboard. I spent an average of fourteen hours writing each weekend at Starbucks. I started writing regularly at the Starbucks store inside of the Safeway located on Southeast 39th and Powell Boulevard. Later, I moved to the Starbucks located at Northeast Halsey and 102nd Avenue. My favorite Starbucks, where I finally completed my manuscript, is located on the corner of North Lombard Street and North Philadelphia Avenue in St. Johns. My special thanks go to the people of Starbucks who served me coffee, water, bagels, sandwiches, and juice.

LaVergne, TN USA
20 January 2010

170669LV00001B/230/P